Development During the Transition to Adolescence

Minnesota Symposia
On Child Psychology
Volume 21

Development During the Transition to Adolescence

Minnesota Symposia
On Child Psychology
Volume 21

edited by

MEGAN R. GUNNAR
W. ANDREW COLLINS
The University of Minnesota

LEA LAWRENCE ERLBAUM ASSOCIATES, PUBLISHERS
1988   Hillsdale, New Jersey   Hove and London

Lawrence Erlbaum Associates, Inc., Publishers
365 Broadway
Hillsdale, New Jersey 07642

Library of Congress Cataloging-in-Publication Data

Development during the transition to adolescence.

"The Minnesota Symposia on Child Psychology, volume 21."
Papers presented at the 21st Minnesota Symposia on
Child Psychology, held Oct. 23–25, 1986 at the University
of Minnesota, sponsored by the Institute of Child
Development of the University of Minnesota.
Includes bibliographies and indexes.
1. Adolescent psychology—Congresses. 2. Puberty—
Congresses. I. Gunnar, Megan R. II. Collins, W. Andrew,
1944–   . III. University of Minnesota. Institute of
Child Development. IV. Minnesota Symposia on Child
Psychology (21st : 1986 : University of Minnesota.
[DNLM: 1. Adolescence—congresses. 2. Adolescent.
Psychology—congresses. 3. Child Development—
congresses. W3 MI607 v.21 / WS 462 D489 1986]
BF724.D44 1988   155.5   87-33217
ISBN 0-8058-0194-4

Printed in the United States of America
10 9 8 7 6 5 4 3 2 1

Contents

7. Commentary: The Role of Conflict in Adolescent-Parent Relationships
Catherine R. Cooper

8. Commentary: Developmental Issues in the Transition to Early Adolescence
J. Brooks-Gunn

Preface

This volume contains the papers presented at the 21st Minnesota Symposium on Child Psychology, held October 23–25, 1986, at the University of Minnesota, Minneapolis. As has been the tradition for this annual series, the faculty of the Institute of Child Development invited internationally eminent researchers to present their work and to consider problems of mutual concern.

The theme of the 21st Symposium, and the present volume, was development during the transition to adolescence. The adolescent years are increasingly receiving research attention, but the nature and course of changes from childhood to adolescence have rarely been addressed in empirical studies. In recent years, however, several major research efforts on physical, social and cognitive transitions during this period have begun to focus on issues and processes of change. The goal of the 21st Symposium was to assemble a group of active scholars from several disciplines who had in common an interest in the processes of change during the transition from childhood to adolescence.

We were fortunate to have as contributors to the symposium some of the most outstanding current scholars in this area. The speakers were Christopher Coe, Glen Elder, John Hill, Roberta Simmons, and Judith Smetana. They discussed a variety of issues pertinent to our understanding of this transition period, including the role of gonadal hormones, the impact of menarche and social-cognitive development on familial conflict, and the influence on the adolescent of social and historical change. In addition to these speakers, we were also fortunate to have three scholars with us who took on the task of providing a framework for discussion of the presentations: W. Andrew Collins who served as the keynote speaker and provided an overview of the current state of research in this area; Catherine R. Cooper who focused our attention on the issue of conflict, its definition and its role in adolescent-parent relationships, and J. Brooks-Gunn who in her commentary addressed the question of whether and to what extent the early adolescent period is either distinct or unqiue.

In all, the three days of the symposium were intellectually exciting and stimulating: The excitement and the challenge of the symposium are reflected clearly, I believe, in the chapters in this volume. In addition to the presenters and discussants, a number of people contributed their ideas and time to various roundtables and conversation hours which were a part of the 21st Symposium: Ann Masten, Willard Hartup, Geoffery Maruyama, Phillip AuClaire, William Sonis, June Tapp, Alan Sroufe, Barry Garfinkel, Charles Nelson, Eugene Borgida, Marty Erickson, Susan Perry, Ellen Berscheid, David Olson, Mark Snyder, Harry Hoberman, Gloria Leon, Ora Pescovitz, and Norman Garmezy. My thanks to all of these participants and to the staff and students of the Institute of Child Development.

Finally, I would like to acknowledge financial support for the symposium from the NICHD: 1 R13 HD 21906.

Megan R. Gunnar

Research on the Transition to Adolescence: Continuity in the Study of Developmental Processes

W. Andrew Collins
Institute of Child Development,
University of Minnesota

The contributors to the 21st annual Minnesota Symposium represent a growing number of developmental scholars who are turning their attention to the transition to adolescence. There have been numerous studies of children in the elementary school years (Collins, 1984) and a sizable number involving teenagers, as well (Petersen, in press); but by and large, those literatures have not focused on the processes of change that bridge the two periods. We chose the term *transition to adolescence* for this Symposium to underscore a focus on the processes by which individuals organize their experiences around the biological, behavioral, and social events of the second decade of life.

For most of the past two decades, considerable attention has been given to development during infancy and early childhood. The growing interest in middle childhood and adolescent development is less a reaction against the remarkably productive emphases of those years than an extension of the study of developmental processes to the later and, in some respects, more complex transitions of the school years. Although there is apparent discontinuity in the population under study, there is considerable continuity in the developmental issues that drive research on the transition to adolescence and those that were central to the study of early development.

The authors in this volume are researchers whose work represents especially compelling attempts to examine significant issues of developmental process in the phenomena of the transition to adolescence. In this introductory chapter, I note three themes that not only characterize their work, but illustrate the intellectual impetus behind a developmental perspective on the changes of middle childhood and adolescence.

BIOLOGICAL MATURATION
AND DEVELOPMENTAL PROCESSES

The first theme is the reason that is both the most obvious and, to many scholars, the most compelling reason for studying the transition to adolescence: namely, to take advantage of the salient changes of puberty to examine the nature of biological maturation and its interactive role in individual development.

Studies of pubertal changes illustrate why developmentalists now generally acknowledge that biological differences affect development through diverse processes. For example, a predictable recurring theme in research on puberty has been to specify the organizing and activating roles of gonadal hormones on sexually dimorphic behavior. The goal has been to estimate the nature and extent of biological contributions to behavioral differences between males and females that emerge at adolescence. The yield from this correlational approach has been enlightening, but largely by suggesting that pubertal change per se does not exert a strongly deterministic influence on behavioral change at adolescence. Ford and Beach (1951) and Money (Money & Ehrhardt, 1972) long ago demonstrated that the biological substrate for sexually dimorphic reproductive behavior was laid down prenatally or immediately postnatally, leaving for puberty primarily an activating role in sexual behavior. In another domain, attempts to find an association between pubertal hormone changes and brain lateralization differences that would explain spatial skill differences have resulted in ambiguous findings (Newcombe & Dubas, 1987). Even in the area of emotional functioning, there is not yet evidence of direct links with gonadal hormone variations, despite the general increase in affective disorders during the adolescent years (Masten, 1986). In all of these instances, we may yet find further evidence of hormonal influences, but the information we now have indicates that accounts based solely on variations in pubertal indicators are inadequate.

It is not surprising, consequently, that research on pubertal change has increasingly focused on social-mediational models of the link between biological change and individual adaptation. Here the yield has been more positive. Take, for example, the extensive work on correlates of timing of maturation. During the transition to adolescence, physical maturity status is correlated with predictions and ratings of social success and of social and emotional maturity by adults and peers, with late-maturing boys and early-maturing girls being rated less favorably than early-maturing boys and on-time or late-maturing girls (e.g., Blyth et al. 1981; Faust, 1960; Jones, 1965; Jones & Bayley, 1950; Jones & Mussen, 1958; Simmons, Blyth, & McKinney, 1983). Furthermore, self-esteem and satisfaction with body tend to be lower for the former groups (Blyth, Simmons, & Zakin, 1985; Duncan, Ritter, Dornbusch, Gross, & Carlsmith, 1985; Mussen & Jones, 1957; Simmons et al., 1983). Thus, there is ample reason to seek explanations of timing effects on self-evaluation that incorporate perceptions of others' responses to physical-maturity cues and young persons' own self-perceptions of deviations from norms of appearance.

An even finer grained picture of the implications of the social context for individual adaptation emerges from studies of menarche. The gist of these studies is that this salient pubertal event elicits different reactions from adolescent females, depending on several contextual influences that appear to change the understanding and emotional significance of menstruation. For example, girls from families with negative, secretive attitudes toward sexuality often experienced menarche more negatively than girls from families with more positive, open attitudes. Girls who had little or no information about their bodies and the nature and significance of menarche tended to respond with more fear and distaste than those who were better prepared (Brooks-Gunn & Ruble, 1982, 1983; Greif & Ulman, 1982; Rierdan & Koff, 1985). Girls who experienced menarche very early were more likely to find it fearsome and negative than those who were on time or late, perhaps because early maturers were less likely to have been given adequate information about what to expect (Ruble & Brooks-Gunn, 1982). Thus, the emotional and perceived physical effects of menarche varied in comprehensible ways as a function of contextual variables. These findings buttress the point that the subjective experience of physical change is significant in determining individuals' responses to pubertal transitions.

Such findings put considerable pressure on those who study the transition to adolescence to provide new models to guide research on the interaction of biological, individual, and social factors. The prevailing view is that the interplay among these factors occurs as a *transaction,* in which changes in the individual produce concomitant reactions from others, which in turn alter the influences on further developmental change. For example, signs of physical maturation may trigger age-graded behavioral expectations from others that later maturers of the same age do not face so intensely. These reactions and expectations create a different set of environmental opportunities and demands for early and late maturers, which, in turn, affect their subsequent development (e.g., Lerner, 1985).

This general model is not a new one in developmental psychology or in psychobiology, nor is it unique to an interest in older children and adolescents (e.g., Sameroff, 1975). In the 1957 conference on the concept of development that was a forerunner of the Minnesota Symposium series, T. C. Schneirla (1957) described a similar pattern, which he called a *circular function:*

An indispensable feature of development is that of circular relationships . . . as the processes of each given stage open the way for further stimulus-reaction relationships depending on the scope of the instrinsic and extrinsic conditions then prevalent. (p. 86)

Then, as now, the difficulties of documenting the implicit action-reaction phases implied by transactions or circular functions were obvious. Schneirla noted, in fact, that:

> As an abstract operation, for heuristic purposes, (maturation and experience) may be conceptualized disjunctively in their effects upon development . . . . But realistically, the two concepts must be considered as standing for complex systems of intervening variables closely integrated at all stages of development. (p. 86)

The data we now have from the transition to adolescence are indeed disjunctive, to use Schneirla's word, from the perspective of a transactional model. For example, there is evidence that adults and peers perceive individuals of different pubertal statuses differently and that self-evaluation tends to be lower for the groups that traditionally are rated as less socially successful or desirable, but relatively little is known about the processes by which self and others' perceptions may affect psychosocial outcomes. Similarly, girls' perceptions and reported emotional responses to menarche vary with contexts, but as yet there is no information about the part of the transactional process by which these variations would affect adaptation in the general population. At present, researchers may be said to be following an implicit strategy of examining the various segments of hypothesized transactions in a more or less piecemeal fashion in hopes of aggregating a network of evidence that will eventually bear on the more complex dynamic process; but we are far from reaching that goal.

As in other periods of life, the transactional model of development must become more integral to research designs in the study of the transition to adolescence if it is to be more than an appealing metaphor for developmental change. As we accumulate more evidence, the pressure builds for more elaborate designs to analyze the transactions that may help to account for some of the phenomena. For example, a team at the National Institutes of Health (Nottelman et al., 1987) have recently found that levels of adrenal androgens and sex steroids, relative to age, show different patterns of association to four categories of psychosocial measures: competence; self-image; behavior problems; and affective states, such as depression and anxiety. In sorting out the linkages that explain these general correlations, these researchers intend to track the associations between different hormones and changes in physical morphology and capabilities on one hand and changes in social context and interpersonal reactions. A design that addresses, over time, the possible transactions between hormonal changes in the individual and the possible pathways in the social context is the minimal requirement for an adequate analysis of correlations between hormonal concomitants of puberty and social and emotional characteristics.

At this point, the study of pubertal change virtually stands alone as a vehicle for analyzing the role of differential rates of biological maturation in human development. One reason for this is that biological change in adolescence is clearly discernible and its social significance is widely—albeit implicitly—agreed upon. Consequently, the often subtle interplay between primary biological change, social mediating factors, and behavior and adjustment can be tracked more readily during pubescence than at other times in the life cycle. The chapters in this volume take us farther in both of the classic directions of research on pubertal change: in understanding how gonadal hormones may and may not be implicated in intensified gender differences in behavior at puberty (Chapter 2), and in what we know about the processes through which pubertal status may affect psychosocial functioning and adaptation in interpersonal relationships (Chapters 3 and 5). These chapters provide some of the best current examples of the thoughtful incorporation of biological markers into the study of developmental processes.

ENVIRONMENTAL CHANGE AND INDIVIDUAL DEVELOPMENT

A second theme deals with an aspect of developmental transitions that is somewhat more gradual than the biological changes of puberty, but nonetheless distinctively marked in the experience of most children: namely, normative and historical changes in the environment. Let me hasten to add that behavioral and social scientists in general—and psychologists, in particular—still have rudimentary concepts and skills for characterizing environmental influences as richly and precisely as we might wish (e.g., Magnusson, 1981). Yet there are clear signs that environmental change is an essential element in understanding developmental transitions. In the case of the transition to adolescence, let me note briefly several emerging lines of research on the sources of environmental change and their role in development.

Changes in Age-Related Behavioral Expectations

The first is an interest in environmental changes that stem from age-graded expectations for behavioral and emotional functioning. Two examples ilustrate this point. First, data from the Human Relations Area Files show that the age of 12 or 13 is a major demarcation point for age-related expectations across cultures, signifying the time when adultlike physical capability, combined with greater cognitive and social maturity, produces a qualitative shift in typical behaviors (Rogoff, Sellers, Pirrotta, Fox, & White, 1975). This work documents a general change in expectations at the beginning of adolescence that contrasts with expectations for younger children. It may be, of course, that this apparently age-related change actually reflects a presumed association with biological change. Hence, my second example.

In research at the Institute of Child Development (Collins, Schoenleber, &

Westby, 1987), we have attempted a more finely grained analysis of the expectations held by middle-class adults in the United States for children of different ages within the transition to adolescence. Using a Behavioral Expectations Inventory for assessing behaviors that are commonly thought to change between the ages of 11 and 16, we had adults—none of whom were themselves parents of adolescents—indicate whether each of the 28 items was "characteristic" or "not characteristic" of each of three age groups: 11- to 12-year-olds, 13- to 14-year-olds; and 15- to 16-year-olds. There were separate instruments for boys and for girls, and each group of adults rated only one sex. We found that the extent to which items in these categories were expected followed linear patterns, with expectations for 11- to 12-year-olds and 15- to 16-year-olds at the extremes and expectations for 13- to 14-year-olds in the middle. In some categories, of course, adults expected more abrupt changes in behavior within this span of ages. For example, behaviors having to do with communication and sensitivity, like "is moody" and "responds in a surly way to parents' comments," were thought to be characteristic of the older two groups, but not of the younger. A few items, mostly those concerning heterosexual activity and seriousness, were expected for 15- to 16-year-olds, but not the younger two groups. There was, then, quite extensive differentiation of expectations on the basis of age alone, divorced from any cues about individual physical or personal characteristics.

How may expected differences of this sort contribute to environmental change in the transition to adolescence? Some recent studies suggest one way: age-related changes may elicit different attributions about child behaviors than parents have made at earlier points in development. For example, Dix, Ruble, Grusec, and Nixon (1986) compared adults' responses to hypothetical misbehaviors by children and adolescents and found that the older the child, the more likely parents were to infer that that child understood that certain behaviors are wrong, that the transgression was intentional, and that the behavior indicated negative dispositions in the child. Furthermore, when parents inferred that the child was capable of self-control and that the misbehavior was intentional, they were more upset with the child, and they thought punishment, rather than discussion and explanation, was a more appropriate response. Clearly, transgressions by adolescents have a different significance than transgressions by younger children; they trigger a complex of parental judgments and responses to behavior that effectively change the environment. Age-related expectations may be thought of as setting up a process of change that is similar in its implications for subsequent development to the processes described earlier as being triggered by physical maturation.

The influence of age-related changes in expectations is evident in a recent study of age versus pubertal status as a determinant of when adolescents begin to date. Dating is a behavioral transition that has usually been thought to be linked to pubertal change, but Sanford Dornbusch and his colleagues (Dornbusch et al., 1981) used data from the U.S. National Health Examination Survey of 12- to 17-

year-olds to compare pubertal status and age as predictors of whether adolescents had yet had a date. Pubertal status, assessed by physicians according to Tanner's widely accepted criteria, added less than 1% to the variance in dating behavior explained by age. Among adolescents between 12 and 15, all of whom were at the middle stage of pubertal development by Tanner's criteria, the percentage of those who had ever had a date increased linearly and steadily across ages. To address a transactional hypothesis, we still need evidence that this association with age is mediated either by general norms for behavior or by the proximal expectations of others, rather than by physical-maturity status. Dornbusch et al.'s analysis reminds us that, although physical maturation is a change of unquestionable relevance to the development of sexual behavior, many concomitants of social roles and behaviors associated with sexuality are linked to environmental influences, invoked by age-group membership. The pioneering work of Roberta Simmons and her colleagues (Chapter 5) provides evidence that the convergence of biological and environmental changes in age-graded school structures is a particularly significant source of influence on adolescent functioning during the transition to adolescence (Simmons, Blyth, Van Cleave, & Bush, 1979).

Diversity of Environmental Influences

Another common source of environmental change in developmental transitions is a change in the diversity of social contexts and influences to which individuals are exposed. Most of our information on the changing social world of early adolescents is anecdotal and fragmentary, but we know that a larger proportion of time is spent outside of the home than in earlier developmental periods; a larger proportion of out-of-home time, in turn, is spent in situations in which peers are primary (Hartup, 1983; Maccoby & Martin, 1983). The major out-of-home setting of childhood, the school, effectively changes as well; the social field for the elementary school child is usually the self-contained classroom, whereas in junior high and high school the social field broadens to include the school as a whole (Minuchin & Shapiro, 1983). The addition of extracurricular activities and part-time work settings further changes the environment in adolescence (Czikszentmihalyi & Larson, 1984).

Research on children's and adolescents' perceptions of the family and peer systems provides examples of how these increasingly diverse environments are experienced in the transition to adolescence. Consider three findings:

1. Emmerich, Goldman, & Shore (1971) showed that young elementary-school children tend to conceive of their adult and child contacts as part of a single social system, in which higher standards are expected in conduct with adults than with peers; whereas adolescents treat rules of conduct as

though they were governed by two different social systems—one involving adults, and one peers—each of which requires high conduct standards.

2. Hunter (1984, 1985a, 1985b) has recently reported that adolescents distinguish between the nature of their discussion with parents and friends, perceiving discussions with parents to be constructed upon the greater authority and expertise of the parent and conversations with peers as more consistently serving as opportunities to share experiences and perceptions. It is important to note, however, that Hunter (1985a) and a number of other researchers find that adolescents, by their own report, continue to discuss a variety of personal and general topics with parents throughout the adolescent years. The issue is not whether they talk, or even the emotional tenor of the conversations, but the social and personal functions being perceived.

3. Berndt (Berndt & Hoyle, 1985) have documented that expectations regarding relationships with peers—particularly friendships—increase during the transition to adolescence, in the sense that adolescents believe friends are obligated to provide mutual support, caring, and responsibilities to a greater extent than younger children do.

From the perspective of environmental change, these three findings seem to indicate that the parent and peer social systems become more differentiated in the transition to adolescence, but they are also complementary to each other. The relations between them may actually be reciprocal in some important ways. Hartup (1979) has recently suggested that the family system serves a gating function for smooth, successful peer relationships, and Youniss (1980) has argued, in turn, that children may bring to their families from their peer groups knowledge, expectations, and behavioral tactics that enable their families to adjust to the demands of interaction with a rapidly maturing child. Thus, it may not be only the fact of change in each social system that matters for the experiences of the child, but also the ways in which the systems are interrelated.

As in the case of biological changes, it may be that the nature and salience of such changes make the transition to adolescence an especially propitious time to examine changing environments as an element of developmental transition. This is true for school and out-of-school institutional influences as well as the more personal contexts of family and friendships. Simmons' studies of the interplay of family, peer, and school components of the transition to adolescence (Chapter 5) illustrate some effects of increasing diversity of settings that impinge on development during the transition to adolescence.

Historical Milieu and Individual Development

A third, effectively superordinate, theme in the study of environmental change in development concerns the effect of historical milieu on the operative environmental changes that young people experience in the transition to adolescence.

There is now compelling evidence that ontogenetic change in the individual is inextricably embedded in the interpersonal relationships of which he or she is a part and which are themselves colored by ambient economic, cultural, and political forces. This point constrains our analyses of developmental change throughout the life span. For example, research on nutritional deprivations in infancy has indicated that the effects of economic hardships can be significant and persistent. In the life history research by Glen Elder (Chapter 6), the adolescent years have provided a valuable focal point for demonstrating how the impact of a life period can be different, depending on the larger social context.

Let me make a final point about the potential for studying the impact of environmental change in connection with developmental transitions, drawing from the perspective of research on the shift into adolescence. A major difficulty with regard to this or any life period is how to specify the characteristics of relevant environments. So far, our approaches have been relatively impoverished. We usually adopt the notion of a local "learning environment" for socialization and intellectual stimulation. In research we vary environmental features as we understand them one at a time, as in studies of basic learning or perceptual processes, or we treat them in an undifferentiated global fashion, as when social class is used as a summary indicator for what is actually a constellation of social, cultural, and economic variables (Collins, 1984).

A richer conceptual framework is needed to capture the nature of changing external forces on the developing individual, not only the immediate, ambient sources of stimulation that impinge on individuals, but also the culturally normative responses and the survival pressures that form the context for, and give meaning to, experience. Anthropologists have adopted the concept of the ecocultural niche to encompass this broader view. The term pertains to the cumulative historical, social, and economic structures and experiences that give significance to mundane events, as well as to pivotal transitions, in a child's life. Such factors as urban versus rural residence, family status, parental and nonparental child care arrangements, tasks typically assigned to children and adolescents, and the role of women in the society have all been demonstrated to affect important dimensions of developmental transitions across cultures (Weisner, 1984).

One effect of underdeveloped concepts of environment is a paucity of research in which variations in environments are integral to conceptualization and design. Neither in the transition to adolescence nor in other developmental periods is there adequate information on ethnicity and socioeconomic variations. Although there is some evidence of group differences, there is not yet an array of workable methods for examining the changing expectations, opportunities, and demands that impinge upon children in different sociocultural settings during developmental transitions. Similar lacunae exist with respect to variations in family structures. Redressing these deficiencies is essential to gaining knowledge of processes through which environments impinge upon transitions in development.

CONTINUITY AND DISCONTINUITY IN DEVELOPMENT

Finally, the study of biological and environmental changes in the transition to adolescence raises an issue that has long been central to the study of development generally: How are continuity and change balanced in the processes of development?

An illustration of the issue as it emerges in the transition to adolescence comes from the study of parent-child relationships. There are two lines of evidence to support the assumption that family relations constitute a primary context for development well into the adolescent years. First, studies of reported influence show consistent high regard for parents and differentiation between parents and peers in areas to which their influence is pertinent (Hill, 1980). For example, in the Isle of Wight study of 14- to 15-year-olds and their parents (Rutter, Graham, Chadwick, & Yule, 1976), adolescents reported overwhelmingly that they continued to go on outings with their families and that parents approved of their friends; relatively few reported communication difficulties, rejection of mother, and physical withdrawal, although the incidence of these behaviors was higher in psychiatric populations. Parents' reports were concordant with adolescents'.

Second, findings from a number of studies indicate that differences in families are correlated with differences in adolescent adjustment and behavior in much the same way that family and child differences are associated in earlier periods. Such characteristics as positive emotional expression, openness to communication, but firm guidelines for behavior and a teaching orientation are associated both with continuing positive relationships with parents and with patterns of competence (Baumrind, 1968; Cooper, Grotevant, & Condon, 1984; Elder, 1963; Hauser et al., 1984). Although these studies of families do not include a temporal dimension or specific ties to developmental change, comparisons across age periods imply that the functions of parents in the lives of their offspring are similar to their functions in earlier periods.

It is clear, however, that there is a major change during this transition in the nature and content of interactions and in relative influence of child in family decision making. Decrease in positive affective expression is common in the 10- to 12-year-old period (Maccoby, 1984; Papini & Datan, 1983). If you extrapolate an age curve from many reports of contentiousness between parents and children in different age periods, it looks quite curvilinear, with an increase between 10 and 13 and a decrease beginning about 16 or 17 (Montemayor, 1983). The rising curve of contentiousness appears in parallel to increases in assertiveness and attempts at dominance. For example, in a short-term longitudinal study, Steinberg (1981) found that patterns of conflict changed as a function of boys' pubertal status, with assertiveness, as assessed by interruptions and refusal to yield, peaking at mid-puberty. Furthermore, there was a decline in mother's influence relative to son in family decision making over the course of the longitudinal study. The family interactions of girls show somewhat different, but no less pronounced, differences as a function of pubertal status (Hill, Holmbeck, Marlow, Green, & Lynch, 1985). What we know about parent-child relationships in the early adolescent years thus far implies that change is taking place, but that a fair amount of functionally significant continuity exists across these years. The notion of a *transformation,* but not a disjunction or rupture, in relationships seems to fit the evidence.

As the term implies, the transformation in family relationships involves both continuity and discontinuity, both of which may well be necessary to the various adjustments and realignments that are required as one member of the family moves from childhood toward adulthood. The idea that discontinuity is essential for developmental change has been a major theme in the study of the transitions of early life. Certainly, cognitive-developmental theories such as Piaget's (1981) imply that moderate inconsistency provides the impetus for change. In the study of adolescence, Anna Freud (1958) and Peter Blos (1962) are among several theorists who have argued that perturbation is a feature of healthy growth. The questions are, how much and what kinds of discontinuity are optimal, and under what conditions is one at risk from marked discontinuity? These themes are at the heart of several chapters in this volume: in Hill's and Smetana's concern with the concept of conflict in family relationships (Chapters 3 and 4), in Simmons' notion of an "arena of comfort" in times of precipitous environmental change (Chapter 5), and in Elder's discussion of the developmental impact of deprivation in the Great Depression (Chapter 6).

The continuity-discontinuity issue is of most interest with regard to the transition to adolescence for the reason that it has preoccupied students of early development: because it bears on the likelihood of altered developmental trajectories for individuals. How malleable are human beings in the face of the changing experiences, opportunities, and demands of the transition to adolescence? The question of whether malleability is greater before adolescence is difficult to address, because there are only a few studies of samples that have been studied longitudinally from an age that pre-dates adolescence. The findings that we do have imply that malleability declines—but by no means disappears—with age (Lerner, 1984). And in some cases, the longitudinal evidence linking adolescent development to adult status on a variety of psychosocial variables indicates that conditions that appear to be dysfunctional in adolescence may actually be associated with greater flexibility and competence in later life (Elder, 1980; Livson & Peskin, 1980). Glen Elder's work indicates how historical period may interact with adolescent maturational patterns to produce these findings. Specifying the cross-time linkages between adolescent development and events in both earlier and later life periods carries a number of methodological difficulties and some conceptual challenges, as well (Connell & Furman, 1984; Hinde & Bateson, 1984). Neither approaches that emphasize change nor those that focus exclusively on documenting continuities are likely to illuminate the simultaneity of continuity and change in development. Elder's work (Chapter 6) is unique in the lens it provides on the forces that affect developmental trajectories in adolescence.

SOME FINAL WORDS

These points are meant to show how the study of the transition to adolescence has grown out of, and how it is now helping to extend, our knowledge of basic issues in development. To be sure, despite considerable progress in general in the study of developmental processes during this period, progress has been somewhat uneven across developmental domains. The greatest advances have come in the study of biological changes and psychosocial development, with a considerable lag in areas such as cognitive functioning. This gap must be closed, lest ability to advance in other areas of transitional change eventually be impaired. To date, however, the study of the transition to adolescence should be viewed as enriching our understanding of issues that transcend adolescence or any single period of life and that stimulate our thinking about the study of human development generally.

REFERENCES

Baumrind, D. (1968). Authoritarian vs. authoritative parental control. *Adolescence, 3*, 255–272.

Berndt, T., & Hoyle, S. (1985). Stability and change in childhood and adolescent friendships. *Developmental Psychology, 21*, 1007–1015.

Blos, P. (1962). *On Adolescence*. New York: Free Press.

Blyth, D., Simmons, R., Bulcroft, R., Felt, D., Van Cleave, E., & Bush, D. (1981). The effects of physical development on self-image and satisfaction with body image for early adolescent males. In R. Simmons (Ed.), *Research in community and mental health* (Vol. 2), Greenwich, CT: JAI Press.

Blyth, D., Simmons, R., & Zakin, D. (1985). Satisfaction with body image for early adolescent females: The impact of pubertal timing within different school environments. *Journal of Youth and Adolescence, 14*, 207–225.

Brooks-Gunn, J., & Ruble, D. (1982). The development of menstrual-related beliefs and behaviors during early adolescence. *Child Development, 53*, 1567–1577.

Brooks-Gunn, J., & Ruble, D. (1983). The experience of menarche from a developmental perspective. In J. Brooks-Gunn & A. Petersen (Eds.), *Girls at puberty: Biological and psychosocial perspectives* (pp. 155–178). New York: Plenum.

Collins, W. A. (1984). The status of basic research on middle childhood. In W. A. Collins (Ed.), *Development during middle childhood: The years from six to twelve* (pp. 398–421). Washington, DC: National Academy of Sciences Press.

Collins, W. A., Schoenleber, K., & Westby, S. (1987). *The Behavior Expectations Inventory: Middle-class adults' expectations for 11–16 year olds*. Unpublished manuscript, Institute of Child Development, University of Minnesota.

Connell, J., & Furman, W. (1984). The study of transitions: Conceptual and methological issues. In R. Emde & R. Harmon (Eds.), *Continuities and discontinuities in development* (pp. 153–174). New York: Plenum.

Cooper, C., Grotevant, H., & Condon, S. (1984). Individuality and connectedness in the family as a context for adolescent identity formation and role-taking skill. In H. Grotevant & C. Cooper (Eds.), *New directions for child development: Adolescent development in the family* (pp. 43–60). San Francisco: Jossey-Bass.

Czikszentmihalyi, M., & Larson, R. (1984). *Being adolescent: Conflict and growth in the teenage years.* New York: Basic Books.

Dix, T., Ruble, D., Grusec, J., & Nixon, S. (1986). Social cognition in parents: Inferential and affective reactions to children of three age levels. *Child Development, 57,* 879–894.

Dornbusch, S., Carlsmith, J., Gross, R., Martin, J., Jennings, D., Rosenberg, A., & Duke, P. (1981). Sexual development, age, and dating: A comparison of biological and social influences upon one set of behaviors. *Child Development, 52,* 179–185.

Duncan, P. Ritter, P., Dornbusch, S., Gross, R., & Carlsmith, J. M. (1985). The effects of pubertal timing on body image, school behavior, and deviance. *Journal of Youth and Adolescence, 14,* 227–235.

Elder, G. H., Jr. (1963). Parental power legitimation and its effect on the adolescent. *Sociometry, 26,* 50–65.

Elder, G. H., Jr. (1980). Adolescence in historical perspective. In J. Adelson (Ed.), *Handbook of adolescent psychology* (pp. 3–46). New York: Wiley.

Emmerich, W., Goldman, K. S., & Shore, R. E. (1971). Differentiation and development of social norms. *Journal of Personality and Social Psychology, 18,* 323–353.

Faust, M. (1960). Developmental maturity as a determinant of prestige in adolescent girls. *Child Development, 31,* 173–184.

Ford, C., & Beach, F. (1951). *Patterns of sexual behavior.* New York: Harper & Row.

Freud, A. (1958). Adolescence. In R. Eissler, A. Freud, H. Hartman, & M. Kris (Eds.), *Psychoanalytic study of the child* (Vol. 13). New York: International Universities Press.

Greif, E., & Ulman, K. (1982). The psychological impact of menarche on early adolescent females: A review of the literature. *Child Development, 53,* 1413–1430.

Hartup, W. (1979). Two social worlds of childhood. *American Psychologist, 39,* 944–950.

Hartup, W. (1983). Peer relations. In E. M. Hetherington (Ed.), *Handbook of child psychology: Vol. 4. Socialization, personality, and social development* (pp. 103–196). New York: Wiley.

Hauser, S., Powers, S., Noam, G., Jacobson, A., Weiss, B., & Follansbee, D. (1984). Familial contexts of adolescent ego development. *Child Development, 55,* 195–213.

Hill, J. (1980). The family. In L. Steinberg (Ed.), *Toward adolescence: The middle school years NSSE yearbook* (pp. 32–55). Chicago: University of Chicago Press.

Hill, J., Holmbeck, G., Marlow, L., Green, T., & Lynch, M. (1985). Menarcheal status and parent-child relations in families of seventh-grade girls. *Journal of Youth and Adolescence, 14,* 301–316.

Hinde, R., & Bateson, P. (1984). Discontinuities versus continuities in behavioral development and the neglect of process. *International Journal of Behavioral Development, 7,* 129–143.

Hunter, F. T. (1984). Socializing procedures in parent-child and friendship relations during adolescence. *Developmental Psychology, 20,* 1092–1099.

Hunter, F. T. (1985a). Adolescents' perceptions of discussions with parents and friends. *Developmental Psychology, 21,* 433–440.

Hunter, F. T. (1985b). Individual adolescents' perceptions of interactions with friends and parents. *Journal of Early Adolescence, 5,* 295–305.

Jones, M. C. (1965). Psychological correlates of somatic development. *Child Development, 36,* 899–911,

Jones, M. C., & Bayley, N. (1950). Physical maturing among boys as related to behavior. *Journal of Educational Psychology, 41,* 129–148.

Jones, M. C., & Mussen, P. H. (1958). Self-conceptions, motivations and interpersonal attitudes of early and late maturing girls. *Child Development, 29,* 491–501.

Lerner, R. (1984). *On the nature of human plasticity.* New York: Cambridge University Press.

Lerner, R. (1985). Adolescent maturational changes and psychosocial development: A dynamic interactional perspective. *Journal of Youth and Adolescence, 14,* 355–372.

Livson, N., & Peskin, H. (1980). Perspectives on adolescence from longitudinal research. In J. Adelson (Ed.), *Handbook of adolescent psychology* (pp. 47–98). New York: Wiley.

Maccoby, E. (1984). Middle childhood in the context of the family. In W. A. Collins (Ed.), *Development during middle childhood: The years from six to twelve* (pp. 184–239). Washington, DC.: National Academy of Sciences Press.

Maccoby, E., & Martin, J. (1983). Socialization in the context of the family. In E. M. Hetherington (Ed.), *Handbook of child psychology: Vol. 4. Socialization, personality, and social development* (pp. 1–102). New York: Wiley.

Magnusson, D. (1981). Problems in environmental analysis: An introduction. In D. Magnusson (Ed.), *Toward a psychology of situations: An interactional perspective* (pp. 3–10). Hillsdale, NJ: Lawrence Erlbaum Associates.

Masten, A. (1986, October). *Psychopathology in early adolescence.* Paper delivered at a conference on development during early adolescence, Charleston, SC.

Minuchin, P., & Shapiro, E. (1983). The school as a context for social development. In E. M. Hetherington (Ed.), *Handbook of child psychology: Vol. 4. Socialization, personality, and social development* (pp. 197–274). New York: Wiley.

Money, J., & Ehrhardt, A. (1972). *Man and woman, boy and girl.* New York: Mentor.

Montemayor, R. (1983). Parents and adolescents in conflict: All families some of the time and some families most of the time. *Journal of Early Adolescence, 3,* 83–103.

Mussen, P., & Jones, M. C. (1957). Self-concepts, motivations, and interpersonal attitudes of late and early maturing boys. *Child Development, 28,* 243–256.

Newcombe, N., & Dubas, J. (1987). Individual differences in cognitive ability: Are they related to timing of puberty? In R. Lerner & T. Foch (Eds.), *Biological-psychosocial interactions in early adolescence* (pp. 249–302). Hillsdale, NJ: Lawrence Erlbaum Associates.

Nottelman, E., Susman, E., Blue, J., Inoff-Germain, G., Dorn, L., Loriaux, D., Cutler, Jr., G., & Chrousos, G. (1987). Gonadal and adrenal hormone correlates of adjustment in early adolescence. In R. Lerner & T. Foch (Eds.), *Biological-psychosocial interactions in early adolescence* (pp. 303–324). Hillsdale, NJ: Lawrence Erlbaum Associates.

Papini, D., & Datan, N. (1983, April). *Transitions into adolescence: An interactionist perspective.* Paper presented at the biennial meetings of the Society for Research in Child Development, Detroit, MI.

Petersen, A. (in press). Adolescence. In *Annual Review of Psychology.*

Piaget, J. (1981). *Intelligence and affectivity: Their relationship during child development.* Palo Alto, CA: Annual Reviews, Inc.

Rierdan, J., & Koff, E. (1985). Timing of menarche and initial menstrual experience. *Journal of Youth and Adolescence, 14,* 237–244.

Rogoff, B., Sellers, M., Pirrotta, S., Fox, N., & White, S. (1975). Age of assignment of roles and responsibilities to children: A cross-cultural survey. *Human Development, 18,* 353–369.

Ruble, D., & Brooks-Gunn, J. (1982). The experience of menarche. *Child Development, 53,* 1557–1566.

Rutter, M., Graham, P., Chadwick, O., & Yule, W. (1976). Adolescent turmoil: Fact or fiction? *Journal of Child Psychology and Psychiatry, 17,* 35–56.

Sameroff, A. (1975). Transactional models in early social relations. *Human Development, 18,* 65–79.

Schneirla, T. C. (1957). The concept of development in comparative psychology. In D. Harris (Ed.), *The concept of development* (pp. 78–108). Minneapolis: University of Minnesota Press.

Simmons, R., Blyth, D., & McKinney, K. (1983). The social and psychological effects of puberty on white females. In J. Brooks-Gunn & A. Petersen (Eds.), *Girls at puberty; Biological and psychosocial perspectives* (pp. 229–272). New York: Plenum.

Simmons, R., Blyth, D., Van Cleave, E., & Bush, D. (1979). Entry into early adolescence: The impact of school structure, puberty, and early dating on self-esteem. *American Sociological Review, 44,* 948–967.

Steinberg, L. (1981). Transformations in family relations at puberty. *Developmental Psychology, 6*(17), 833–840.

Weisner, T. (1984). Ecocultural niches of middle childhood: A cross-cultural perspective. In W. A. Collins (Ed.), *Development during middle childhood: The years from six to twelve* (pp. 335–36). Washington, DC: National Academy of Sciences Press.

Youniss, J. (1980). *Parents and peers in social development.* Chicago: University of Chicago Press.

2 Hormones and Behavior at Puberty: Activation or Concatenation

Christopher L. Coe
University of Wisconsin

Kevin T. Hayashi
Stanford University School of Medicine

Seymour Levine
Stanford University School of Medicine

It is often assumed that the behavioral changes observed during adolescence are strongly influenced by the hormonal events of puberty. A number of researchers have suggested, for example, that increasing testosterone levels enhance a predisposition for aggression in adolescent males or stimulate parent-offspring conflict (Kreuz & Rose, 1972; Olweus, Mattson, Schalling, & Low, 1980; Steinberg, in press). Similarly, observations of the behavior of children with abnormal hormone conditions, such as precocious puberty or the 5α-reductase deficiency, have led investigators to conclude that pubertal hormones play an important role in the development of eroticism and adult, sex-typical behavior (Imperato-McGinley, Peterson, & Gautier, 1981; Money & Ehrhardt, 1972). However, we must remain cautious about attributing a direct hormone causation to all behavioral changes at puberty because a correlation between hormonal and somatic change may partly underlie some of the behavioral effects. Studies on adolescents have shown that body appearance is an important determinant of both self-image and the reactions of others (Simmons, Blyth, & McKinney, 1983; Tobin-Richards, Boxer, & Petersen, 1983), and many of the physical changes at puberty, including body hair and breast development, are directly caused by the increasing secretion of steroid hormones from the gonads and adrenals (Gupta, Attanasio, & Raaf, 1975; Olweus, Mattson, Schalling & Row, 1980; Tanner, 1962).

In this chapter we provide additional evidence that questions the antecedent role of pubertal hormones in inducing the behavioral changes observed during adolescence. Our studies suggest that the pubertal changes in physiology and behavior should be viewed as co-occuring processes that parallel one another because of a common trajectory laid down in fetal life. The coincidental timing of physical, hormonal, and behavioral events at puberty leads one naturally to conclude that they are causally linked, when some of the temporal association may actually be due to a similar maturational clock started in the CNS during sexual differentiation. This hypothesis is based on detailed study of the physical and behavioral maturation of developing monkeys across the pubertal transition. Half of the monkeys were gonadectomized prior to puberty in order to evaluate how gonadal hormones control the timing and expression of behavioral and morphological change at puberty.

Money and Ehrhardt (1972) provided the most widely used theoretical framework for explaining the emergence of adult, sex-typical behavior (Fig. 2.1). According to their model, gender identity is established in infancy when the social environment reinforces a biological disposition created by the hormonal milieu in fetal life. Subsequently, this juvenile "gender identity receives further confirmation from the hormonal changes of puberty" (p. 4) that induce eroticisim and morphological changes in the adolescent. Money and Ehrhardt's thinking was strongly influenced by extensive animal research indicating that hormones exert an "organizational" influence on the fetus during sexual differentiation and an "activational" influence on phenotypic expression during adult life. This two-stage model of hormone action was originally proposed to account

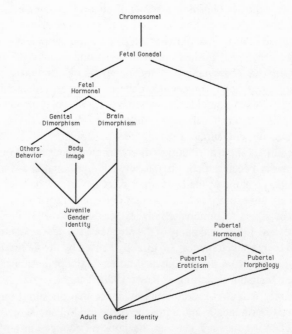

FIG. 2.1.   Model proposed by Money and Ehrhardt (1972) for understanding the influence of gonadal hormones on behavior. Reprinted from *Man & Woman, Boy & Girl*, Baltimore: The Johns Hopkins University Press, p. 3.

for sexually dimorphic anatomy, and was later applied to behavioral processes (Beach, 1948; Young, 1961). Notwithstanding some interesting exceptions in lower vertebrates (Crews, 1987), the organizational and activational model of hormone action has received broad support when applied to the mediation of sexual behavior. For example, androgens in the mammalian fetus and neonate usually establish a predisposition for mounting behavior, which is stimulated by the presence of a receptive partner and facilitated by appropriate gonadal hormone levels in the adult. However, we believe that a simple application of the activational component of the model will continue to be inadequate to account for the emergence of more complex behavior patterns, especially in the higher primates and humans.

The coincidental timing of hormonal and behavioral changes in the normal adolescent makes it difficult to distinguish hormone activation of behavior at puberty from a common maturational process that could induce parallel changes (i.e., chronological age). This point can best be illustrated with some behavioral data that we collected on our closest evolutionary relative, the chimpanzee. Observations on the behavior of 9 male chimpanzees ranging from 1 to 14 years of age were recorded over a 3-year period (Coe & Levine, 1983). The data of interest here are the frequency of male displays shown while the chimpanzees lived relatively undisturbed in two social groups within large outdoor enclosures (1.5 acres) at the Stanford Primate Facility (Fig. 2.2). Male displays are used to convey aggressive intent, and males must become proficient with the charging display before they have to employ it in adult dominance interactions. Figure 2.2 presents the average hourly number of displays shown by males at 1-year age intervals (1–4 subjects per point). Rudimentary motoric elements of the display began to appear more frequently at 5–6 years of age, when testosterone titers were beginning to rise, and charging displays were regularly shown by 9- to 11-year-old males, coinciding with the onset of gonadal puberty (Martin, Swenson, & Collins, 1977). By 13–15 years of age, we have observed dominance struggles and ultimately outright aggression between previously friendly males (Coe & Levin, 1980). The timing of these behavioral changes would certainly appear to implicate an activational effect of the rising testosterone titers.

A reasonable interpretation would be that testosterone is capable of activating a neural substrate for aggression and dominance-related behavior. Similarly, annual variation in the level of aggression shown by seasonally breeding monkeys has led investigators to believe that rising testosterone levels stimulate increased fighting between males as the mating season approaches (Holloway, 1974). Problems with a causal model emerge, however, when one tries to incorporate findings from other types of studies. If testosterone underlies aggressiveness, then castration should markedly reduce aggression in adult males. However, the natural occurrence of an agonadal condition in the dominant male of a rhesus monkey group did not lead to a fall in his rank, nor did castration of the dominant males in groups of squirrel monkeys (Bernstein, Gordon, & Peterson,

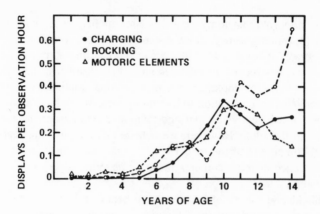

FIG. 2.2.   Maturational changes in the expression of display behavior by male chimpanzees. Increases in display frequency were observed across the pubertal transition into adulthood (from Coe & Levine, 1983).

1979; Green, Whalen, Rutley, & Battie, 1972). Studies on aggression toward an unfamiliar intruder indicated that castrated tamarin monkeys were just as likely as intact monkeys to attack the introduced subject (Epple, 1978). Further, castrated squirrel monkey males can have a higher dominance rank than intact subjects when housed in mixed groups (Fig. 2.3), and testosterone levels in intact males cannot be used to predict the dominance position that will be attained in newly formed social groups (Mendoza, Coe, Lowe, & Levine, 1979). Pharmacologically elevating testosterone levels also did not lead to a increase in aggression in male rhesus monkeys and chimpanzees (Bielert, 1978; Doering, McGinnis, Kraemer, & Hamburg, 1980; Gordon, Rose, Grady, & Bernstein, 1979). Although these findings may come as a surprise to some readers, it should be noted that castration in human males has not reliably resulted in decreased hostility in sex offenders or even necessarily in decreased libidinal drive (Chatz, 1972; Field & Williams, 1970; Heim & Hursch, 1979; Kalin, 1979).

It is also erroneous to assume that sex differences in the behavior of primates emerge for the first time at puberty. Differences in the level of play, exploratory and sociosexual behavior can be readily observed in male and female juvenile monkeys while gonadal hormone levels are low prior to puberty (Caine, 1986; Smith, 1978). In addition, studies on female rhesus monkeys that were exposed to androgen treatment *in utero* have indicated that the sex differences in the behavior of juvenile monkeys are largely mediated by the prenatal, organizational action of gonadal hormones (Goy, 1968; Young, Goy, & Phoenix, 1964). Castration of male and female monkey infants at birth also did not alter the predisposition for sex-typical behavior (Goy & McEwen, 1980). These studies evaluated the play and sexual behavior of infant rhesus monkeys through the first year of life. Our studies were designed to extend these observations to include the pubertal transition that occurs at 2.5–3.5 years of age in the squirrel monkey.

The transition from the juvenile to the subadult (adolescent) stage in the monkey is also a time when one can evaluate the emergence of adult sociality and partner preferences. Just as in human adolescence, the subadult monkey must accomplish a number of developmental tasks. In many species of monkeys, the maturing female must shift her orientation from the juvenile peer group to the maternal part of the troop after she reaches menarche. Subadult males face an even more difficult transition in most monkey species because they are forced to emigrate from the natal group, either becoming solitary or joining bachelor male bands for a period of time. This demographic pattern serves to prevent incestuous mating and provides a means of genetic exchange between neighboring troops. It may also provide one explanation for the longer period of adolescence in the male primate, given the dangers involved in this social transition. As long as a male is perceived as immature, he will not be harassed or peripheralized by the resident adult males. He will also not have to compete as vigorously for a position in the adult male dominance hierarchy. Possibly because of the risks involved in male transfer, there has been an interesting reversal in this adolescent social pattern in the great apes. In both the chimpanzee and the gorilla, it is the menarcheal female that emigrates to a new group, not the adolescent male (Goodall et al., 1979; Harcourt, 1979). Our studies on pubescent squirrel monkeys focused on this developmental change in the social affiliation of male and female monkeys. In the squirrel monkey, females remain within the natal group and the maturing female shows an increasing preference for associating

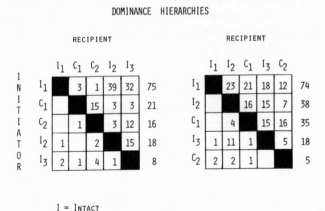

FIG. 2.3. Dominance hierarchies for two groups of squirrel monkeys, each containing 3 intact and 2 castrated males. Note that castrated (C) males ranked higher than some intact (I) males.

with other female members of the troop (Baldwin, 1985). Female interactions with males decrease as the subadult males become increasingly involved in dominance interactions, and eventually the males end up as peripheral members of the troop. In the hopes of delineating a role for gonadal hormones, our behavioral observations focused on the same-sex and opposite-sex partner preferences of the intact and gonadectomized subjects as they matured.

EXPERIMENTAL DESIGN AND METHODS

The puberty studies spanned a 10-year period and involved multi-year assessments of 8 social groups containing a total of 94 subjects (see Table 2.1). Study 1 involved the physical, hormonal, and behavioral assessment of 24 wild-born monkeys that were brought into captivity as juveniles and used to establish the basic measures and experimental paradigm (Coe, Chen, Lowe, Davidson, & Levine, 1981). Study 2 involved the evaluation of puberty in one group of 12 lab-reared subjects to verify that they would show a normal developmental pattern comparable to that of wild-born subjects. This verification was essential because we wanted to assess the pubertal pattern of laboratory-reared subjects in the absence of adult influence and role models. It is known that adult animals can have a strong influence on the development of puberty in primates, and we wanted to remove this complicating factor in the initial studies (Rose, Bernstein, Gordon, & Lindsley, 1978; Ziegler, Savage, Scheffler, & Snowdon, 1987). All lab-reared subjects in Studies 2, 3 and 4 were initially raised in small mother-infant groups containing 4–5 adult females. At 6 months of age, they were weaned into juvenile peer groups, where they remained until 1 year of age when the study groups were established. Thus, all of the sex differences that we describe emerged in the absence of adult influence: No subject ever observed an

TABLE 2.1
Subject Population for the Puberty Studies

		Composition				
Designation	Groups	Intact Males	Castrates	Intact Females	Ov-x Females	N
1. Wild-born juveniles	3	3	0	5	0	24
2. Lab-born juveniles	1	5	0	7	0	12
3. Males with intact females	2	4–5	4	6	0	29
4. Males with ov-x females	2	4–5	4	0	6	29
						94

adult male and none of the juveniles lived with an adult female after 6 months of age.

The subject population of interest for this report derives from Studies 3 and 4. These 4 groups were composed of intact and gonadectomized subjects that were evaluated from 1 to 3.5 years of age. Two of the groups consisted of intact males and castrated males that lived with intact females (combined N = 9,8, and 12, respectively). In contrast, the intact males and castrated males of Study Groups 4 grew up in the presence of ovariectomized females (combined N = 9,8, and 12, respectively). The latter rearing condition was chosen in order to investigate whether male puberty and the normal expression of sex-typical behavior was dependent upon the availability of female hormonal stimuli, a variable known to be of importance in rodents. The gonadectomies were performed on the juvenile monkeys when they reached 1 year of age. At this point, each group was established in a separate animal room at the Stanford Primate Facility where they remained for the duration of the study. The cage environment consisted of 2 pens (12 × 6 × 6 feet high) that were connected by a small doorway. Separating the cages into two distinct units permitted the monkeys to selectively avoid or approach certain group members by choosing a particular cage location. Their social behavior was recorded unobtrusively from within a one-way glass viewing booth that was located at the juncture of the two units. Food and water were available *ad libitum;* fresh fruit and vitamin supplements were provided twice a week. They were purposefully exposed to natural light and climatic conditions of California through large windows behind their cages in order to facilitate the normal development of a seasonal orientation in their reproductive behavior.

The behavioral data are based on focal animal observations in which each monkey in the social group was observed for 5 min on each test day. The 5-min intervals were divided into ten 30-sec intervals, and the frequency and duration of predefined behaviors were scored. Our presentation focuses on social affiliation (spatial proximity that was defined as within 6 in. of another monkey), partner preference and frequency of social play (rough-and-tumble and chase play), and dominance-related behavior (manual grabbing, active and passive displacement, and a species-specific genital display). The data were summarized into annual totals by combining the tallies from 18 observations on each of the 14–15 monkeys in the group, and arranging the group data into a sociogram matrix (initiator rows and recipient columns, as illustrated in Fig. 2.3). The observations spanned the period from December to April each year, the time when we expected the monkeys to undergo pubertal increases in gonadal hormones. Blood samples (1.0 ml) were collected at monthly intervals during this period to verify that the monkeys showed hormone levels characteristic of puberty. For this report, only testosterone data have been presented to show that the intact males were indeed pubescent. During the blood sampling, the monkeys were lightly anesthetized with ether, which allowed us to collect data on changes in body weight and skeletal length (head-rump and knee-heel).

PUBERTAL ONSET
IN LAB-BORN SQUIRREL MONKEYS

As indicated above, one group of 5 male and 7 female squirrel monkeys was established initially to verify that the lab-rearing condition would be conducive to the development of a normal pubertal pattern. The physical and reproductive development of this group of squirrel monkeys from Study 2 is illustrated in Fig. 2.4. As can be seen, a clear sex difference in body weight emerged in the juvenile stage prior to puberty. Males became progressively larger than females after 2 years of age, when females showed a slowing of growth coincident with the onset of puberty. The complete cessation of growth in the postpubertal squirrel monkey female is characteristic of the smaller New World monkeys, although it does differ from Old World monkey females that may show a slow rate of weight gain for several years after menarche (Watts, 1985). The continuation of growth in the male squirrel monkey for several years after puberty is similar to the pattern observed in most primates. Significant weight gain was observed for 2 more years after gonadal puberty, and then the first annual weight fluctuations typical of the adult male were observed (i.e., the so-called fatting response at 4.5 years of age). Postpubertal growth in the male facilitates the development of a sexually dimorphic appearance, and across the Primate Order, it is directly correlated with ultimate body weight and life span for each species (Leutenegger, 1982; Schultz, 1969). That is, larger primate species tend to show more sexual dimorphism in body size, which is associated with a longer period of adolescent growth and a longer overall life span.

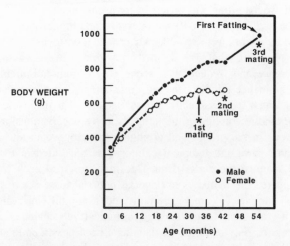

FIG. 2.4. Physical growth of intact male and female squirrel monkeys (Study 2). Lab-reared subjects showed typical sex differences in growth, and the emergence of a normal reproductive pattern.

Figure 2.4 also shows that the monkeys in Study 2 became pubertal at the correct age of 2.5 years, and the first mating period followed the appropriate seasonal orientation for this species. Most monkeys are seasonal breeders and, thus, the first onset of cycling in the female must be coordinated with the adult mating season that occurs at annual intervals. Even in the absence of adults, there were obviously sufficient internal and external *zeitgebers* to correctly orient the onset of puberty in these lab-reared subjects. Fertile mating occurred during this pubertal period, as well as at annual intervals for the next 2 years of the study. Assessment of the males' testosterone levels indicated that the first major increase in gonadal secretion was oriented to the initial breeding period and that it rose and declined in a seasonal pattern thereafter. A seasonal pattern of hormone secretion is characteristic for seasonally breeding monkeys, which do not show a continuous, progressive rise to adult levels like that observed in the great apes and humans. Of particular importance for our subsequent studies, behavioral observations of the group verified that the developing males and females also showed an increasing preference for same-sex partners as they passed through the pubertal transition.

PLASMA TESTOSTERONE LEVELS
IN PUBESCENT MALES

Plasma testosterone levels were analyzed by radioimmunoassay for the 9 intact males that lived with intact females (Study Groups 3) and for the 9 intact males that lived with ovariectomized females (Study Groups 4). Monthly values are portrayed during the first winter period that we anticipated a pubertal increase (December–March) and for the subsequent season (Fig. 2.5). In addition, testosterone titers are portrayed for the month of July when we expected that the pubertal males would show a normal seasonal decline in hormone levels. As can be seen, males showed an increase to pubertal levels of testosterone during the first period, an out-of-season decline, and then a subsequent rise to higher levels during the second winter period. Statistical evaluation by analysis of variance indicated a highly significant effect of age and season, F $(9,144)$ = 13.8, p < .0001. There was not a significant overall effect of the type of female available, although many of the males reared with intact females did have higher testosterone values than those reared with ovariectomized females during the second winter period. Statistical evaluation of the average testosterone values indicated that intact males living with intact females had significantly higher levels at this older age ($t(16)$ = 2.12, p < .05). We conclude that the male squirrel monkey does not require stimulation from cycling females in order to undergo a normal pubertal sequence in testosterone. The age at puberty and the magnitude of the initial testosterone rise must be determined by internal factors in the squirrel monkey. However, there may be a greater effect of female stimuli

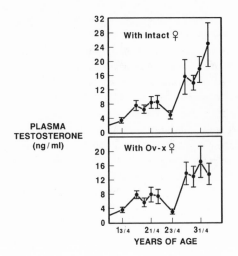

PLASMA
TESTOSTERONE
(ng / ml)

FIG. 2.5. Plasma testosterone levels in intact males before and after puberty (from Studies 3 and 4). The pubertal increase followed a normal, seasonal pattern: higher levels were observed at the correct age and time of year.

on male hormone output during later adulthood. In earlier studies we (Coe et al., 1981; Mendoza et al., 1979), have found that adult males can re-orient their annual testosterone cycle to track the ovarian activity of females. Fertile reproductive activity with intact females and the absence of sexual activity with ovariectomized females may have accounted for the emergence of a difference in the testosterone values of intact males during the Subadult stage that was not apparent in the pubescent males.

PHYSICAL GROWTH IN PUBERTAL MALES AND FEMALES

The body weight data for the 18 intact males and 16 castrated males were analyzed across the same 2-year period. Mean body weights have been presented at 6-month intervals corresponding to the periods shown for the testosterone data above (Fig. 2.6). Analysis of variance revealed a main effect for gonadectomy, indicating that castrated males were significantly lighter throughout the study, $F (1,32) = 6.76, p < .014$. However, both intact and castrated subjects did show a progressive increase in body weight across the 2 years that was clearly of the male pattern. That is, although the weight achieved by castrated males was lower, their growth was sustained even in the absence of a testicular puberty. In this regard, it is noteworthy that the difference in body weight between intact and

castrated subjects was already evident before the first pubertal surge in testosterone, suggesting that the testes may have a general effect on growth even in the
so-called latent period. One other aspect of the data warrants comment. Although
the presence of intact females did not differentially affect the testosterone levels
of intact males during the Pubescent stage and only a small increase occurred in
some males with intact females during Subadult stage, we were surprised to see
that the intact males living with intact females did grow to be somewhat heavier
by 3.25 years of age, $F (3,96) = 21.02, p < .0001$. This difference in the weight
of intact males in the two housing conditions was relatively small (31 g) during
the Subadult stage, but it took on greater significance in the following year when
only intact males that had been reared with intact females showed the annual
weight gain typical for adult males (i.e., the fatting response at 4.5 years of age).
As with the testosterone finding, we believe that the difference may be accounted
for by the occurrence of sexual activity with the intact females, which was not
observed with the ovariectomized females.

The body weight and growth of females were analyzed across the same time
period and led to a similar conclusion about the limited effect of gonadal hormones on the timing of weight gain. As observed in the males, there was a
general effect of gonadectomy on body weight, but it was already apparent
before the onset of cycling in the intact females, $F (1,22) = 4.09, p < .055$.
Intact females weighed on the average 30–50 g more than their ovariectomized
counterparts across the study. Nevertheless, the temporal pattern of growth was
similar in intact and ovariectomized females, and all females showed a general
cessation of growth by 2.75 years of age (Fig. 2.7). The cessation of growth in

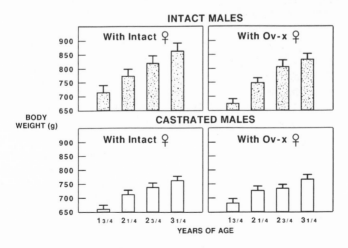

FIG. 2.6. Physical growth in intact and castrated males that lived with
either intact or ovariectomized females. Castrated males were smaller,
but showed a pattern of growth like that of intact males.

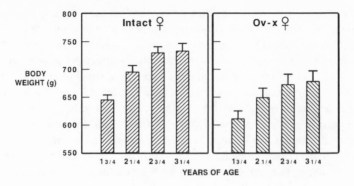

FIG. 2.7.   Physical growth in intact and ovariectomized (ov-x) females.
Note that ov-x females showed an age-appropriate cessation of physical growth.

females is often attributed to the influence of estrogen on fusing the epiphyses of
the long bones. Although this is undoubtedly true, there must also be an additional physiological factor underlying the cessation of growth in order to account
for the data on the ovariectomized females. After the correct chronological age
for menarche, the ovariectomized females showed almost no increase in weight:
an average 7 g increase in weight between 2.75 and 3.25 years of age. In keeping
with these data, Goy and Kemnitz (1983) have reported that rhesus monkey
females exposed to androgen *in utero* have a masculinized temporal pattern of
growth and continue to grow for 3 years longer than the normal female (i.e.,
more malelike). Interestingly, the body weight of these androgenized rhesus
females is like that of normal females during the juvenile stage: They do not
weigh more than the normal female until the period of extended growth. We have
rechecked the weight of the our ovariectomized squirrel monkey females recently
now that they are mature adults, and they truly showed a cessation of growth at
the correct age for normal females. Again, these data suggest that the temporal
pattern of body weight growth is established earlier in life and is not controlled
by the concomitant changes in gonadal hormones at puberty.

    One factor underlying body weight in the squirrel monkey is skeletal matura-
tion because weight is strongly correlated with skeletal length in this species.
Figure 2.8 portrays data on skeletal length for all males and females obtained
during the Pubescent period. The correlation between body weight and head-
rump length was even stronger in females than in males. The strength of this
correlation in the squirrel monkey may be partly due to the fact that the achievement of adult skeletal length is closely associated with the onset of puberty. This
differs from humans, who show a dissociation between time of puberty and final
adult height, especially in the case of males (Watts, 1985). As mentioned above,
male squirrel monkeys do continue to gain weight after the onset of testicular

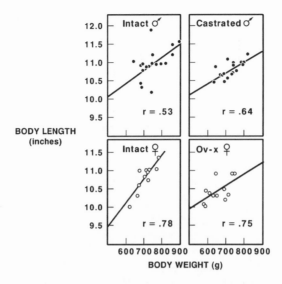

FIG. 2.8. Correlation between body weight and skeletal length in pubescent male and female squirrel monkeys.

puberty, but the additional weight reflects greater girth rather than length. It is during this period of extended male growth that an effect of gonadectomy becomes more apparent because intact males ultimately weigh several hundred grams more than do castrates as mature adults. Moreover, when intact males grew to be somewhat larger between 3.5 and 4.5 years of age, the effect of living with intact females became more evident than during the Pubescent stage.

SOCIAL RELATIONS OF PUBERTAL AND SUBADULT MONKEYS

The social behavior of the 4 monkey groups of Studies 3 and 4 has been summarized into two annual blocks to facilitate presentation. The first period has been designated as Pubescent and the second as Subadult. The data were collected between December and March and analyzed by summing the 18 tallies per subject into sociograms for each group. Social affiliation, as reflected by spatial proximity, provided a good index of the developing social dynamics within each group. The proximity data portrayed in the graphs are based on 180 scores per subject when any monkey located within 6 inches was noted on the data sheet. Males and females, intact or gonadectomized, did not differ significantly in their relative level of spatial proximity to other monkeys. On the average, monkeys spent an average of 6%-10% of the time proximal to other monkeys. This comparable baseline in the pubescent monkey was advantageous for the follow-

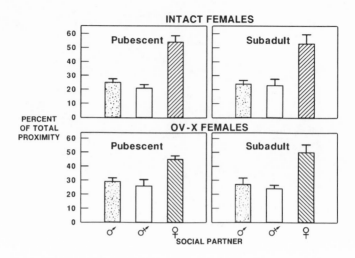

FIG. 2.9. Partner preferences of intact and ovariectomized females based on spatial proximity scores. Both types of females showed the species-appropriate preference for same-sex partners.

ing analysis of partner preferences. The time that each monkey spent in proximity to another monkey was divided according to the number of possible partners (e.g., an intact female had the choice of associating with five other intact females, four intact males, or four castrated males). Figure 2.9 shows the partner preferences of intact and ovariectomized females. Female monkeys showed a clear preference for associating with other females, and a relative avoidance of intact or castrated males, F (2,44) = 40.36, $p <$ .00001. Approximately 50% of the time that a female was observed proximal to another monkey, she was near another female monkey. This social bias of females was already strongly apparent by the Pubescent period, and continued during the Subadult stage. Of greater interest was the fact that both intact and ovariectomized females showed this preference. In addition, neither intact nor ovariectomized females appeared to distinguish between the intact and castrated males. That is, both intact and ovariectomized females reacted to the castrated males as if they were normal males and were less likely to choose to sit near them when a female partner was available.

A complementary pattern of partner preference was apparent in the male data (Fig. 2.10). Males also showed a strong preference for associating with their own sex and the social bias was already clearly established by the Pubescent stage, F (2, 64) = 37.91, $p <$ 00001. Castrated males showed an avoidance of females that was equivalent to that of intact males in both years. Castrated males also appeared to react equivalently to intact and castrated males. However, there was an interesting bias in intact males, who chose to associate somewhat more often

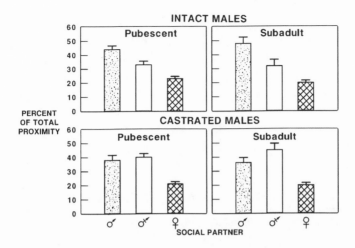

FIG. 2.10.   Partner preferences of intact and castrated males based on spatial proximity scores. Both types of males showed the species-appropriate preferences for same-sex partners.

with their intact counterparts than with castrated males. This social tendency was apparent in both the Pubescent and Subadult stage, and may reflect an influence of their slightly higher levels of rough-and-tumble play behavior shown by intact males (see below).

SOCIAL PLAY IN PUBESCENT AND SUBADULT MONKEYS

As others have observed (Caine, 1986; Goy & McEwen, 1980), social play is one of the best behavioral indices for evaluating sex differences in the developing primate. Males show a stronger predisposition for rough-and-tumble play than do females, and this sex difference becomes more and more pronounced as maturing females withdraw from the increasingly frenetic play bouts of the males. Figure 2.11 shows the percentage of the observation intervals in which monkeys were observed to engage in social play. For each monkey there were at least 360 opportunities for it to be observed in social play during the Pubescent or Subadult stage (180 intervals while it was the focal subject and 180 intervals as a potential partner during observations of another monkey). The analysis of variance indicated a strong sex difference in the overall occurrence of social play, $F (3,54) =$ 11.58, $p < .00003$. Lower levels of female play were already apparent by the Pubescent stage, and although ovariectomized females did play a little more than intact females in the Pubescent stage, they showed similarly low levels of play by the Subadult stage. Castrated males played about three times as much as females,

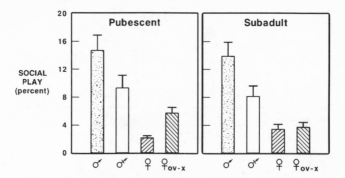

FIG. 2.11. Percent of the observation intervals in which males and females were observed playing. Both intact and castrated males played more than did intact and ovariectomized females.

but less than intact males. The highest levels of rough-and-tumble play were observed in the intact males, and this pattern was consistent across groups and years of observation. It is this continuation of social play in the subadult male that has provoked some theorists to suggest that adolescence may be primarily a male phenomenon in the nonhuman primate species. In most primate species, females cease playing with the onset of the maternal stage after menarche.

Evaluation of the distribution of play across potential partners further emphasized this basic sex difference (Fig. 2.12). Males showed a clear preference for

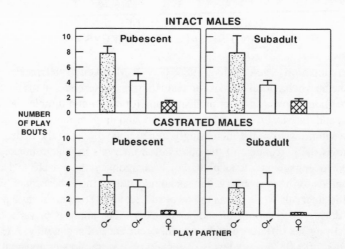

FIG. 2.12. Play partner preferences of intact and castrated males. Both types of males chose to play with males more than females, although intact males showed an even stronger bias for playing with intact counterparts.

choosing other males over females as play partners, F (2,64) = 17.25, p < .00001. Castrated males also chose to play primarily with other males, and were as likely to be observed playing with another castrated male as with an intact male. Thus, prepubertal castration clearly did not feminize the behavioral disposition of the castrated males. In the choice of partners, however, there was a suggestion that castrated males differed somewhat from the intact males. An interaction in the ANOVA between Type of Male and Choice-of-Partner suggested that intact males showed a bias for playing with their own kind, F (2,64) = 2.79, p < .067. The statistics were not overwhelming, and castrated males certainly did play more than females, but intact males were about twice as likely to choose another intact male as a partner when compared to a castrated male. The reason for this choice pattern is not readily apparent and may simply reflect the fact that the intact males played somewhat more. In support of this suggestion is the observation that females also showed a small preference for engaging in social play with the intact males. Although females did not play frequently, when they did play, it was often because they became involved in one of the regular play bouts between the intact males.

EXPRESSION OF DOMINANCE BEHAVIOR IN PUBERTAL MONKEYS

The final behavior category is concerned with the manifestation of dominance in the pubertal monkeys. As monkeys develop, they show an increasing tendency to engage in stratified social relations. Assertive monkeys tend to displace more timid and subordinate monkeys, and during moments of competition, one can discern evidence of a dominance hierarchy. Under normal, noncompetitive circumstances this dominance-related behavior is subtle, but it can transform quickly and result in aggressive behavior when the monkeys are provoked by limited or desired incentives. During our undisturbed observations, we tallied the frequency of several behaviors including manual grabbing, active spatial displacement, avoidance, and the occurrence of a species-specific genital display. For this chapter, we have used these tallies to convey a basic sex difference in the initiation and receipt of dominance behavior.

Pubescent and subadult males clearly expressed more of these behaviors than did females, F (3,54) = 12.04, p < .00001. By the Pubertal stage of development, intact males were nearly three times more likely than females to show dominance-related behavior toward another monkey (Fig. 2.13). To convey a real sense of the disposition in intact males, these data indicate that they engaged in a dominance-related behavior about once every 15 minutes. Castrated males engaged in dominance interactions less frequently than did the intact males, but showed dominance behavior more frequently than females. Intact and ovariec-

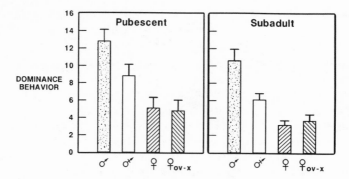

FIG. 2.13. Expression of dominance behavior by intact and gonadectomized monkeys.

tomized females showed the lowest levels of grabbing and spatial displacement,
and they were similar across the 2 years of observation.

Evaluation of the complementary side of this relationship, receipt of dominance behavior, indicated that there was also a clear sex difference. Females
were more likely to be on the receiving end of dominance behaviors than were
males, F (3,54) = 6.96, $p < .01$. There was no influence of gonadectomy (Fig.
2.14). Both intact and castrated males were less likely to be a recipient of
dominance behavior than were females, and ovariectomized females and intact
females were treated similarly. These data should not be interpreted to mean that
females do not show dominance behavior or a hierarchical ranking of their social
relationships; it simply reflects the frequency at which these behaviors are expressed and the relatively higher level of male-to-female interaction at this stage
of development. Indeed, some primatologists have suggested that this type of

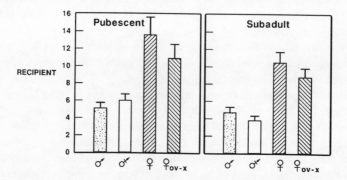

FIG. 2.14. Receipt of dominance behavior by intact and gonadectomized monkeys.

rough behavior on the part of subadult males is so disruptive of group relations that it may be one of the reasons why they are peripheralized from the troop for a period of time (Bernstein & Ehardt, 1985). Further, it has been suggested that one important social function of the adult males is to inhibit the behavior of the subadult males. This inhibition results in a lower level of aggression until the maturing males ultimately acquire a stable rank within the adult male hierarchy. The pubescent and subadult monkeys in our studies showed more variable dominance rankings than are usually seen in adult groups and it is for that reason that we have not presented a linear rank hierarchy for each group.

GENERAL CONSIDERATIONS

These data illustrate that puberty cannot be considered to be purely a hormonal and reproductive event even in animals. Although this conclusion is certainly not novel to the readers of this volume, it is a point that must continually be reiterated. Much of the theorizing about the hormonal control of behavior has emanated from studies of sexual behavior in rodents. Even in nonhuman primates, the pubertal transition must be viewed as a multidimensional process involving complex changes in physical growth and social behavior, in addition to the onset of gonadal puberty. From this perspective, one must question the placement of gonadal activity as the antecedent event underlying all of the associated behavioral and somatic changes. Our findings on the effects of prepubertal gonadectomy suggest that many of the developmental changes progress in a normal manner even in the absence of normal hormonal stimulation at puberty. We believe that the major period of hormone influence is actually the fetal stage, rather than in the adult organism. As mentioned previously, the studies by Goy (1968) on the effects of prenatal androgen exposure in female rhesus monkeys are in keeping with this conclusion. Support for this view can also be gathered from another interesting group of nonhuman primates, the monogamous callithricid monkeys. In these primates, developing monkeys are inhibited from showing any hormonal changes indicative of the pubertal transition as long as they remain in the presence of their parents. Nevertheless, it appears that their hypothalamus and behavior can develop independently of gonadal development, and they can virtually become sexually active overnight when the inhibitory adult social influence is removed (Ziegler et al., 1987).

In our studies the gonadectomies were performed at 1 year of age, 1.5 years before the onset of puberty, and the loss of gonadal hormones did not interfere with the normal development of sex differences in behavior. Our findings are extremely similar to those on rhesus monkeys gonadectomized at birth (Goy & Kemnitz, 1983). This would certainly indicate that the major time of hormone action is during the period of sexual differentiation in fetal life. The period of hormone influence may extend post-natally to include the prolonged period of high testosterone secretion during the first year of life in the young primate male (Plant, 1986; Robinson & Bridson, 1978). A clear function for this postnatal period of high gonadal activity has not been established, but it may partially explain why just prenatal androgen treatment of the female primate fetus does not completely masculinize her endocrine physiology. Unlike androgenized female rodents, the androgenized female primate treated prenatally ultimately begins to cycle in adulthood and continues to show many aspects of feminine behavior (Thornton & Goy, 1986). Of relevance to our studies, she does show a delay in the timing of menarche that is more appropriate to the male temporal pattern (Goy & Kemnitz, 1983). This observation and our data indicate that there is a maturational clock that can be masculinized or feminized. We were struck by the fact that the ovariectomized females and castrated males showed a normal temporal pattern of growth in spite of a general decrease in their body weight.

Another striking aspect of our results was the relatively normal unfolding of the developmental sequence in the absence of adult influence or role models. Not only did the developing monkeys achieve a normal onset of puberty, but even the normal developmental sequence of social behaviors was maintained. Clearly, human adolescence is more complex than the pubertal transition in animals, and other contributors to this volume have written extensively on the social expectations and roles that must be fulfilled (e.g., Hill & Lynch, 1983). However, one is reminded of the comments in Maccoby and Jacklin (1974) that, even in the human, sex differences in behavior seem to appear with minimal adult facilitation. Here we can only speak by analogy and note the possible legacy that our animal heritage has left us.

These comments should not be taken to suggest that the presence of adults would have been without influence. Indeed, we purposely chose to remove this variable because it added another layer of complexity that might have obscured our delineation of a gonadal hormone influence. There are several studies on nonhuman primates that have shown that adults can influence the pubertal progression in developing monkeys (e.g., Rose et al., 1978; Ziegler et al., in press). In particular, adult males may have an inhibitory influence on the development of young males. Under natural conditions, adult males certainly have a major behavioral influence and would be one of the primary forces compelling the developing male to emigrate from the natal troop. Adult males also have a significant controlling influence over the behavior of the subadult males remaining within the group and would probably have reduced the level of dominance behavior directed toward females in our groups. Indeed, a major social function of adult males is to inhibit the behavior of the subadult males, and subadults may become hyperaggressive in the absence of this inhibitory influence (Bernstein & Ehardt, 1985).

In this chapter we also have not considered all of the possible factors that can affect pubertal onset. For example, psychological and environmental influences on behavioral or physiological development may be mediated nonspecifically via general stress effects. Sustained adrenal activation can interfere with normal gonadal development (Kime, Vinson, Major, & Kilpatrick, 1980); similarly, psychological factors that affect diet and food intake can influence the onset of puberty by affecting growth. We have not addressed the latter issue in this paper, but the influence of body weight on the onset of puberty in nonhuman primates is similar to that observed in humans (Frisch, 1983). In previous studies on chimpanzees, we have documented that females in captivity achieve an earlier menarche, show a shorter period of adolescent sterility, and have a shorter inter-birth interval because of the influence of diet and body weight on reproductive function (Coe, Connolly, Kraemer, & Levine, 1979). Table 2.2 summarizes the results of an interesting comparison between the reproductive development of larger and faster growing female chimpanzees at the Stanford Primate Facility and wild chimpanzees under natural conditions in Gombe, Tanzania. Further, female dominance status can interact with this relationship between reproductive physiology and body weight. We have observed that subordinate squirrel monkey females, especially those of smaller stature, come to puberty at an older age than do more dominant, larger females (Coe et al., 1981). The literature on the effects of female dominance status on reproductive success is well established in nonhuman primates (Drickamer, 1974).

It should also be emphasized that the choice of an appropriate animal model for the studies on puberty is a complicated issue. We are sure that the reader was struck by the many unique characteristics of the squirrel monkey. There are over 55 genera within the Primate Order and there is considerable variation around the general developmental pattern (Rowell, 1977). In particular, any study on monkeys must incorporate the fact that these species are seasonal breeders and, therefore, they will not show a simple, linear development of the reproductive system with age (Glick, 1979). Instead, the pattern is punctuated by seasonal

TABLE 2.2
Effect of Body Weight and Diet on Reproductive
Development in the Female Chimpanzee. Years of
Age When Captive-Reared (Stanford) and Wild
(Gombe) Chimpanzees Reached Each
Reproductive Phase

	Stanford	Gombe
Adolescent swellings	5.5–7	8.5–9.5
Menarche	7.7–9.5	10.5–12
Adolescent sterility	0.4–1.4 years	2.5 years
First conception	8.2–10.7	12–14
First birth	8.9–11.5	13–15
Cycle resumption	12.2–13	17–19
Second conception	12.8–14.1	18.5–21
Second birth	13.4–14.8	19–22

surges of gonadal activity superimposed upon a linear aging process. In this regard, the chimpanzee and gorilla would provide a better animal model than would the monkey. In addition, the larger apes show a more similar elongation of the adolescent phase associated with their longer life span. Whereas the monkey may show a subadult stage lasting 2–3 years, adolescence in the great apes is extended for 5–6 years. The prolonged period of social immaturity in apes is probably related to the interesting shift from male emigration to female transfer as one looks from monkey to ape society. No one fully understands what motivates the female ape to undertake the risky journey into a neighboring group where she is often reacted to with considerable aggression, especially by the resident females (Goodall et al., 1979). However, it is of interest that the female chimpanzee makes this transition in adolescence just after she begins to cycle, a time in her reproductive life when she is optimally attractive to the adult males.

Notwithstanding the uniqueness of any animal model, there are several generalities that can be drawn from these primate studies. First, it is apparent that the the emergence of sex differences in the behavior of infant and juvenile monkeys does not depend on adult influence. Assessment of social affiliation, play behavior, and dominance-related behavior provide some of the best indices for studies of this type in nonhuman primates. Here it is of interest to note that rough-and-tumble play is also one of the distinguishing features of boys and girls in the preschool environment. We believe that these sex differences will follow a developmental pattern that parallels, but is not dependent upon, the normal sequence of gonadal activation. Objections to this conclusion could be raised on the basis of behavioral changes observed in children with precocious puberty. However, one must remain open to the possibility that several aspects of the CNS could be maturing more rapidly in this human condition, with both physiology and behavior moving along an accelerated trajectory together. It is only in the case of sexual behavior that we have clear evidence of direct hormone action on behavior, and even here, it is difficult to delineate strong, linear correlations when the hormones are within the normal range. In many studies it has been easier to show that psychological variables can affect hormone activity, than it has been to show the reverse influence. Moreover, in humans the strong correlation between hormones and somatic change always presents a potential confounding variable given the obvious importance of appearance for determining self-image and the reactions of others. It is probably more correct, therefore, to approach the question of hormone-behavior relationships with a model of co-occurring processes than to postulate a causal model based on a unidirectional hormone influence.

ACKNOWLEDGMENTS

This research was supported by HD02881 from NICHD to S. Levine. C. Coe is supported in part by MH41659 from NIMH, N00014-87-K-0227 from the Office of Naval Research, and RR00167 from the Animal Resources Branch of NIH. S. Levine has a PHS Research Scientist Award (MH19936). We also wish to acknowledge the invaluable assistance of H. Hu, E. Lowe, and I. Melonas in the data collection and analysis.

REFERENCES

Baldwin, J. D. (1985). The behavior of squirrel monkeys (*Saimiri*) in natural environments. In L. A. Rosenblum & C. L. Coe (Eds.), *Handbook of squirrel monkey research* (pp. 35–54). New York: Plenum.

Beach, F. (1948). *Hormones and behavior*. New York: Paul B. Hoeber.

Bernstein, I. S., & Ehardt, C. L. (1985). Age-sex differences in the expression of agonistic behavior in rhesus monkey (*Macaca mulatta*) groups. *Journal of Comparative Psychology, 99* (2), 115–132.

Bernstein, I. S., Gordon, T. P., & Peterson, M. (1979). Role behavior of an agonadal alpha-male rhesus monkey in a heterosexual group. *Folia primatologica, 32*, 263–267.

Bielert, C. F. (1978). Androgen treatments of young male rhesus monkeys. In D. J. Chivers & J. Herbert (Eds.), *Recent advances in primatology* (V. 1, pp. 485–488). London: Academic Press.

Caine, N. G. (1986). Behavior during puberty and adolescence. In J. Erwin (Ed.), *Comparative primate biology: Behavior, conservation and ecology* (V. 2A, pp. 327–361). New York: A. R. Liss.

Chatz, T. L. (1972). Recognizing and treating dangerous sex offenders. *International Journal of Offender Therapy, 16*, 109–115.

Coe, C. L., Chen, J., Lowe, E. L., Davidson, J. M., & Levine, S. (1981). Hormonal and behavioral changes at puberty in the squirrel monkey. *Hormones and Behavior, 15*, 36–53.

Coe, C. L., Connolly, A. C., Kraemer, H. C., & Levine, S. (1979). Reproductive development and behavior in captive female chimpanzees (*Pan troglodytes*). *Primates, 20*, 571–582.

Coe, C. L., & Levin, R. N. (1980). Dominance assertion in male chimpanzees. *Aggressive Behavior, 6*, 161–174.

Coe, C. L., & Levine, S. (1983). Biology of aggression. *Bulletin of the American Academy of Psychiatry and the Law, 11*(2), 131–148.

Crews, D. (1987). *Psychobiology of reproductive behavior*. Englewood Cliffs, NJ: Prentice-Hall.

Doering, C. H., McGinnis, P. R., Kraemer, H. C., & Hamburg, D. A. (1980). Hormonal and behavioral response of male chimpanzees to a long-acting analogue of gonadotropin-releasing hormone. *Archives of Sexual Behavior, 9*, 441–450.

Drickamer, L. C. (1974). A ten-year summary of reproductive data from free-ranging *Macaca mulatta*. *Folia primatologica, 21*, 61–80.

Epple, G. (1978). Lack of effects of castration on scent marking, displays, and aggression in a South American primate (*Saguinus fuscicollis*). *Hormones and Behavior, 11*, 139–150.

Field. L. H., & Williams, M. (1970). The hormonal treatment of sexual offenders. *Medicine, Science and the Law, 10*, 27–34.

Frisch, R. E. (1983). Fatness, puberty and fertility: The effects of nutrition and physical training on menarche and ovulation. In J. Brooks-Gunn & A. C. Petersen (Eds.), *Girls at puberty* (pp. 29–51). New York: Plenum.

Glick, B. B. (1979). Testicular size, testosterone level and body weight in male *Macaca radiata:* Maturational and seasonal effects. *Folia primatologica, 32*, 268–289.

Goodall, J., Bandora, A., Bergmann, E., Busse, C., Matama, H., Mpongo, E., Pierce, A., & Riss, D. (1979). Intercommunity interactions in the chimpanzee population of the Gombe National Park. In D. A. Hamburg & E. R. McCown (Eds.). *The great apes* (pp. 13–55). Menlo Park: Benjamin/Cummings.

Gordon, T. P., Rose, R. M., Grady, C. L., & Bernstein, I. S. (1979). Effects of increased testosterone secretion on the behavior of adult male rhesus living in a social group. *Folia primatologica, 32,* 149–160.

Goy, R. W. (1968). Organizing effects of androgen on the behaviour of rhesus monkeys. In R. P. Michael (Ed.), *Endocrinology and human behaviour* (pp. 12–31). London: Oxford University Press.

Goy, R. W., & Kemnitz, J. W. (1983). Early, persistent, and delayed effects of virilizing substances delivered transplacentally to female rhesus fetuses. In G. Zbinden (Ed.), *Application of behavioral pharmacology in toxicology* (pp. 303–314). New York: Raven.

Goy, R. W., & McEwen, B. S. (1980). *Sexual differentiation of the brain.* Cambridge, MA: MIT Press.

Green, R., Whalen, R. E., Rutley, B., & Battie, C. (1972). Dominance hierarchy in squirrel monkeys (*Saimiri sciureus*). Role of the gonads and androgens on genital display and feeding order. *Folia primatologica, 18,* 185–195.

Gupta, D., Attanasio, A., & Raaf, S. (1975). Plasma estrogen and androgen concentration during adolescence. *Journal of Clinical Endocrinology and Metabolism, 40,* 636–643.

Harcourt, A. H. (1979). The social relations and group structure of wild mountain gorillas. In D. A. Hamburg & E. R. McCown (Eds.), *The great apes* (pp. 187–192). Menlo Park: Benjamin/ Cummings.

Heim, N., & Hursch, C. J. (1979). Castration for sex offenders: Treatment or punishment? A review and critique of recent European literature. *Archives of Sexual Behavior, 8,* 281–304.

Hill, J. P., & Lynch, M. E. (1983). The intensification of gender-related expectations during early adolescence. In J. Brooks-Gunn & A. Petersen (Eds.), *Girls at puberty* (pp. 201–228). New York: Plenum.

Holloway, R. L. (1974). *Primate aggression, territoriality and xenophobia.* New York: Academic Press.

Imperato-McGinley, J. Peterson, R. E., & Gautier, T. (1981). Male pseudohermaphroditism secondary to 5α-reductase deficiency: A review. In M. J. Novy & J. A. Resko (Eds.), *Fetal endocrinology* (pp. 359–382). New York: Academic Press.

Kalin, N. H. (1979). Genital and abdominal self-surgery. *Journal of the American Medical Association, 241* (20), 2188–2189.

Kime, D. E., Vinson, G. P., Major, P. W., & Kilpatrick, R. (1980). Adrenal-gonad relationships. In I. C. Jones & I. W. J. Henderson (Eds.), *General and clinical endocrinology of the adrenal cortex* (V. 3, pp. 183–264). London: Academic Press.

Kreuz, L. E., & Rose, R. M. (1972). Assessment of aggressive behavior and plasma testosterone in a young criminal population. *Psychosomatic Medicine, 34,* 321–332.

Leutenegger, W. (1982). Scaling of sexual dimorphism in body weight and canine size in primates. *Folia primatologica, 37,* 163–176.

Maccoby, E. E., & Jacklin, C. N. (1974). *The psychology of sex differences.* Stanford, CA: Stanford University Press.

Martin, D. E., Swenson, R. B., & Collins, D. C. (1977). Correlation of serum testosterone levels with age in male chimpanzees. *Steroids, 29,* 471–481.

Mendoza, S. P., Coe, C. L., Lowe, E. L., & Levine, S. (1979). The physiological response to group formation in adult male squirrel monkeys. *Psychoneuroendocrinology, 3,* 221–229.

Money, J., & Ehrhardt, A. A. (1972). *Man & woman, boy & girl.* Baltimore: Johns Hopkins University Press.

Olweus, D., Mattson, A., Schalling, D., & Low, H. (1980). Testosterone, aggression, physical and personality dimensions in normal adolescent males. *Psychosomatic Medicine, 42*(2), 253–269.

Plant, T. M. (1986). A striking sex difference in the gonadotropin response to gonadectomy during infantile development in the rhesus monkey (*Macaca mulatta*). *Endocrinology, 119*(2), 539–545.

Robinson, J. A., & Bridson, W. E. (1978). Neonatal hormone patterns in the macaque. I. Steroids. *Biology of Reproduction, 19,* 773–778.

Rose, R. M., Bernstein, I. S., Gordon, T. P., & Lindsley, J. G. (1978). Changes in testosterone and behavior during adolescence in the male rhesus monkey. *Psychosomatic Medicine, 40,* 60–70.

Rowell, T. E. (1977). Variation in age at puberty in monkeys. *Folia primatologica, 27,* 284–296.

Schultz, A. H. (1969). *The life of primates.* London: Weidenfeld & Nicolson.

Simmons, R. G., Blyth, D. A., & McKinney, K. L. (1983). The social and psychological effects of puberty on white females. In J. Brooks-Gunn & A. Petersen (Eds.), *Girls at puberty* (pp. 229–272). New York: Plenum.

Smith, E. O. (1978). *Social play in primates.* New York: Academic Press.

Steinberg, L. (in press). Pubertal maturation and family relations: Evidence for the distancing hypothesis. In G. Adams, R. Montemayor, & T. Gullotta (Eds.), *Advances in adolescent development* (V. 1). Beverly Hills, CA: Sage Publications.

Tanner, J. M. (1962). *Growth at adolescence.* Oxford: Blackwell Scientific.

Thornton, J., & Goy, R. W. (1986). Female-typical sexual behavior of rhesus and defeminization by androgens given prenatally. *Hormones and Behavior, 20,* 129–147.

Tobin-Richards, M. H., Boxer, A. M., Petersen, A. C. (1983). The psychological significance of pubertal change: Sex differences in perceptions of self during early adolescence. In J. Brooks-Gunn & A. Petersen (Eds.), *Girls at puberty* (pp. 155–178). New York: Plenum.

Watts, E. S. (1985). Adolescent growth and development of monkeys, apes and humans. In E. S. Watts (Ed.), *Nonhuman primate models for human growth and development* (pp. 41–65). New York: A. R. Liss.

Young, W. C. (1961). *Sex and internal secretions.* Baltimore: Williams & Wilkins.

Young, W. C., Goy, R. W., Phoenix, C. H. (1964). Hormones and sexual behavior. Broad relationships exist between the gonadal hormones and behavior. *Science, 143,* 212–218.

Ziegler, T. E., Savage, A., Scheffler, G., & Snowdon, C. T. (1987). The endocrinology of puberty and reproductive functioning in female cotton-top tamarins (*Saguinus oedipus*) under varying social conditions. *Biology of Reproduction, 37(3),* 618–627.

3 Adapting to Menarche: Familial Control and Conflict

John P. Hill
Virginia Commonwealth University

In 1978, Larry Steinberg and I advanced some initial cross-sectional data on adaptation to pubertal change in families of boys. A two-wave follow-up of the same families (Steinberg, 1977, 1981) confirmed a period of temporary perturbation in mother-son relations at the apex of pubertal growth. In a structured family interaction task (SFIT) (Ferreira, 1963), sons interrupted mothers more and mothers interrupted sons more at the apex of pubertal growth than before or after this point in development. After the apex of pubertal growth, mothers' interruptions of sons were less frequent, but sons' interruptions of mothers continued to increase in frequency and were more effective. Mothers' yielding to sons' interruptions were more frequent. Over the first part of the pubertal cycle, the utterances of mothers and sons were increasingly more "restricted" (Bernstein, 1964); both mothers and sons advanced assertions without elaborating them. Over the latter part of the cycle, boys continued to provide fewer elaborations of declarative statements whereas mothers' assertions once again became more elaborated. In addition, sons gained more influence over final family decisions in the structured task and mothers lost influence. In terms of conventional interpretations of data from such tasks, sons gained in power in the family and this occurred at the expense of mothers. Whether the pattern of findings around the apex of pubertal growth in mother-son relations (both parties interrupting more and elaborating their assertions less) can be termed conflictual is addressed below.

The data on fathers and sons did not raise the issue of conflict. Over the pubertal cycle, sons interrupted fathers less often, fathers interrupted sons more often, and fathers (but not sons) were more successful in their interruptions. All of these were linear effects. What is seen here may be a dominance-submission display not unlike that observed in other primate species; the newly pubertal male is an adult member of the tribe but low in the dominance hierarchy (much like the status of a newly elected member of the Senate of the United States). At the same time, by virtue of the son's new status, deference from females in the tribe increases (one would hope not like the Senate).

Whatever the interpretation, findings similar to these now have been reported in subsequent, albeit cross-sectional, studies by Steinberg (in press), me (Hill, Holmbeck, Marlow, Green, & Lynch, 1985b), and other investigators (Anderson, Hetherington, & Clingempeel, 1986; Papini & Datan, 1982; Papini & Sebby, 1985; Savin-Williams & Small, 1986). I conclude that pubertal status and changes in pubertal status in males are associated both with behavior of family members and with changes in the behavior of family members. There is a phenomenon here worthy of further study and interpretation. As yet, however, we do not know how puberty impacts family relationships, family interaction, or the family as a system, as opposed to its impacts on frequencies of behavior of individual family members. (I am indebted to Grotevant and Cooper, 1986, for their clarification of these distinctions.) Some more serious assessments of mother-child and father-child attachments prior to puberty, for example, might usefully be included in future research with an eye toward tracking transformations in family relationships over the duration of the pubertal cycle (Hill & Holmbeck, 1986a). Taking interaction seriously means some attention given either to sequential analyses (Bakeman, 1978; Holmbeck, 1986) or to analyses of selected interaction sequences, as, for example, Vuchinich (1984) has essayed for oppositional interchanges. One approach to the family as a system may be to examine relations between dyadic subsystems, an approach whose rich possibilities are suggested in work on the families of younger children by Sroufe, Jacobvitz, Mangelsdorf, DeAngelo, and Ward (1985). Research on pubertal effects is not yet that sophisticated, however. In turning to the principle content of this chapter—menarche and its relations to the behavior of individual family members—it is important to bear in mind that data about the behavior of individual family members have implications for, but not data about, family relationships, family interaction, or the family as a system.

We approached the study of relations between menarcheal status and the behavior of individual family members with the conviction that biological change surely must imply transformations in parent-adolescent relations for girls as well as boys. This conviction was based on our studies of pubertal effects in boys; pubertal effect studies of others; the Berkeley studies of early- and late-maturing girls (e.g., Clausen, 1975; Jones & Mussen, 1958); theoretical statements about the significance of menarche for increased internal and familial conflict; and, earlier empirical work on menarcheal effects, however sparse and unsophisticated.

Before going on to detail the nature of our expectations about impacts of biological change in girls on family behavior, it is important to understand why we chose to focus initially on menarche rather than on some other pubertal events, or an overall measure of pubertal change as we have employed with boys. Given the likelihood of curvilinear relations in many instances between pubertal measures and behavioral measures, given the complexities of intraindividual variations in timing and tempo of pubertal change (asynchronicity), and given interindividual variability, we decided that tracking more than one pubertal event in an initial study was too Byzantine a task to manage effectively. Why not consider overall pubertal status, as with boys? Although we did obtain overall ratings of pubertal status, as well as daughter and parent reports of figural and other developments, we chose menarche as the focus of our initial analyses principally because several other research groups had begun to be interested in menarcheal effects (e.g., Brooks-Gunn & Ruble, 1983; Petersen, Tobin-Richards, & Boxer, 1983; Rierdan & Koff, 1980). It seemed more useful to work in the presence of a growing interpretative context. Furthermore, there was the possibility that menarche was somehow "special" in that earlier studies comparing undifferentiated premenarcheal with undifferentiated postmenarcheal groups have yielded differences and they should not have if earlier pubertal events have strong effects (Greif & Ulman, 1982). Finally, most of the events that comprise biological change in adolescence do unfold gradually (Tanner, 1962). Menarche, on the other hand, is a punctate developmental event. It signals reproductive maturity with a definitive and culturally consensual quality not associated with any event in the maturation of boys.

Menarche

There is some current controversy about the extent to which menarche is as "usually traumatic" as was claimed, for example, by Helene Deutsch (1944) in her classic work on the psychology of women. The bulk of the information suggests that when menarche occurs on time, negative attitudes, negative emotions, and physical symptoms *do* emerge but are probably not so severe as to warrant the traumatic label. Ruble and Brooks-Gunn (1982), for example, report that postmenarcheal girls are a little bit upset, and a little bit excited, and they perceive parents as having "slightly negative" feelings. About one fifth of the girls used exclusively positive terms and another one fifth used exclusively negative terms to describe their initial experience. Most girls expressed at least one "worry" (mostly uncertainty about the meaning of the event or possible embarrassment). Fifty percent of Ruble and Brooks-Gunn's sample reported experiencing at least one symptom (most frequently cramps or nausea) during the first period. When interviewed after several periods, 56% reported physical discomfort or pain, and 22% reported moodiness/fatigue before or during their periods. Eighty percent of the girls followed longitudinally by Ruble and Brooks-Gunn told somebody immediately or soon after menarche, most often (82%) their mothers. Secretiveness decreases rapidly. After two or three periods, most girls report not only that their girls friends "know" but also that they talk about symptoms.

Premenarcheal girls anticipate telling more people than postmenarcheal girls actually do tell. Premenarcheal girls expect more pain and more negative feelings than postmenarcheal girls experience. However, postmenarcheal girls are more surprised by the event than premenarcheal girls expect to be. As one of Whisnant and Zegans' (1975) subjects said, "You thought you know [sic] but you didn't." Unprepared girls expressed more negative feelings, fewer positive feelings, and more surprise, and reported more frequent and severe symptoms as well.

Studies of personality characteristics of pre- and postmenarcheal girls are rare. They suggest, especially among seventh graders (i.e., when most girls experience menarche) and in the first 6 months after menarche, an increased focus on body changes. On the Draw-a-Person Test, for example, there is greater sexual differentiation in the pictures of seventh- than eighth-grade girls (Koff, Rierdan, & Silverstone, 1978; Rierdan & Koff, 1980). Apparently, the "amount of time elapsed since onset of menstruation is an important variable in assessing the impact of menarche" (Greif & Ulman, 1982). Simple premenarcheal *versus* postmenarcheal comparisons will not do. Post menarcheal girls feel more womanly. "They go from having very little sense of themselves as female, a fairly undifferentiated sense of their bodies, to a sense of themselves as womanly, as mature, as being distinct from men in a positive way" (Rierdan, 1982, p. 9). Other investigators report more interest in self-adornment and in heterosexual behavior in postmenarcheal than premenarcheal girls (Stone & Barker, 1939).

For early-maturing girls, menarche appears to be much more than inconvenient, ambivalent, and confusing. Although criteria for definition of on-time and off-time vary from study to study, thus posing interpretative problems, the menarcheal experience of early-maturing girls probably warrants the traumatic label. Compared to other girls, early maturers have the most negative attitudes toward menarche, report increasing global dissatisfaction with their bodies, and manifest greater depression, more anxiety, more external locus of control, and greater fear of social disapproval (Brooks-Gunn & Ruble, 1983; Greif & Ulman, 1982; Rierdan & Koff, 1983; Simmons & Blyth, in press). Similar negative effects of early menarche on self-esteem have been reported when menarche is coincident with other transitions, as into junior high school (Simmons & Blyth, in press), and when girls experiencing it perceive themselves to have little power in family decision making (Miller & Taylor, 1986). How school, peer, and family contexts might mediate or modulate the earlier reported findings on depression, anxiety, and the like has not been investigated.

Menarche and Family Behavior

Theoretical Views.   The impact of girls' entry into the pubertal cycle and of menarche on family behavior has been the object of considerable speculation but little study. Much of the effort is psychoanalytic or inspired by psychoanalysis. The contemporary psychoanalytic view, which owes much to the clinical work and writings of Peter Blos (1962, 1979), is most systematically, compellingly, and elegantly expressed by Louise J. Kaplan in her recent book, *Adolescence: The Farewell to Childhood.* For an adolescent to complete the passage from childhood into adulthood, Kaplan argues, a form of displacement of libidinal desire called *removal* is required. In *removal,* the sexual hunger once attached to the infantile images of the parents is converted from incestuous longing to adult genital desire (Kaplan, 1984). A variety of defensive strategies may be expected in the service of coming to terms with adult genital sexuality and at the same time renouncing parents as erotic objects:

> In the more usual course of the adolescent passage, at various times, in various combinations, bodily asceticism, uncompromising ideation, transfer of love desire, reversal of love into hate will be employed to ease the anxiety of incest. Suffering from bouts of self-hate, the average adolescent is frequently rejecting of everything her parents represent. And there are moments when she would wish to escape from her conflicts by handing her body and soul to the parents. . . . And even the average adolescent will occasionally entertain the notion that her parents are persecuting oppressors. (p. 141)

Both Kaplan and Blos have emphasized what Freud in his later work called the negative Oedipus Complex; that is, the child's love for the parent of the same sex: "The crucial sexual and moral issues are to preserve the tender and affectionate ties to the parent of the same sex, to de-eroticize the passions that are attached to that parent and to transfer them elsewhere, and to humanize the exalted idealizations that had been attributed to that parent" (Kaplan, 1984, p. 163). This business of humanization is fraught with further difficulty. At the same time, the (young) adolescent must struggle with the wish to return to the past: to surrender body and soul to an ever-present and magical caregiver "who will mirror everything one wishes to be" (p. 165).

According to Kaplan, this backward pull is a greater complication for girls than for boys and the result is that "the emotional dissension between mothers and daughters can assume wild proportions. The struggle . . . is always exacerbated by the subtle social message that girls are better off if they remain child-like" (p. 169). Although bouts of yearning and disparagement characterize the relationship with the mother, the father remains a symbol of power and authority and usually is not the target of denigration. "During puberty, it is Mother who pays" (p. 172). Denigration of the mother counteracts the erotic pull, but exposing the clay feet of the idol also exposes the worthlessness and powerlessness of the identificand. New identifications of adolescence are drawn from one or two friendships or a crush. These help the young woman to bear the realization that "the woman on whom she had modeled herself is far from a divine creature fashioned in heaven" (p. 181). Kaplan suggests that this process lasts until the assumption of adult responsibilities when the adolescent's own conceptions of who she is and who she is not are consolidated and a less stridently independent and more realistic appraisal of the mother begins to occur.

Other views place emphasis upon the mother's reactivity to biological change in the daughter rather than on intraindividual change in the daughter. Magrab (1979), for example, argues that "menstruation is perhaps the most significant event in the life of the adolescent daughter in her relationship with her mother" (p. 120). Menarche means that the daughter's sexuality can no longer be denied; the daughter is more beautiful, more sexual, and suddenly a clear rival for the territory of womanhood. Friday (1977) asserts that it is the rare mother who can believe that there is enough sexuality to go around and whose daughter's sexuality cannot threaten hers. From this perspective, we might expect changes in maternal attributions and behavior both toward daughters and spouses. Attributing rivalry to the daughter's behavior and responding in kind may predispose to conflict in the mother-daughter dyad. Attributing fathers' warmth toward daughters as a signal of (greater) sexual interest may predispose to conflict in the spousal dyad.

Yet another line of argument suggests that puberty (and perhaps, especially menarche) instigates greater parental control over daughters than before. Suddenly there is less latitude for behaving "like a boy" and more vigilance and "chaperonage" lest virginity be lost (Block, 1979; Hill & Lynch, 1983; Katz, 1979; Lott, 1981; Newson & Newson, 1968). This lessened permissiveness may be more characteristic of fathers:

> [F]athers have, for the most part, regarded their daughters as the responsibility of their wives. To the extent that they have taken interest in their daughters' development, their concern has been with the attainment and maintenance of conformity to traditional sex roles. For their own good fathers believe girls must learn their place in the world and beware of being overly assertive or competent lest they make themselves unattractive marriage partners. (Lamb, Owen, & Chase-Lansdale, 1979, p. 89)

A complementary set of views was advanced initially by Deutsch (1944), subsequently by Parsons and Bales (1955), and later extended by Johnson (1963). This "reciprocal role learning" model discriminates between two socialization processes believed to be present in father-daughter interaction. The daughter is held to be attentive in interactions with the father to cues signifying the ways in which he expects her to behave. Such cues might be evident in the types of behaviors fathers elicit as well as in their responses to daughters' behaviors. This differential reinforcement is held to be accompanied in father-daughter interaction by role complementation; that is, "learning feminine behavior by interacting with and complementing the behavior of a masculine 'anti-model' " (Lamb et al., 1979, p. 108). There is no special claim made about these processes with respect to menarche but they might attain special importance at menarche if the gender intensification hypothesis is valid and if fathers are more concerned with the daughter's "femininity" than are mothers.

This speculative *largesse* implicates both conflict and control in familial adaptation to menarche but is not matched with much in the way of empirical investigation. The available information can be summarized in terms of (a) what is known, in general, about parent-adolescent relations without regard to puberty or menarche, and (b) what is known, more specifically, about family relations around the time of menarche.

Related Empirical Work.   Most studies of parent-adolescent relations have been focused upon families of high-school rather than middle-school age children (Hill, 1980). Information from these studies therefore bears only indirectly upon younger adolescents and their families.

Five summary statements are useful here: First, the mother is the central figure in the socialization of adolescents in terms of time spent in face-to-face interaction and in terms of responsibility for dealing with day-to-day "issues" within the family and without.

Second, three fourths (or more) of adolescents and their mothers report that daughters have close, positive, warm relations with their parents (Hill, 1980; Montemayor, 1983) and this overall positive emotional tone does not appear to change over the high-school years (see, for example, Kandel & Lesser, 1972). However, relationships with parents have been inadequately assessed with respect to contemporary criteria for understanding relationships (Grotevant & Cooper, 1986; Hill & Holmbeck, 1986a; Kelley et al., 1983). With the exception of one recent study (Atkinson & Bell, 1986), there is no serious empirical basis for assertions about the differential attachments of young adolescents to their mothers or fathers or about the changes in such attachments during middle childhood or pubescence. Atkinson and Bell assessed need for ready access, desire for proximity in terms of stress, comfort in the presence of the parent and discomfort when not present, security and trust in the relationship, strength of affectional bonds, defensive proximity avoiding, and ambivalence in proximity. Both male and female eighth and ninth graders rated mother attachment higher than father attachment. Sons were more attached to fathers than were daughters and daughters were more attached to mothers than were sons. This exceptional study deserves replication and the measure further validation.

Third, when family conflicts occur—mostly about mundane matters, garbage and galoshes—for both sexes, they are more common with mothers than with fathers. Conflicts between mothers and adolescent daughters are more common than conflicts between mothers and adolescent sons (Hill, 1980; Montemayor, 1983).

Fourth, there are intimations in the empirical literature that fathers of adolescent daughters, despite their lesser quantitative involvement in the rearing of girls, may play a substantial role in the socialization of their daughters. Relevant studies here include Hetherington's (1972) work on the avoidant and/or seductive behavior toward adult males of adolescent girls experiencing earlier paternal loss through death and divorce; Block's (1979) work on gender differences in mothers' and fathers' socialization efforts; and work by others suggesting that masculinity in fathers is positively associated with femininity in daughters (Lamb et al., 1979; Lynn, 1969). In addition, laboratory studies contrasting mothers' behaviors toward daughters with those of fathers suggest that the latter are more likely to stress expressive than instrumental matters on achievement tasks (Lamb et al., 1979; Lynch, 1981). Fathers may well be more invested in gender-role differentiation than mothers and the key process may be some kind of role-complementation.

Fifth, there is one variable set that emerges in the literature on parent-child and parent-adolescent relations as somehow critical to (a) compliance to parental expectations; (b) instrumental competence; and (c) prosocial behavior. Parents who "explain" rearing decisions or allow some "say" in making rules are more effective than those who do not in producing socialization outcomes of which most "experts" and middle-class parents would approve. Whether we are to understand such effects in terms of (a) elaborated versus constricted communications (Bernstein, 1964), (b) power-assertion and internalization (Hoffman, 1975), or (c) the development of role- or perspective-taking skills is unclear. Explanation may be more important in adolescence than in childhood, however. In the face of greater cognitive sophistication on the part of the adolescent, naked assertion of parental power may delegitimate parental authority (Baumrind, 1968).

Studies of Menarchael Impact.   In 1939, Stone and Barker reported what appear to be the first data on the topic; namely, that home conflicts were greater for postmenarchael than premenarchael girls. Whisnant and Zegans (1975) concluded from their clinical study that postmenarcheal girls reported changes in relationships with their parents and more than 50% with their mothers. In 1979, Garwood and Allen found that postmenarcheal girls reported more "home and family" problems than did premenarcheal girls. Rierdan (1982) informally reports her impressions of family behavior in relation to menarche as follows:

> In terms of family relationships, the girls very much look to their mothers for information, for support in making this transition to womanhood; and very many pull away from their fathers. The girls' wish is that their father not know or that if he knows hopefully he would have the good sense not to say anything. They anticipate themselves as wanting to pull away from him and anticipate a wish that he would pull away from them. So there is a suggestion of real difficulty in family relationships around the time of the onset of menstruation for girls. (p. 9)

THE QUESTIONNAIRE STUDY

Initially, we planned to collect both observational and questionnaire data from all of our subjects. Unfortunately, the demands placed upon our subject families were too great and subject loss became a problem. Therefore we embarked on two simultaneous streams of data collection, one field/questionnaire based and the other laboratory/observation based. So as to reduce our ignorance prior to dealing with the laboratory/observational data, our initial analyses focused upon the questionnaire data (Hill, Holmbeck, Marlow, Green, & Lynch, 1985a). Analyses of these data were designed to address the following questions: could we find impacts of biological change on family behavior similar to those identified earlier (Steinberg, 1981; Steinberg & Hill, 1978) when we examined (a) girls instead of boys, (b) self- and parental reports of menarcheal status rather than observers' reports of pubertal status, and (c) questionnaire reports of family behavior instead of observational data?

We reasoned that if temporary perturbations in family relations were characteristic of adapting to menarche, and these involved conflict and control, they ought to be reflected in reports of parental acceptance, parental influence, disagreements over rules, daughters' involvement in family activities, family rules and standards, and, perhaps, oppositionalism. Mindful of the possible importance of early maturing, we examined time since menarche instead of simply contrasting family behavior in premenarcheal versus postmenarcheal girls.

Method

Subjects. One hundred seventh-grade girls, recruited through the cooperation of several school districts in a large midwestern city, served as subjects for this study. The girls were the oldest children in their families and were living with both of their natural parents. On the Duncan Socio-Economic Index (SEI) (Duncan, 1977), ratings based upon paternal occupation ranged from 8 to 97 (where ratings around 50 are assigned to occupations such as foreman, bookkeeper, and telephone lineman). Fathers' mean SEI score was 56.80 (*SD* = 20.07). Seventy-five percent of the fathers in the sample had at least some college education. Twenty fathers were between 31 and 35 years old; 51 between 36 and 40; 19 between 41 and 45; 8 between 46 and 50; and 2 over 50. Sixty-four mothers worked outside the household in paid positions. Their mean SEI score was 46.95 (*SD* = 22.03). SEI scores ranged from 2 to 84. Twenty-six mothers worked part-time and 38 worked full-time. Fifty-five of the mothers had some college education or beyond. One mother was under 30 years old, 46 were between 31 and 35 years old, 36 were 36 to 40 years old, and 1 was over 50 years old. About half of the families contacted agreed to participate. A random sample of the latter compared with those refusing to participate showed no differences in father SEI ratings.

Procedure.   Research assistants brought child and parent questionnaires to the family's home at a time when they could all be together to fill them out. The assistants remained with the family to answer questions, monitor independent response, baby-sit younger children, and ensure completion of the questionnaire.

Measures.   Girls and their parents were asked to indicate whether menstruation had not yet begun, had begun within the past 6 months, within the past 12 months, or longer than 12 months ago (hereafter referred to as the 0, 0–6, 6–12, and 12+ groups). Correlations between respondent pairs ranged from .87 to .91, and all pairs achieved 80% agreement or above. In the analyses reported below, the report of menarcheal status employed is that of the parent whose reported or perceived behavior is being examined. For frequencies in each menarcheal group, as reported by mothers and fathers, see the Fig. 3.1 caption.

Scales labeled Parental Acceptance and Family Rules and Standards came from Spence and Helmreich's (1978) Parental Attitudes Questionnaire and were included in our child questionnaire. Girls reported separately for each parent on Parental Acceptance but on families as a whole for Family Rules and Standards. Items for what became Oppositionalism, Involvement in Family Activities, Disagreements over Rules, and Parental Influence Scales were borrowed from a variety of sources or developed by our own staff. Alphas were satisfactory for all scales except Oppositionalism: data on this scale are not reported.

Analyses.   Relations between menarcheal status and the other variables were assessed with multiple regression analyses. Months since menarche was treated as a continuous variable and was entered into the regression equation as a set of power polynomial terms (that is, the terms were entered separately and hierarchically). This analytic approach allowed us to test for linear and nonlinear relations (Cohen & Cohen, 1983). Given that our menarche status variable had four levels, we entered linear, quadratic (one bend), and cubic (two bends) terms. As it turned out, the percentage of variance accounted for ranged from 0% for Oppositionalism (father-daughter) to 16% for Involvement in Family Activities (mother-daughter).

Results and Discussion

Mother-Daughter Dyad.   In general, the more physically mature girls saw themselves as less accepted and as less influenced by their mothers than did the less physically mature girls (see Fig. 3.1). These cubic trends describe less perceived acceptance and influence in the 0–6 group and in the 12+ group than in the other two groups. Ignoring the 12+ group, for daughters' perceptions of

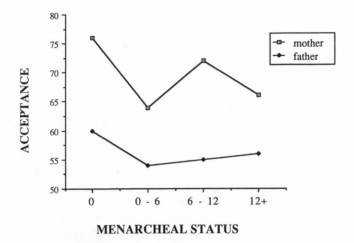

MENARCHEAL STATUS

FIG. 3.1. Menarcheal status and perceived acceptance: The negative linear and the negative cubic trends are statistically significant for mothers. The negative linear effect is statistically significant for fathers. N (0 group) = 62 (mother report) and 61 (father report); N (0–6 group) = 11 (mother report) and 13 (father report); N (6–12 group) = 17 (mother report) and 19 (father report); N (12+ group) = 10 (mother report) and 7 (father report).

mothers, we may say that there is a temporary effect of menarche not unlike the quadratic trends that played such a key role in the earlier longitudinal study of boys (Steinberg, 1981) and in our later extension, using questionnaire measures (Hill et al., 1985b). We argue that such curvilinear effects are consonant with notions of adaptation to pubertal change.

However, the trends *are* cubic and not quadratic. For perceived acceptance and influence, significant cubic trends mean that our 0–6 group and our 12+ group look much the same. What are we to make of the second turn toward negativity present here? Our interpretation—and it is only that—takes into account that the 12+ group is a group of early-maturing girls. Based upon what we know of the difficulties encountered by girls who experience menarche early rather than being temporary, initial negative impacts of puberty on family relations may be likely to persist. In short, given a longitudinal study, we would predict temporary perturbations of menarche on family relations for on-time girls and persistent perturbations for early maturers. Although we favor such an interpretation of these cubic trends, there are alternative interpretations. Regular menstrual periods apparently do not begin until about 6 months after menarche (Tanner, 1962). Thus, the onset of regular menstrual periods may account for a second round of perturbations in family relations. Perhaps the advent of premenstrual syndrome or even the synchronization of mother-daughter periods are implicated in these effects. Some (not-as-yet-understood) hormonal effects that are cyclical in nature may be at work. Because our subjects are all seventh graders, the great majority of whom begin dating and having nonintercourse sexual behavior prior to menarche (Murphy, 1986), onset of such behaviors does not appear to account for the effect.

As may be seen in Figs. 3.3 and 3.4, maternal reports of daughters' involvement in family activities showed a negative cubic relation to months since menarche, and maternal reports of disagreements over rules showed a positive cubic trend. Maternal and daughter reports both imply that mother-daughter relations take a temporary turn for the worse after menarche. Both mothers and daughters report some distancing (less acceptance, influence, involvement) and some heightened conflict (more disagreements).

A recent study by Steinberg (in press) is relevant here. Physically mature girls reported more intense but not more frequent conflicts with mothers than did less physically mature girls. The more physically mature girls also reported less cohesion with the mother, less "calm communication," and less acceptance from her (although these effects were qualified when chronological age was entered into the equations). Maternal reports yielded mostly parallel findings. Physical maturity measurement in this Steinberg (in press) study is based upon observer judgment of general pubertal status and not specifically upon age at menarche. Thus, although the results are by no means directly comparable, they are certainly compatible with the general hypothesis that perturbations in the mother-daughter dyad are associated with pubertal events just as they are for the mother-son dyad.

Steinberg found no curvilinear effects for relations between a global measure of pubertal status in girls and mother-daughter relations. Our preliminary examination of relations between overall measures of pubertal status for girls and behavior of family members suggests the same conclusion. Given that menarche is a late event in the pubertal cycle and that some worsening in the mother-daughter dyad's relations appears to occur before menarche (Steinberg's data), the fact that investigators report significant comparisons between premenarcheal girls and postmenarcheal girls in the direction of poor adjustment after menarche (e.g., our data) suggests that menarche has some special significance for mother-daughter relations. What is needed is an analysis that simultaneously takes menarche and other pubertal events into account; an analysis that, given our current level of understanding, is likely to be more ideal in prospect than in practice.

Father-Daughter Dyad.   Daughters perceived their fathers to be less accepting of them after menarche (Fig. 3.1). For all postmenarcheal groups, lower acceptance is reported than for the premenarcheal group. Daughters also see fathers as less influential after menarche than before (see Fig. 3.2). Both of these effects are linear. Within the bounds of the age and pubertal cycle studied here, our data

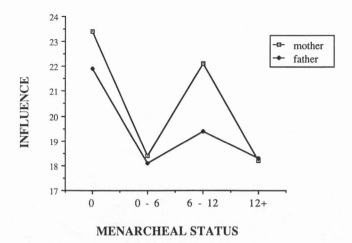

MENARCHEAL STATUS

FIG. 3.2. Menarcheal status and daughters' reports of maternal and paternal influence: The negative linear and cubic trends are statistically significant for perceived maternal influence and the negative linear trend is statistically significant for perceived paternal influence.

suggest a longer-lasting change in father-daughter relations than in mother-daughter relations. Interestingly, fathers do not perceive daughters to be less involved in family activities (Fig. 3.3) nor are there differences in fathers' reports of disagreements over rules as a function of menarcheal status (Fig. 3.4). Similar results have been reported informally by Rierdan (1982), Steinberg (in press), and Armentrout and Burger (1978). The latter investigators report less perceived acceptance by fathers for seventh graders than for younger or older daughters. Steinberg (in press) found the more physically mature girls perceived their fathers to be less accepting of them after menarche than before. Daughters also reported less cohesion, less calm communication, but not more conflict in relationships with fathers, as a function of pubertal status. Fathers reported less cohesion but no less calm communication nor more conflict with increased biological maturity. In general, over the adolescent era, conflicts are most common in the mother-daughter dyad (Montemayor, 1983); apparently conflicts associated specifically with puberty and menarche are no exception.

Why no relations between puberty/menarche and reported conflict with fathers? Steinberg has suggested three reasons. First, adolescents may find it easier to "act out" against the lower status parent (Weisfeld & Berger, 1983). Second, both young adolescent girls and boys may have a stronger need to individuate from the mother than from the father (Blos, 1962; Chodorow, 1978; Kaplan, 1984). Third, conflict with fathers may be rare because adolescent-father relationships are emotionally flat (Youniss & Smollar, 1985). A fourth reason, suggested by Montemayor (1983), is that adolescents of both genders interact

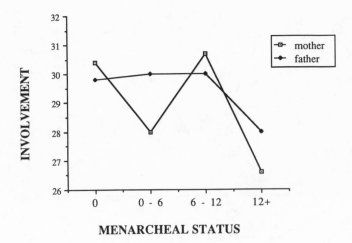

FIG. 3.3. Menarcheal status and parental report of daughters' involvement in family activities: The negative linear and the negative cubic trends are statistically significant for maternal report.

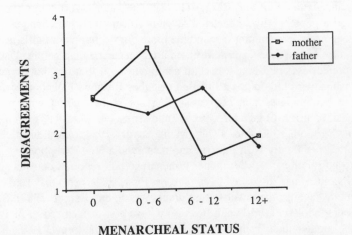

FIG. 3.4. Menarcheal status and parental report of disagreements over rules: The positive cubic trend for mothers is statistically significant.

more with mothers than with fathers, given that mothers have more supervisory responsibility: more interaction breeds greater opportunity for conflict. A fifth reason, consistent with the Gender-Intensification Hypothesis, is that early adolescence may be a period when socializing agents permit less latitude in nontraditional role performances with respect to gender. Parents and peers may expect more ladylike ladies and more manly men, and such templates for behavior may be especially appealing to young adolescents undergoing rapid biological and social change (Hill & Lynch, 1983). Such a tendency may be more apparent in the behavior of fathers than mothers if it is the case, as many claim, that fathers' expectations and sanctions in child-rearing are more influenced by gender than are those of mothers (Johnson, 1963; Lynn, 1969; Heilbrun, 1965; Hetherington, 1965). Overt conflict with males, especially fathers and other authorities, simply is less tolerable than before; "it just isn't feminine."

In a subsequent study (Hill & Holmbeck, in press), where pubertal and menarcheal effects were not considered, we found no differences between numbers of disagreements over rules with mothers and fathers in contrast to the general finding in the literature that conflicts with mothers are more prevalent than conflicts with fathers (Montemayor, 1983). Our results probably differ from those reported earlier because our measure of conflict is based on disagreements over *specified* rule situations and not some more global assessment. In addition, our data are based upon parent and not child report. Parents and adolescents agree only half the time about whether a conflict has occurred (Montemayor & Hanson, 1985). These results suggest that the content and context of disagreement or conflict require attention in future studies.

We found that perceived parental acceptance was negatively correlated with disagreements over rules in the father-daughter (but not in any other) dyad. This finding affirms the notion that open disagreement may be especially problematical in this dyad where preservation of father's masculinity and of daughter's femininity are both threatened by assertive, open disagreement(s). Disagreements over rules accounted for no more than 5% of the variance in perceived acceptance. However, one other source of variance in perceived paternal acceptance may be actual decreases in paternal behaviors indicative of acceptance after menarche. Given the advent of sexual reproductivity, generally believed to be signaled by menarche, everyday expressions of affection on the part of the father may actually decrease in frequency. Only one bit of empirical information supports this argument. Fathers in Steinberg's (in press) study reported less cohesion with physically mature daughters than with less mature girls but no differences were found in related measures of fathers' perceptions of closeness and calm communication with daughters. My own informal conversations with several fathers of young adolescent girls have resulted in descriptions of changes in fathers' expressions of affection toward daughters during early adolescence. Conversations with pediatricians affirm the view that puberty may be associated with lessened physical affection. However, fathers believe that their behavioral change is tied to figural, especially breast, development, rather than to menarche.

Factors other than paternal behavior change may also be implicated in daughters' perceptions of less acceptance by fathers following menarche. Negative attitudes toward menarche (especially for early-maturing girls) may lead to transformed or even distorted conceptions of parental behaviors; those behaviors that once signified acceptance may no longer do so. Douvan (1970) has claimed that adaptation to menarche involves looking increasingly to the outer world for self-definition at a point when inner change is so dramatic. Thus, the normally "shallow" father-daughter relation may no longer be satisfactory. Peskin (1973), on the other hand, claims that menarche, especially when early, leads to an intrapersonal, inward-looking, rather than interpersonal, stance. Although their views are directly contradictory, both theorists point to the potential for transforming views of parents without much parental participation in the process (see also Hill & Lynch, 1983).

Family Standards and Rules.   Information about the relations between menarcheal status (as perceived by mothers and fathers) and family rules and standards is presented in Fig. 3.5. Daughters perceived more control in the family shortly after menarche than before or after; both quadratic trends were statistically significant. We have some evidence here for the kind of difference in the rearing of pre- and postmenarcheal girls that Block (1979), Katz (1979), and Newson and Newson (1968) had in mind when they spoke of increased chap-

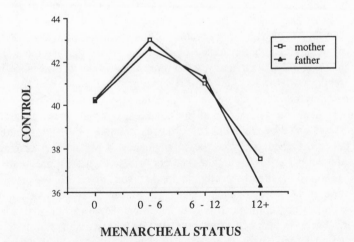

FIG. 3.5. Menarcheal status and daughters' perceptions of family control: Both negative quadratic trends (one based upon maternal, and the other based upon paternal, report) are statistically significant.

eronage, vigilance, and less permissiveness during early adolescence. What is interesting is the apparent temporary nature of increased control shortly after menarche; the mean for family rules and standards was not high for the early-maturing group; there was no cubic trend. Perhaps "vigilance" does persist longer for early maturers but decreases once menstruation becomes modal (Petersen, 1983).

Overall, this study suggests that menarcheal status is associated with changes in both parents' and daughters' perceptions of family relations. Effects for the mother-daughter dyad appear to be both more temporary and more conflictual than do effects for the father-daughter dyad. All postmenarcheal groups of daughters saw their fathers as less accepting than did premenarcheal girls. Girls experiencing early menarche may be at some special risk for chronically disordered mother-daughter relations, although there are other interpretations possible for the cubic effects obtained. Longitudinal studies will certainly be necessary to resolve the issues involved.

In our observational work, we then expected that for on-time girls conflict would increase around menarche with mothers but not fathers and after menarche more power assertion by both mothers and fathers would be noted. We expected that conflict with mothers would be high for the early-maturing group as well. Thus cubic trends were anticipated. Given the gender intensification hypothesis (Hill & Lynch, 1983) and the work of Hetherington, Stouwie, and Ridberg (1971), we did not expect linear positive effects of menarche on assertiveness nor did we expect girls to gain in overall influence on family decision making.

THE OBSERVATIONAL STUDY

The analyses from our observational study of girls reported here deal only with associations between months since menarche and frequency data on family behavior in the family interaction task. Perhaps particular measures we deploy speak better to control (power or assertiveness) issues than to issues of conflict (a point to be addressed in greater detail in the final section of this paper). Control or power in the family has been defined as "the ability . . . of individual members to change the behavior of other family members" (Cromwell & Olsen, 1975, p. 5). Among the components of control that are delineated are power processes, or the techniques individuals use as they attempt to gain and keep control of negotiations or decision-making processes. The most common measures of power processes in family interaction research are amount of talking time and number of successful and unsuccessful interruptions. Influence over the "final decision" made by the family in a task such as SFIT may be regarded as an outcome measure of power or control.

Another aspect of behavior in family interaction situations related to control is the assertion advanced without benefit of justification or elaboration akin to what

Raven and French (1958) labelled *direct power*. We code utterances for explanation; that is for the presence of the elaboration of assertions (e.g., "we should do this" vs. "we should do this because . . ."). We have found, in families of boys, that unelaborated assertions *are* more frequent at the apex of pubertal growth for sons and for mothers. In this first cross-sectional, observation study of family behavior around menarche we examined time-since-menarche in relation to a variety of variables that are thought to reflect attempts at control: talking time, interruptions, decision influence, and unelaborated assertions (represented in our coding scheme in terms of the presence of explanations).

As for the measurement of *conflict* in family interaction tasks, frequencies of initial disagreement and interruptions have received the most empirical attention. We examine some variables based upon counts of initial (dis)agreements and interruptive behavior. Initial disagreements in the SFIT task index *conflicts of interest,* choices that have the potential for interfering with the actions of others but that do not necessarily imply or necessarily lead to contentious interchange in laboratory or "real-world" situations.

In the family interaction literature, frequencies of individual family members' interruptions have been treated as indices of family conflict as well as control. In our view, serious inferences about family conflict require more stringent criteria than are involved in reporting simple frequencies of interruptions by individual family members. This issue is treated in greater detail below; minimally it would appear that mutual interruptions (a power struggle) would be necessary to invoke the term *conflict.*

Method

A more detailed description of methods and results of this study may be found in Hill, Cantara, Holmbeck, Lynch, and Green (1987). This report also includes consideration of other variables and of spousal interaction not considered here.

Subjects. Subjects for this study were 115 seventh-grade girls and their parents recruited from the same population as in the questionnaire study. All families were biologically intact and all of the target girls were firstborn children. Socioeconomic, work, and educational status did not differ from that of families in the questionnaire study.

General Procedure. All families came to the Boys' Town Center for the Study of Youth Development to complete several laboratory interaction tasks (only the SFIT is considered here) and to complete brief questionnaires designed to elicit information about demographic issues, pubertal status, and other variables not relevant to the present chapter. The SFIT was the first of the interaction tasks to be completed and was videotaped.

Menarcheal Status.   Daughters' reports of menarcheal status are used in the analyses reported below. As in the questionnaire study, family members were asked to indicate whether menstruation had not begun, had begun within the past 6 months, within the past 12 months, or longer than 12 months ago. About 80% agreement in placing the time of menarche was characteristic of each pair of respondents (mother-father, mother-daughter, father-daughter). Correlations between pairs ranged from .87 to .91. By daughters' reports, menarcheal status placements were as follows: premenarcheal (N = .62); 0–6 months (N = 20); 6–12 months (N = 17); and 12+ months (N = 16).

SFIT.   Each family member was given a list of five multiple-choice questions and asked to indicate a preferred first and second choice. The questions dealt with fairly innocuous matters such as vacation destinations, restaurant preferences, and preferences for family purchases. Following independent completion of preference questions, family members were brought together and asked to decide on a joint response. Individual preferences were left to individuals to reveal in the context of the interaction.

The videotaped sessions were transcribed in conformity to a detailed set of instructions. All sessions were transcribed in the form of utterances (defined in terms of a complete thought unit—a spoken simple sentence). Interruptions were noted on the transcripts in such a way that they could be counted and their "success" (the other's yielding) could also be scored. Who spoke before whom, speech by speech, also was counted, thus providing a rough estimate of dyadic interchanges. In addition, individual family members' initial preferences and final consensus preferences were recorded. This permitted initial agreements between the various family dyads to be counted. Decision influence was assessed by comparing individuals' initial preference with the consensus preference. Talking time was measured by counting number of words spoken. (In a subsample of 20 families, talking time and number of words spoken were highly correlated [r = .94]. Counting words was more efficient and more reliable.)

Explanations were coded from the transcripts by two coders working independently; discrepancies were resolved by an expert coder who reviewed all coded transcripts. *Kappa* for coding explanations was .74.

Analyses.   As in our questionnaire study, menarcheal status is treated as a continuous variable and entered into multiple regression equations as a set of power polynomial terms. The terms are entered hierarchically, beginning with the linear term and continuing with the terms that test for, first, quadratic and, then, cubic trends.

Results and Discussion

Father-Daughter Dyad.   With increasing maturity, there was less initial agreement between fathers and daughters (Fig. 3.6). For both fathers and daughters,

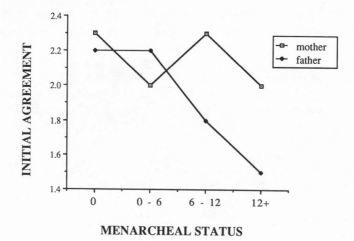

FIG. 3.6.   Menarcheal status and initial agreement in mother-daughter and father-daughter dyads: The negative linear trend is significant for the father-daughter dyad.

talking time was higher for those families where girls had reached menarche sometime during the past year than in the 0 and 12+ groups (Fig. 3.7). Father-daughter interaction sequences were higher for the 0-6 group and for the 12+ group than for the other two groups (Fig. 3.8). Fathers' interruptions of daughters were greater shortly after menarche but then less common with increasing maturity. There were no corresponding changes in daughters' interruptions (Fig. 3.9). After menarche, however, daughters yielded progressively less to fathers' interruptions; that is to say, fathers' interruptions became less successful (Fig. 3.10). Frequencies of explanation for individual family members were not affected by menarcheal status; however, total family explanations were higher with increasing maturity (a significant linear effect; Fig. 3.11) and tended to be higher (cubic effect) for the immediately postmenarcheal and the 12+ than in the other two groups ($p = .06$). Menarcheal status proved to be unrelated to daughters' influence on overall family decision making. (A more complete description of results may be found in Hill et al., 1987).

In the face of more frequent conflicts of interest (initial disagreements), both fathers and daughters made increased attempts to control the decision-making process through talking more and more to each other. Fathers' interruptions of daughters were more frequent. Daughters did not interrupt more but they did yield less. These findings suggest a transformation in father-daughter relations following menarche characterized by what might be labeled passive-assertiveness on the part of the daughter. Shortly after menarche, fathers interrupt their

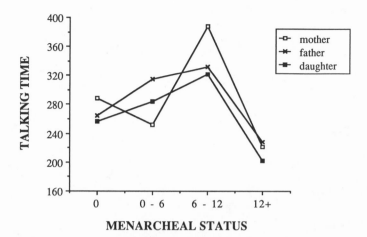

FIG. 3.7. Menarcheal status and talking times for fathers, mothers, and daughters: The positive quadratic trends are statistically significant for fathers and daughters. The negative cubic trend for mothers is statistically significant.

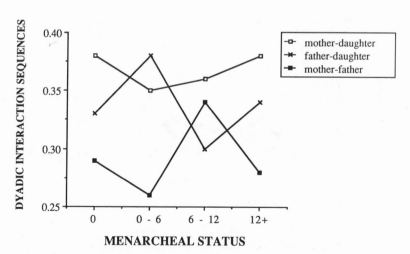

FIG. 3.8. Menarcheal status and dyadic interaction sequences: The positive cubic trend for father-daughter interaction sequences is statistically significant.

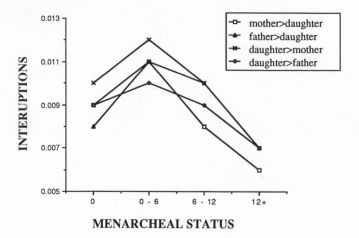

FIG. 3.9.   Menarcheal status and interruptions by dyad: Both negative quadratic trends for the mother-daughter dyad are statistically significant. The quadratic trend for interruptions of daughters by fathers also is statistically significant.

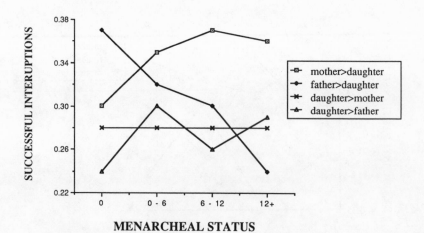

FIG. 3.10.   Menarcheal status and successful interruptions: The negative linear trend for fathers' interruptions of daughters is statistically significant.

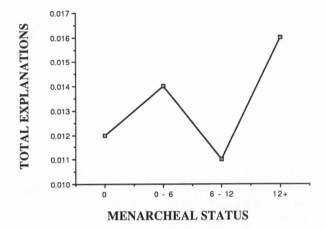

MENARCHEAL STATUS

FIG. 3.11. Menarcheal status and total family explanations: The positive linear trend is statistically significant and the cubic trend approaches statistical significante ($p = .06$).

daughters more but the girls do not interrupt their fathers more. Instead, they yield less, displaying a kind of passive resistance to fathers' control attempts. This pattern of results centering around menarche is quite different from that observed for boys in the earlier interaction studies that centered around the apex of pubertal growth (Steinberg, 1981; Steinberg & Hill, 1978). (Given the different pubertal measures employed, gender comparisons are risky but, nonetheless, suggestive of avenues for future research.)

Fathers of boys interrupted them more and boys yielded to them more with increasing maturity in what seems to be a dominance-submission display. Boys did not interrupt fathers more with increasing maturity nor were there changes in frequencies of initial agreement, talking time, or dyadic exchanges. When set against the backdrop of the findings for boys, there is a more evident negotiatory quality in father-daughter interactions than in father-son interactions. Even while conflicts of interest (initial disagreements) are more common with increasing maturity for girls, and fathers and daughters talk more to each other, frequencies of interruptions for both parties (suggesting contentious interchanges) do not increase. Interruptions for fathers do not increase in linear fashion; the data imply only a temporary elevation of such behavior on the part of fathers alone. That dyadic interchanges between fathers and daughters are more common after menarche than before and that daughters yield less to fathers' interruptions (rather than interrupting fathers more) may be the most striking phenomena here.

Mother-Daughter Dyad.   Frequencies of initial agreement between mothers and daughters were not affected by menarcheal status (Fig. 3.6). Mother-daughter sequences of dyadic interaction were consistently high for each of the groups, accounting at each menarcheal level for more than a third of all sequences (Fig. 3.8) despite less maternal talking time (and increased daughter talking time) in the 0–6 group (Fig. 3.7). However, a greater proportion of both mother and daughter utterances involved interruptions of one another immediately after menarche than prior to it or 6–12 months afterward (Fig. 3.9). No menarcheal status affects were observed for yielding to interruptions.

Shortly after menarche, both mothers and daughters were more assertive in their interactions with one another, and not passively so either. The findings appear to be the behavioral counterpart of the maternal report of greater disagreements over rules just after menarche than before or later in the questionnaire study. They are similar to our results for mothers and sons at the apex of pubertal growth in that mothers are interrupting children more *and* children are interrupting their mothers more—a pattern not observed for fathers and children of either sex. Effects for fathers of children of both sexes tend to be more linear. Were these longitudinal data, we might say that the effects are more long-lasting, whereas those for mothers and daughters (and sons) are more short-lived and *conflict* may be an appropriate label for them.

General Discussion.   The differential pattern of results for mother-daughter and father-daughter relations just after menarche in the observational study may be understood in terms of gender role socialization through complementation, provided we broaden the interpretative context for the observational categories somewhat. From the observational literature on fathers' roles in the development of achievement motives in (generally younger) daughters, we know that fathers tend to behave more expressively than instrumentally on laboratory tasks they are asked to perform with daughters. Fathers behave as though success in the task for them were more a matter of maintaining an enjoyable affective (and, probably, deferential) relationship than of facilitating their daughters' independent achievement. There may even be a flirtatious style about fathers' interventions (Lamb et al., 1979). If we view talking time in terms of doing what it takes to try to maintain or display a pleasant, positive affective relationship, the talk-time results for fathers begin to make new sense. Despite greater initial disagreements, there are no indications of mutually interruptive behavior between fathers and daughters and they talk more to one another (dyadic sequences).

At the same time, family explanations are higher in the immediately postmenarcheal group for the family as a whole (a marginal finding also compatible with the notion of keeping father-daughter relations on an even keel, especially under conditions of constraint and observation). That fathers' active attempts at control just after puberty are met with less yielding and not more interrupting also may serve the same function, perhaps exacerbated by the laboratory environment. As I watch the videotapes, my impression is that fathers are irritated when initial agreements are exposed and that fathers try to charm daughters into compliance.

That my view is not totally subjective is suggested by a set of ratings completed by Cantara (1983). Undergraduate assistants rated affiliativeness and dominance in terms of their initiations for a subsample ($N = 81$) of our families. All possible pairs were rated separately by different pairs of observers for each dyadic combination. No menarcheal effects were observed for the dominance ratings for any dyad but there were two such statistically significant (cubic) effects for the initiation of affiliativeness. Mothers of the 0–6 group and of the 12+ group, compared to the other two groups, were seen as less affiliative toward daughters whereas fathers were seen as more so. These results and interpretations would be cleaner were the observational situation itself focused upon dyads rather than triads. The results are, nonetheless, consonant with the notion of a paternal investment in maintaining an expressive and deferential role for daughters—an aim which, if present, is only partially realized, given that postmenarcheal daughters yield less and not more to fathers' interruptions. Nonetheless, an increased influence of daughters on the family consensus is not associated with advanced menarcheal status.

Unfortunately, our data do not permit us to select from among the available explanations for greater apparent conflict around menarche in the mother-daughter dyad. It seems likely that only longitudinal designs and treatments of the data at relationship, interaction, and system levels will permit satisfying interpretations. It is possible, for example, that events in the father-daughter dyad show initial reactivity to menarche and events in the mother-daughter dyad are, in turn, reactive to changes in father-daughter interaction. This is the chain of events suggested if paternal intensification of gender role expectations is the central issue. It is also possible that initial reactivity to menarche appears in the mother-daughter dyad and changes in father-daughter interaction are secondary to these, as is suggested by Friday (1977) and Magrab (1979), when they argue that menarche establishes the daughter as a sexual rival to the mother.

Our questionnaire and observational results are compatible in that neither disagreements over rules nor daughters' and fathers' interruptions of one another were related to menarche. As noted, it appears that overt conflict is not characteristic of this dyad after menarche. But the operative word here may turn out to be *overt*. There was greater disagreement between fathers and daughters in initial individual choices in our laboratory task, which translates into open disagreement as soon as family members reveal their own preferences. Although we have interpreted daughters' lesser yielding behavior as part of a pattern of passive assertiveness, it could be considered as conflictual as well in light of interference definitions of that term.

Still comparing the questionnaire and observational results, we note also the contrast between daughters' perceptions of less paternal warmth after menarche and observers' ratings of more frequent initiations of affiliative behavior by fathers of the 0–6 and 12+ groups. Only from comparing both kinds of data from the same families will we obtain any satisfying answers but some possibilities can be suggested. First, it may be that the more frequent initiations of affiliativeness on the part of the father are a situational adaptation to the demands of a laboratory task (to "charm" into compliance daughters who ought not to be disagreeing in public). If so, what of the mirror image results for mothers' affiliativeness? Mothers may have less to lose than fathers in public conflicts with daughters. Second, daughters' perceptions of warmth may be more influenced by decreases in paternal physical affection of the sort we have presumed occur around this time than by fathers' verbal affiliative behavior. Third, daughters' perceptions of less paternal warmth may be more related to increased paternal control attempts than to affiliative behavior per se.

Results for father and daughter talking times and father-daughter dyadic sequences add further to the richness of the observational as compared to the questionnaire data for fathers. Talking time has traditionally been viewed as a manifestation of attempted control over interaction. From this perspective, both fathers and daughters in the 0–6 and 12+ groups are higher in power assertiveness than the other two groups. There is a kind of equality implied here, a power sharing; fathers and daughters around menarche talk things over in ways not common to any other dyad. Through role complementation, it appears that sons may learn assertiveness toward mothers (women?) and daughters learn interpersonal skills helpful in relationships with fathers (men?).

Early Versus On-Time Maturing.   Thus far, I have ignored the issue of early versus on-time maturing in presenting the results from our observational efforts. In general, cubic trends were less often present than in the questionnaire study. However, they were obtained for mothers' talking time (negative cubic trend indicating less maternal participation in the 0–6 and 12+ groups), father-daughter dyadic sequences (positive cubic trend), total family explanations (positive cubic trend, $p = 06$), and observer ratings of affiliativeness initiated by fathers (positive) and by mothers (negative). Indices of conflict and control are not directly implicated in these results but they are consistent with our questionnaire results in suggesting greater emotional distance in the mother-daughter dyad in the 0–6 and 12+ groups. We conclude that an empirical base continues to be present for longitudinal investigation of this issue.

Generalization from this Work.   Before turning to a discussion of conflict, it is useful to discuss limits to the generalization of this work. Although the decision to focus on white, firstborn, seventh graders living with their natural parents still makes sense to us, some of its implications and consequences warrant further consideration. We chose to study firstborn children and their parents because it seemed that familial experience at the onset of adolescence would not be the same another time around and that it would complicate our design (and increase our sample size) to take prior experience into account. In the absence of much information about intraindividual biological change and family behavior, it seemed important to provide a base for further study.

A recent paper offers some confirmation of our decision and suggests its limitations (Cohen, Adler, Beck, & Irwin, 1986). In their questionnaire study of 900 parents of sixth and seventh graders, they found that first born children were perceived by their parents as more interpersonally negative (more quick to talk back and argue, more temperamental, more angry at parents, more bossy, and more too-sure-of-themselves) than were later-born children. Parents of firstborn children also reported more negative feelings (angry, confused, frustrated, out of control, guilty) toward adolescents than did parents of later-born children. These results support our strategy in that they confirm differences between parenting of firstborn and later-born children and, at the same time, suggest that generalizing to later-born children from our findings is risky.

Our decision to use seventh graders alone was motivated by avoidance of analytical complexities that would have been involved by having to take chronological age into account (complexities magnified by the likelihood of curvilinear effects of pubertal and menarcheal status on the family behaviors of interest). Although an appropriate range of pubertal and menarcheal statuses among seventh graders was assured by this decision (given individual differences in the onset, duration, and termination of pubertal events), the decision was a better one for girls than for boys because any boys well into the pubertal cycle in the seventh grade are, in fact, early maturers. Comparisons of our data from families of boys and girls, already suspect since the biological point of reference for boys is apex pubertal growth and for girls is menarche, carry the additional risk of comparing (mostly) on-time girls with (mostly) early-maturing boys.

Finally, our decision to study white adolescents living with both of their natural parents means that our data speak to an increasing minority of families in the United States. The limitations to generalization here are obvious. There is, as well, a pressing need to extend this kind of work, and family research in general during the adolescent era, to populations of families that differ in color, family structure, or both, from the population that we have sampled (Hill, in press).

CONFLICT

Thus far, I have used the term *conflict* conditionally in relation to the results of our observational study of girls (as well as boys). Removing the conditional requires addressing a question often ignored in family interaction research: How is conflict to be defined? Recently Peterson (1983) has defined conflict as "an interpersonal process that occurs whenever the actions of one person interfere with the actions of another" (p. 365). Interference is considered "to include not only outright obstructions of activity, but any reduction in effectiveness or benefit of one person's activity that is causally related to the actions of another" (p. 365).

Two possible attributes of conflict are missing from Peterson's definition. The definition does not include either affect or contention. The conditions under which interference leads to negative affect or contentious interchanges, on any given occasion or chronically, then become empirical matters. Over the short run, Peterson suggests a branching model wherein the interference is either avoided (one or both parties withdraw before the conflict becomes "open"), or there is engagement in the conflict. Engagement (open conflict), in turn, may lead to either negotiation or escalation. Termination of the conflict, once engaged in, may occur through separation (a form of withdrawal, too, but one that occurs later on in the sequence), domination, compromise, integrative agreement, or some long-term commitment to changing the rules governing interaction (structural improvement).

Montemayor and Hanson (1985) have published some important data that bear upon conflict resolution. They inform us, from their telephone survey of tenth graders, that two conflicts with family members occurred every 3 days on the average for their subjects. Forty-seven percent of the conflicts with parents were marked by avoidance (walking away in the face of interference), 38% by domination, and only 15% by negotiation.

Three issues are raised by Peterson's definition and framework and by Montemayor's data: First, most investigators and reviewers have focused upon heated and contentious interchanges in "counting" conflicts rather than upon interference alone. This means that conflict in the "Peterson" sense is probably more prevalent than most investigators or reviewers have concluded and may even be more prevalent in adolescence than in late childhood. It seems not only plausible but likely that intraindividual changes and increased orientations to peers would provide greater opportunities for interference in meeting life goals of adolescents and parents. Second, what then becomes striking is the percentage of conflict "solved" by domination and avoidance (or "walking away"). Current methods of measuring conflict in parent-adolescent relations may underestimate its frequency because these two modes of conflict resolution are likely to have been counted as instances of "no conflict."

Third, as Montemayor and Hanson (1985) point out, the frequency of conflict avoidance in naturalistic situations requires that we be especially careful in interpreting behavior in laboratory tasks such as the SFIT, wherein conflict-resolution is demanded and conflict-avoidance—in the sense of physical withdrawal—is not permitted.

At first glance, it appears that interruptions fit into "interference" definitions of conflict. Yet we have been wary of inferring conflict from individual frequency data for several reasons. First, one may question the conventional interpretation of interruptions as indicative of conflict. As Marlow (1985) has pointed out, "interruptions may appear at times of high excitement and creativity and may indicate a high level of flexibility in the family's interactions" (p. 27). And, as noted by Holmbeck (1986), "interruptions may occur between two individuals who know each other well simply because these individuals are able to anticipate what the other is going to say before this individual has completed his/her utterance" (pp. 24–25). Second, interruptive frequency of utterance toward a target from one actor in the family drama is not by itself indicative of conflict. We are, perhaps, safer in beginning to use that word with caution when both mother-to-daughter *and* daughter-to-mother utterances are interruptive in nature (Hill & Holmbeck, 1985, 1986b). Third, just because daughters interrupt their mothers more and mothers interrupt their daughters more often after menarche does not yet establish that the interruptions are mutual. When we can establish that the girls who are interrupting their mothers and the mothers who are interrupting their daughters are from the same families, then we will be less cautious.

Establishing spurts of interruptive behaviors emitted sequentially by both parties will move us from simple counts to mutual engagement and, further, to the possibility of discriminating escalation from mere engagement. Still, what we may be observing is mutual spontaneity and anticipatory behavior. Affect has been a missing ingredient in observational studies for too long a time. We are now completing analyses that permit the double-coding of utterances such that mutual interruptions can be examined in their affective contexts. What is of particular interest here is twofold: (a) mutual interruptions in the context of negative affect; and (b) mutual interruptions in the context of the withdrawal of positive affect. Under either condition, the inference of conflict appears to be a legitimate one. The latter condition is of special interest if it is true, as Montemayor and Hanson (1985) and Papini and Datan (1982) have suggested, that the withdrawal and absence of positive affect is far more characteristic of parent-adolescent interchange than is angry contentiousness.

Vuccinich (1984) has shown that direct, indirect, and implicative disagreements in family dinner-table discourse provide substantial information about family status. Another of our analyses in progress will permit both frequency and sequential analyses of disagreements; that is, direct contradiction (M: "Steve Martin is funny"; C: "No he's not"); indirect opposition (M: "Let's go for a pool table"; C: "We already have a pool table"); statements of shock and surprise ("You didn't really say that"); and the like. Analyses of disagreements will provide yet another avenue for obtaining confirmatory information about familial conflict.

Disagreements also are of special interest to us, given that Cooper, Grotevant, and Condon's (1983) work (and the Cooper and Grotevant theoretical scheme) implies that open disagreement may facilitate the development of perspective taking and identity exploration. This is in strong contrast to the traditional stance of family-interaction researchers that healthy families disagree less and agree more (e.g., Jacob, 1975). Tolerance for open expressions of disagreement may well represent a positive force in individuation around puberty provided that they do not escalate into "fights." The potential we possess for discriminating "conflicts of interest" (expressions of disagreement) from "contentious interchanges" (expressions of disagreement that lead to counter-disagreement, negative affect, bursts of mutual interruptions) may be salutary for family interaction research more generally.

At the same time, parent-adolescent relations, in general, may be better characterized by relative absence of positive behaviors than by the presence of overt conflict (Montemayor, 1985). Effects of menarche on global measures of parental acceptance may be less related to control and conflict than to decreases, at menarche, in parental behaviors such as positive affect and gaze. (Menarcheal effects on fathers' and daughters' talking times and dyadic interchanges ought to be illuminated, as well, by affective appraisals.) Currently, frequency and sequential analyses are being performed examining positive affect and gaze.

Adaptation.   However the considerations raised about conflict in families including young adolescents are resolved, research on the transition to adolescence is also unlikely to advance significantly without further attention to conceptual and operational definitions of *adaptation.* Minimally the invocation of that concept must involve the description of some steady state—whether at the individual behavior, relationship, interaction, or system level of analysis—followed by the description of perturbations linked to biological change and, then, by the description of some new steady state. We have, thus far, been content to let curvilinear trends in our findings carry the burden of the meaning of adaptation; yet, some of the effects of biological change in family behavior are linear and it is difficult to believe that they are not part of the adaptational picture as well. Another problem with our current data in relation to *adaptation* is that we have not measured sufficient time since apex pubertal growth or since menarche to offer a satisfactory description of some new steady state. In both cases, searching for solutions will require greater attention to the patterning or organization of the behavior involved. It seems useful to note that all prepubertal steady states in family functioning are unlikely to be the same and that this may provide a fruitful departure point for the future study of adaptation. Identifying some types of usual prepubertal steady states, proposing some differential adaptations to biological change for each type, and testing these propositions appear to hold promise for future research. It is a path that we intend to follow.

ACKNOWLEDGMENTS

The research reported here was supported, in large part, by Father Flanagan's Boys Home and the John D. and Catherine T. MacArthur Foundation. Without the generous cooperation of many school administrators in the Omaha metropolitan area and of seventh graders and parents in their school districts, this research could not have been implemented. Nearly 200 staff members and students have been associated directly with this program of research over the years. I am indebted to each of them for their contributions and, especially to the following, whose intellectual and administrative leadership has been invaluable: Mary Ellen Lynch, Thomas Green, Grayson Holmbeck, Albert Cantara, Lynn Marlow, Michael Jellinek, and Francie Schroeder. A continuing series of conversations with Dale Blyth, W. Andrew Collins, Catherine Cooper, Harold Grotevant, and Laurence Steinberg has provided important stimulation and support.

REFERENCES

Anderson, E. R., Hetherington, E. M., & Clingempeel, W. G. (1986, March). *Pubertal status and its influence on the adaptation to remarriage.* Paper presented at the Biennial Meetings of the Society for Research on Adolescence, Madison, WI.

Armentrout, J. A., & Burger, G. K. (1978). Children's reports of parental child-rearing behavior at five grade levels. *Developmental Psychology, 7,* 44–48.

Atkinson, B. R., & Bell, N. J. (1986, March). *Attachment and autonomy in adolescence.* Paper presented at the Biennial Meetings of the Society for Research on Adolescence, Madison, WI.

Bakeman, R. (1978). Untangling streams of behavior: Sequential analyses of observation data. In G. R. Sackett (Ed.), *Observing behavior: Vol. 2. Data collection and analysis methods.* Baltimore: University Park Press.

Baumrind, D. (1968). Authoritarian vs. authoritative control. *Adolescence, 3,* 255–272.

Bernstein, B. (1964). Elaborated and restricted codes: Their social origins and some consequences. In J. Gumperz & O. Hymes (Eds.), The ethnography of communication. *American Anthropologist Special Publication, 66,* 55–69.

Block, J. H. (1979). Another look at sex differentiation in the socialization behaviors of mothers and fathers. In F. Denmark (Ed.), *Psychology of women: Future directions of research* (pp. 123–152). New York: Psychological Dimensions.

Blos, P. (1962). *On adolescence.* New York: Free Press.

Blos, P. (1979). *The adolescent passage.* New York: International Universities Press.

Brooks-Gunn, J., & Ruble, D. N. (1983). The experience of menarche from a developmental perspective. In J. Brooks-Gunn & A. C. Petersen (Eds.), *Girls at puberty: Biological and psychosocial perspectives* (pp. 155–178). New York: Plenum.

Cantara, A. R. (1983). *Pubertal status and assertiveness in family interaction in early adolescent girls.* Unpublished master's thesis, Virginia Commonwealth University, Richmond, VA.

Chodorow, N. (1978). *The reproduction of mothering: Psychoanalysis and the sociology of gender.* Berkeley, CA: University of California Press.

Clausen, J. (1975). The social meaning of differential physical and sexual maturation. In S. Dragastin & G. Elder, Jr. (Eds.), *Adolescence in the life cycle* (pp. 25–47). New York: Wiley.

Cohen, J., & Cohen, P. (1983). *Applied multiple regression/correlation analysis for the behavioral sciences.* Hillsdale, NJ: Lawrence Erlbaum Associates.

Cohen, M., Adler, N., Beck, A., & Irwin, C. E. (1986). Parental reactions to the onset of adolescence. *Journal of Adolescent Health Care, 7,* 101–106.

Cooper, C. R., Grotevant, H. D., & Condon, S. M. (1983). Individuality and connectedness in the family as a context for adolescent identity formation and role-taking skill. In H. D. Grotevant & C. R. Cooper (Eds.), *Adolescent development in the family* (pp. 43–59). San Francisco: Jossey-Bass.

Cromwell, R. E., & Olsen, D. H. (Eds., 1975), *Power in families.* New York: Wiley.

Deutsch, H. (1944). *The psychology of women* (Vol. 1). New York: Grune & Stratton.

Douvan, E. (1970). New sources of conflict in females at adolescence and early adulthood. In J. M. Bardwick, E. Douvan, M. S. Horner, & D. Gutmann, *Feminine personality and conflict* (pp. 31–44). Monterey, CA: Brooks/Cole.

Duncan, O. D. (1977). A socioeconomic index for all occupations. In A. J. Reiss, Jr. (Ed.), *Occupations and social status* (pp. 109–138). New York: Arno Press.

Ferreira, A. J. (1963). Decision making in normal and pathological families. *Archives of General Psychiatry, 8,* 68–73.

Friday, N. (1977). *My mother/myself.* New York: Delacorte.

Garwood, S. G., & Allen, L. (1979). Self-concept and identified problem differences between pre- and post-menarcheal adolescents. *Journal of Clinical Psychology, 35,* 528–537.

Greif, E., & Ulman, K. H. (1982). The psychological impact of menarche on early adolescent females: A review of the literature. *Child Development, 53,* 1413–1430.

Grotevant, H. D., & Cooper, C. R. (1986). Individuation in family relationships. *Human Development, 29,* 82–100.

Heilbrun, A. B. (1965). An empirical test of the modelling theory of sex-role learning. *Child Development, 36,* 789–799.

Hetherington, E. M. (1965). A developmental study of the effects of sex of the dominant parent on sex-role preference, identification, and imitation in children. *Journal of Personality and Social Psychology, 2,* 188–194.

Hetherington, E. M. (1972). Effects of father absence on personality development in adolescent daughters. *Developmental Psychology, 7,* 313–326.

Hetherington, E. M., Stouwie, R., & Ridberg, E. H. (1971). Patterns of family interaction and child-rearing attitudes related to three dimensions of juvenile delinquency. *Journal of Abnormal Psychology, 77,* 160–176.

Hill, J. P. (1980). The family. In M. Johnson (Ed.), *Toward adolescence: The middle school years. The seventy-ninth yearbook of the National Society for the Study of Education* (pp. 32–55). Chicago: University of Chicago Press.

Hill, J. P. (in press). Research on adolescents and their families: Past and prospect. In W. R. Damon (Ed.), *New directions in child psychology.* San Francisco: Jossey-Bass.

Hill, J. P., Cantara, A. R., Holmbeck, G. N., Lynch, M. E., & Green, T. M. (1987). *Menarcheal status and family interaction.* Unpublished manuscript, Virginia Commonwealth University, Richmond, VA.

Hill, J. P., & Holmbeck, G. N. (1985, April). Familial adaptation to pubertal change: The role of conflict. In W. A. Collins (Chair), *Parent-child relations in the transition to adolescence: Family adaptations to pubertal change.* Symposium conducted at the meeting of the Society for Research in Child Development, Toronto, Ontario.

Hill, J. P., & Holmbeck, G. N. (1986a). Attachment and autonomy during adolescence. In G. J. Whitehurst (Ed.), *Annals of Child Development.* Greenwich, CT: JAI Press.

Hill, J. P., & Holmbeck, G. N. (1986b). Familial adaptation to biological change during adolescence. In R. M. Lerner & T. T. Foch (Eds.), *Biological-psychosocial interactions in early adolescence: A life-span perspective* (pp. 207–224). Hillsdale, NJ: Lawrence Earlbaum Associates.

Hill, J. P., & Holmbeck, G. N. (in press). Disagreements about rules in families with seventh graders. *Journal of Youth and Adolescence.*

Hill, J. P., Holmbeck, G. N., Marlow, L., Green, T. M., & Lynch, M. E. (1985a). Menarcheal status and parent-child relations in families of seventh grade girls. *Journal of Youth and Adolescence, 14,* 314–330.

Hill, J. P., Holmbeck, G. N., Marlow, L., Green, T. M., & Lynch, M. E. (1985b). Pubertal status and parent-child relations in families of seventh grade boys. *Journal of Early Adolescence, 5,* 31–44.

Hill, J. P., & Lynch, M. E. (1983). The intensification of gender-related role expectations during early adolescence. In J. Brooks-Gunn & A. C. Peterson (Eds.), *Girls at puberty* (pp. 201–228). New York: Plenum.

Hoffman, M. L. (1975). Moral internalization, parental power and the nature of parent-child interaction. *Developmental Psychology, 11,* 228–239.

Holmbeck, G. N. (1986). *The role of familial conflict in the adaptation to menarche: Sequential analysis of family interaction.* Unpublished manuscript.

Jacob, T. (1975). Family interaction in disturbed and normal families. *Psychological Bulletin, 82,* 33–65.

Johnson, M. M. (1963). Sex-role learning in the nuclear family. *Child Development, 34,* 315–333.

Jones, M. C., & Mussen, P. H. (1958). Self-conceptions, motivations, and interpersonal attitudes of early- and late-maturing girls. *Child Development, 29,* 491–501.

Kandel, D., & Lesser, G. S. (1972). *Youth in two worlds.* San Francisco: Jossey-Bass.

Kaplan, L. J. (1984). *Adolescence: The farewell to childhood.* New York: Simon & Schuster.

Katz, P. A. (1979). The development of female identity. In C. B. Kopp (Ed.), *Becoming female: Perspectives on development* (pp. 3–28). New York: Plenum.

Kelley, H. H., Berscheid, E., Christensen, A., Harvey, J. H., Huston, T. L., Levinger, G., McClintock, E., Peplau, L. A., & Peterson, D. L. (1983). *Close relationships.* New York: Freeman.

Koff, E., Rierdan, J., & Silverstone, E. (1978). Changes in representation of body image as a function of menarcheal status. *Developmental Psychology, 14,* 635–642.

Lamb, M. E., Owen, M. T., & Chase-Lansdale, L. (1979). The father-daughter relationship: Past, present, and future. In C. B. Kopp (Ed.), *Becoming female: Perspectives on development* (pp. 89–112). New York: Plenum.

Lott, B. (1981). *Becoming a woman.* Springfield, IL: Thomas.

Lynch, M. E. (1981). *Paternal androgyny, daughters' physical maturity level, and achievement socialization in early adolescence.* Unpublished doctoral dissertation, Cornell University.

Lynn, D. G. (1969). *Parental and sex role identification: A theoretical formulation.* Berkeley, CA: McCutchan.

Magrab, P. R. (1979). Mothers and daughters. In C. B. Kopp (Ed.), *Becoming female: Perspectives on development* (pp. 113–132). New York: Plenum.

Marlow, E. L. (1985). *The effect of perceived family harmony and pubertal development on compliance gaining in families of adolescents.* Unpublished doctoral dissertation, Virginia Commonwealth University, Richmond, VA.

Miller, C. L., & Taylor, R. (1986, March). *Pubertal development, self-concept, and behavior: The role of family decision-making practice.* Paper presented at the Biennial Meetings of the Society for Research on Adolescence, Madison, WI.

Montemayor, R. (1983). Parents and adolescents in conflict: All families some of the time and some families most of the time. *Journal of Early Adolescence, 3,* 83–103.

Montemayor, R. (1985). *Some thoughts about conflict and power in the parent-adolescent relationship.* Paper presented at the Third Biennial Conference on Adolescent Research, Tuscon, AZ.

Montemayor, R., & Hanson, E. (1985). A naturalistic view of conflict between adolescents and their parents and siblings. *Journal of Early Adolescence, 5,* 23–30.

Murphy, E. C. (1986). *The onset of dating and sexual behavior in junior high school.* Unpublished doctoral dissertation, Virginia Commonwealth University, Richmond, VA.

Newson, J., & Newson, E. (1968). *Four years old in an urban community.* Harmondsworth, U.K.: Pelican.

Papini, D., & Datan, N. (1982, October). *Mutual regulation in family relations: Parental imperatives and adolescents in transition.* Paper presented at the Fifth Annual Communication, Language, and Gender Conference, Ohio University, Athens, OH.

Papini, D., & Sebby, R. (1985, April). *Multivariate assessment of adolescent physical maturation as a source of change in family relations.* Paper presented at the biennial meetings of the Society for Research in Child Development, Toronto, Ontario.

Parsons, T., & Bales, R. F. (1955). *Family, socialization, and interaction process.* Glencoe, IL: Free Press.

Peskin, H. (1973). Influence of the developmental schedule of puberty on learning and ego functioning. *Journal of Youth and Adolescence, 2,* 273–290.

Petersen, A. C. (1983). Menarche: Meaning of measures and measuring meaning. In S. Golub (Ed.), *Menarche* (pp. 234–268). Lexington, MA: Lexington Books, D. C. Heath.

Petersen, A. C., Tobin-Richards, M., & Boxer, A. (1983). Puberty: Its measurement and its meaning. *Journal of Early Adolescence, 3,* 47–62.

Peterson, D. R. (1983). Conflict. In H. H. Kelley, E. Berscheid, A. Christensen, J. H. Harvey, T. L. Huston, G. Levinger, E. McClintock, L. A. Peplau, & D. R. Peterson (Eds.), *Close relationships* (pp. 360–396). New York: W. H. Freeman.

Raven, B. H., & French, J. R. P. (1958). Legitimate power, coercive power, and observability in social influence. *Sociometry, 21,* 83–97.

Rierdan, J. (1982). Becoming a woman: The meaning of menstruation for adolescent girls. In P. Turner-Smith (Ed.), *What do we know about girls?* (pp. 4–10). Indianapolis, IN: Girls Clubs of America.

Rierdan, J., & Koff, E. (1980). The psychological impact of menarche: Integrative versus disruptive changes. *Journal of Youth and Adolescence, 9,* 49–58.

Rierdan, J., & Koff, E. (1983). *The psychological impact of menarche for young adolescents: Stress or well-being?* Paper presented at the International Congress on Psychosomatic Obstetrics and Gynecology, Dublin, Ireland.

Ruble, D. N., & Brooks-Gunn, J. (1982). The experience of menarche. *Child Development, 53,* 1557–1566.

Savin-Williams, R., & Small, S. (1986). The timing of puberty and its relationship to adolescent and parent perceptions of family interactions. *Developmental Psychology, 22,* 322–347.

Simmons, R., & Blyth, D. A. (in press). *Moving into adolescence: The impact of pubertal change and school context.* Hawthorne, NY: Aldine.

Spence, J. T., & Helmreich, R. L. (1978). *Masculinity and femininity: Their psychological dimensions, correlates, and antecedents.* Austin: University of Texas Press.

Sroufe, L. A., Jacobvitz, D., Mangelsdorf, S., DeAngelo, E., & Ward, M. J. (1985). Generational boundary dissolution in mothers and their preschool children: A relationship systems approach. *Child Development, 56,* 317–325.

Steinberg, L. D. (1977). *A longitudinal study of physical growth, intellectual growth, and family interaction in early adolescence.* Unpublished doctoral dissertation, Cornell University, Ithaca, NY.

Steinberg, L. D. (1981). Transformations in family relations at puberty. *Developmental Psychology, 17,* 833–840.

Steinberg, L. D. (in press). The impact of puberty on family relations: Effects of pubertal status and pubertal timing. *Developmental Psychology.*

Steinberg, L. D., & Hill, J. P. (1978). Patterns of family interaction as a function of age, the onset of puberty, and formal thinking. *Developmental Psychology, 14,* 683–684.

Stone, C. P., & Barker, R. G. (1939). The attitudes and interests of pre-menarcheal and post-menarcheal girls. *Journal of Genetic Psychology, 54,* 27–71.

Tanner, J. (1962). *Growth at adolescence* (2nd ed.) Springfield, IL: Charles C. Thomas.

Vuchinich, S. (1984). Sequencing and social structure in family conflict. *Social Psychology Quarterly, 47,* 217–234.

Weisfeld, G., & Berger, J. (1983). Some features of human adolescence viewed in evolutionary perspective. *Human Development, 26,* 121–133.

Whisnant, L., & Zegans, L. (1975). A study of attitudes toward menarche in white middle-class American adolescent girls. *American Journal of Psychiatry, 132,* 809–814.

Youniss, J., & Smollar, J. (1985). *Adolescents' relations with mothers, fathers, and friends.* Chicago: University of Chicago Press.

4

Concepts of Self and Social Convention: Adolescents' and Parents' Reasoning about Hypothetical and Actual Family Conflicts

Judith G. Smetana
University of Rochester

INTRODUCTION

Developmental psychologists have become increasingly interested in the transformations in family relations that occur in early adolescence. The available evidence suggests that parent-child relations undergo a variety of changes as family members adjust to the biological and psychosocial changes of early adolescence. Affective, behavioral, and cognitive disequilibrium in family relationships have been described or predicted, and although it has been hypothesized that realignments in one sphere provoke realignments in another (Steinberg, 1985), researchers have tended to examine each independently of the others. For instance, some researchers have examined behavioral changes in decision-making, the regulation of behavior, and the amount of time spent with parents versus peers (Csikszentmihalyi & Larsen, 1984; Hunter & Youniss, 1982; Steinberg, 1981; Steinberg & Hill, 1978; Youniss & Smollar, 1985). Others have examined changes in emotional tensions between parents and early adolescents (Hill, 1980; Hill & Holmbeck, 1985, in press; Montemayor, 1982, 1983; Montemayor & Hanson, 1985). Although researchers no longer consider early adolescence a developmental period of strife and rebellion, as was once thought (A. Freud, 1937/1958; Hall, 1904), parent-child relationships, nevertheless, have been found to be characterized by mild bickering, disagreements and conflicts over everyday issues, and emotional stress during early adolescence.

Although changes in adolescents' reasoning capabilities would seem to offer a natural starting point for studying family relations in early adolescence, cognitive or social-cognitive approaches are rare. The development of cognitive structures (Inhelder & Piaget 1958), social-cognitive abilities (Shantz, 1983), and social understanding (Damon, 1977; Selman, 1980; Turiel, 1983) have been studied extensively, but they have not been linked to changing family relations in early adolescence. The family interactions that facilitate social-cognitive development, for instance, role-taking abilities (Cooper, Grotevant, & Condon, 1983; Grotevant & Cooper, 1986) have been examined, but not the reverse, e.g., the effect of developing social understanding on realignments in early adolescents' family relationships. The few studies emerging in this area (Collins, 1985; Dix, 1984; Paikoff, Collins, & Laursen, 1986) have focused on children's views of family relations without concurrently obtaining parents' views or without obtaining more traditional developmental measures of social cognition.

In this chapter it is asserted that alterations in adolescent-parent relationships can be meaningfully understood within a social-cognitive framework that takes into consideration the multifaceted ways that adolescents and parents interpret their social worlds and their competing goals in social situations. It is also proposed that conflicts and development in the social-cognitive realm are related to the affective realignments in parent-child relationships that have been the focus of so much previous research. Thus, developmental changes in adolescents' understanding and construction of expectations and responsibilities within the family social system are seen to have broad implications for understanding family relationships. Furthermore, conflicts between parents and children are seen to emerge as the boundaries of legitimate parental authority are renegotiated during adolescence, and this renegotiation is seen to occur in some conceptual domains (i.e., conventional and personal), but not in others (i.e., moral).

Numerous investigations have reported that the route to autonomy during early and middle adolescence entails minor conflicts over everyday issues such as dress, grooming, chores, schoolwork, use of make-up, and so on (Coleman, 1974; Douvan & Adelson, 1966; Hill & Holmbeck, 1985, in press; Hill, Holmbeck, Marlow, Green, & Lynch, 1985; Montemayor, 1982, 1983, 1986; Montemayor & Hanson, 1985; Offer, 1969; Offer & Offer, 1975; Remmers & Radler, 1962; Steinberg, 1981; Steinberg & Hill, 1978). The issues causing conflict have been viewed as mundane and trivial, resulting in a similar view of the phenomenon itself. Researchers have lacked a framework for conceptualizing these mundane issues found to be at the heart of adolescent-parent conflict.

In the research discussed in this chapter, conflict in parent-child relations is viewed as occurring over the social conventions, social rules, and social system of the family. Changes in parent-child relationships from preadolescence through late adolescence are examined within a domain model of social-cognitive development. Social conventions are considered as a conceptual and developmental domain distinct from other types of social judgments. Previous research using this domain model has focused on the larger social systems of culture and school and their conventions. However, the family is also a constituted social system with a social organization entailing hierarchical structures, patterns of authority, rules, and conventions. In the research presented here, children's (and parents') thinking was examined within this framework. Before describing the study itself, the model of social development and its relevance to adolescent-parent relationships is outlined.

DOMAINS OF SOCIAL-COGNITIVE DEVELOPMENT

Conventions as a Domain of Judgment

Social conventions are one aspect of children's reasoning about social organization and social systems (Turiel, 1975, 1978, 1979, 1983). Conventions have been defined as the arbitrary and agreed-upon behavioral uniformities that coordinate the interactions of individuals within social systems. Conventions (e.g., modes of address, dress, sex roles, manners, or mores regarding sexuality) coordinate interactions by providing individuals with a set of expectations regarding appropriate behavior.

A great deal of empirical research (Davidson, Turiel, & Black, 1983; Nucci, 1981; Smetana, 1981a, 1983, 1985, 1986; Turiel, 1978, 1983; Weston & Turiel, 1980) indicates that concepts of convention and social organization are analytically separable from moral judgments (i.e., judgments regarding how individuals ought to relate to one another). Judgments regarding social conventions serve social-organizational ends, whereas moral judgments are prescriptive, categorical judgments, structured by justice, that pertain to such issues as others' welfare, trust, or the equitable distribution of resources. In contrast to conventions, moral acts are not arbitrary; although moral prescriptions are an aspect of social organization, they are determined by factors inherent in social interactions (i.e., their intrinsic effects on others) rather than by their function in maintaining the social system. It should be noted that this distinction and the working definition of the domains have been partly guided by philosophical works (e.g., Dworkin, 1978; Gewirth, 1978; J. S. Mill, 1863/1963; Rawls, 1971).

Concepts of convention and social organization are also analytically separable from children's understanding of themselves and others as psychological systems (Nucci, 1977, 1981; Smetana, 1982; Turiel, 1983). The psychological domain pertains to children's understanding of self, identity, and personality, and their attributions regarding their own and others' thoughts and behavior. In particular, concepts of convention have been empirically distinguished from personal issues, one aspect of the psychological domain. Personal issues are issues that have consequences that pertain only to the actor, and as such, are viewed as beyond societal regulation and moral concern. They include issues such as the choice of one's friends, the content of one's correspondence, one's recreational activities, and actions that focus on the state of one's body, such as aspects of physical appearance or smoking (Nucci, 1981). (The personal domain thus refers to an epistemological category rather than implying that an actor is selfish, egoistic, or hedonistic.) It has been hypothesized that developing notions of personal choice represent an important aspect of the individual's autonomy or distinctiveness from others (Nucci, 1981).

Social conventions, morality, and personal issues may constitute conceptually and developmentally distinct domains of social judgment. That is, although there may be overlap or intersections among the domains, concepts within each domain form separate, self-regulating developmental systems. (This assumption is part of what has come to be referred to as a "domain" approach to social and cognitive development, e.g., Damon, 1977; Feldman, 1980; Keil, 1986; Smetana, 1982; Turiel, 1983.) The assertion that social knowledge is organized within conceptually distinct knowledge systems or domains, in turn, stems from the proposition that social knowledge is constructed out of individuals' interactions with the social environment. Since social interactions are not of one type, different types of social knowledge are constructed. (For further discussion of the epistemological basis for these domain distinctions, see Turiel & Davidson, 1986).

A great deal of recent writing and research has been directed toward specifying the definitional criteria of the domains and examining whether children distinguish the domains using those criteria. The application of criteria in our research has been discussed extensively elsewhere (Shweder, Turiel, & Much, 1981; Turiel, 1983; Turiel & Smetana, 1984). To summarize briefly, the research indicates that with regard to domain prototypical events, children across a wide age range apply distinctive criteria to events in the different domains. Morality is evaluated as generalizable, wrong independent of rules, and unalterable; conventions are evaluated as contextually relative, contingent on rules, and alterable. In contrast, personal issues are evaluated as independent of societal regulation and moral concern because they pertain only to the individual. Thus, children's social judgments vary according to the type of act under consideration; different types of social orientations are found to coexist in children's social judgments.

Multifaceted Events and Heterogeneity in Social Judgments

Many events and social situations may include both conventional and moral (or personal) components, either in conflict or in synchrony with one another (Smetana, 1983; Turiel & Smetana, 1984). Rather than invalidating the distinctiveness of the domains, as has been suggested (Rest, 1983), this merely reflects the complexity of the social world. Social interactions and behaviors may contain components of more than one domain, individuals may have more than one goal, or individuals may have conflicting goals in social situations. Research on the separation of domains has provided a method for analyzing judgments in such multifaceted situations. Subjects have been presented with situations entailing potential domain conflicts by opposing moral considerations against conventional or personal ones (Smetana, 1981b, 1982, 1983; Turiel, 1983). In such situations, most subjects were aware of different domain considerations. Some subjects emphasized one domain and subordinated the other, whereas others coordinated the two components so that they were reconciled. Alternatively, some subjects experienced conflict between concerns in the two domains. Thus, conflict in judgments may occur when an individual cannot coordinate or reconcile competing concerns in more than one domain.

By extension, it can also be hypothesized that conflict in social judgments can be interindividual. For instance, previous research from the domain perspective on adolescent and young adult women's reasoning and decision making about abortion (Smetana, 1981b, 1982) indicated that individuals conceptualized abortion in fundamentally different ways. Some viewed abortion as a moral issue, whereas others viewed it as an issue of personal jurisdiction. Others coordinated the two domains (or failed to coordinate the domains) in their judgments. Since these different orientations were based on different underlying premises regarding the nature of personhood, the different orientations could not be reconciled. The heated nature of the public debate over abortion appears to stem from these fundamental differences in the way abortion can be conceptualized and the difficulty of reconciling different positions. In addition, the abortion example indicates that interindividual conflict in social judgments is not restricted to the social-cognitive realm, but appears to have a powerful affective component as well.

Changes in parent-child relationships during adolescence can also be characterized in terms of conflicts between domains in social judgments. Family members may have different interpretations of events or rules, and this may lead to conflict. For instance, parents may justify the regulation of certain activities, like television viewing, on the basis of conventional concerns, whereas adolescents might view such issues as under their personal jurisdiction and consider their parents' reasons to be misattributed. Different interpretations of the same event may arise because the event or rule is ambiguous and individuals construct different interpretations of it, or because the rule or expectation is multifaceted, and individuals' conflicting goals in the situation may lead them to subordinate different concerns (Smetana, 1983). Parents may also use "domain-inappropriate" justifications, such as moralizing a primarily conventional event to obtain greater compliance, although previous research has suggested that such messages are considered to be less adequate than those coordinated with the domain of the event (Nucci, 1984). Thus, children and parents may have competing goals in family situations (i.e., maintaining social order versus maintaining personal jurisdiction). This may lead to their different interpretations of events, which, in turn, may lead to conflict and disagreement in parent-child relationships.

The Development of Conventional Concepts

In addition to examining the distinctions between and the coordination of domains, researchers have also examined developmental change within each domain. Consistent with the notion that the domains are separate, self-regulating developmental systems, it has been proposed that concepts within each domain are qualitatively reorganized in development. Furthermore, although the synchronicity of development across these domains requires further study, it is assumed that development in one domain is not a prerequisite for development in another. (This is in contrast to others, who view cognitive development as necessary but not sufficient for moral development [Kohlberg, 1971] or role taking [Selman, 1980].)

Extensive research has been directed toward identifying and specifying developmental changes in children's concepts of conventions as constitutive aspects of social systems. The results of both cross-sectional and longitudinal studies indicate that children's understanding of conventions develops through a sequence of age-related changes (Turiel, 1975, 1979, 1983) entailing a dialectical process of affirmation and then negation of the importance of convention in regulating social life. Each affirmation entails a construction of conceptions of convention and social structure. Each phase of affirmation is followed by a phase negating the validity of the previous phase and a reevaluation of concepts of social organization. Although individuals may advocate adherence to conventions for pragmatic or prudential reasons, negation phases entail reorganizations of the previous mode of thought. These levels are more fully described in Table 4.1. Both cross-sectional (Turiel, 1975, 1978, 1983) and longitudinal (Turiel, 1983) research indicates that all individuals progress through the same sequence of changes in thinking, although the rate and endpoint may vary, and that the process of development entails a process of internal regulation and equilibration.

Changes in adolescent-parent relationships may be related to developmental changes in adolescents' reasoning about social conventions. A salient characteristic of level 4 thinking is the rejection of the necessity for many conventions, as well as criticalness toward the dictates of those in authority. A salient aspect of level 6 thinking is a rejection of convention as "nothing but" social expectation. Nonconformity to rules, resulting in conflict, may be more likely during these two negation phases in the development of conventional concepts.

Previous studies differ as to the ages when conflict and bickering between parents and children are most likely to occur. Conflict has been found to peak in early adolescence (Hill & Holmbeck, 1985, in press; Offer, 1969; Steinberg & Hill, 1978), according to pubertal status (Hill & Holmbeck, 1985, in press; Steinberg & Hill, 1978) and has also been evident or found to persist through middle adolescence (Coleman, 1974; Douvan & Adelson, 1966; Montemayor, 1982). Most studies have sampled a restricted age range, and few studies have examined the quality of parent-child relationships from preadolescence through

TABLE 4.1
Levels of Social-Conventional Concepts

Level 1 (ages 6–7). Conventions are viewed as descriptive of uniformities in behavior; the existence of social uniformities is enough to require their maintenance. Although aware of differences in power status, children have no systematic notions of social organization, and uniformities are not understood to serve functions of coordinating interactions within social systems.

Level 2 (ages 8–9). Empirical uniformity is not a sufficient basis for maintaining conventions. Conventional acts are regarded as arbitrary. Conventions are not seen as part of the structure or function of social interaction.

Level 3 (ages 10–11). Conventions are seen as arbitrary and changeable. Adherence to convention is based on concrete rules and authoritative expectations. Conceptions of conventional acts are not coordinated with conceptions of rules.

Level 4 (ages 12–13). Conventions are now seen as arbitrary and changeable regardless of rules. Evaluations of rules pertaining to conventional acts are coordinated with evaluations of the act. Conventions are seen as "nothing but" social expectations.

Level 5 (ages 14–16). The emergence of systematic and more integrated conceptions of social systems. Conventions are seen as normative regulation in a system with uniformity, fixed rules, and static hierarchical organization.

Level 6 (ages 17–18). Convention is regarded as codified social standards. Uniformity in convention is not considered to serve the function of maintaining the social system. Conventions are "nothing but" societal standards that exist through habitual use.

Level 7 (ages 18–25). Conventions as uniformities that are functional in coordinating social interactions. Shared knowledge, in the form of conventions, among members of social groups facilitates interaction and operation of the system.

---

adolescence. Therefore, developmental patterns, particularly in the transition to adolescence, have been difficult to discern. The above model, however, predicts that the occurrence of adolescent-parent conflict will be curvilinear from preadolescence through late adolescence. Conflicts should be greater in the transition to adolescence (ages 12–13) and again in late adolescence (ages 16–18), when children reject the necessity for conventional regulation, than in preadolescence (ages 10–11) and mid-adolescence (ages 14–16), when conventions are affirmed as arbitrary rules or as integrated aspects of hierarchical social systems.

ADOLESCENT-PARENT CONFLICT:
AN EMPIRICAL INVESTIGATION

These hypotheses and the overall social-cognitive framework have several methodological implications for the study of conflict and transitions in adolescent-parent relationships. First, the developmental hypothesis necessitates studying children across a broad age range so that changes in the transition to and through-

throughout adolescence can be assessed. The need for broad sampling across ages, however, has to be balanced against the need for intensive, semi-structured clinical interviews to identify developmental changes in reasoning, which, for pragmatic reasons, puts restrictions on sample size. Second, parents' as well as adolescents' judgments regarding their relationships must be an integral part of the investigation. This is necessary in order to test the hypothesis that conflict and tensions arise from parents' and children's different interpretations of family expectations. Further. the focus on the match or mismatch between parents' and children's interpretations of everyday situations requires that parents and children be interviewed about actual conflicts. This differs from previous interview studies in which conflict has been assessed primarily by responses to a small set of issues that were predetermined by the investigator and that may be of varying relevance to individual families: conflicts rarely have been assessed on issues generated by the subjects themselves. Finally, an integral aspect of our approach involves going beyond a description of the issues causing conflict to an assessment of their interpretation. The study described below was designed with these considerations in mind.

Study Design and Overview

The results discussed here are based on interviews with a total of 102 children. The children were divided into four age groups: preadolescents (5th and 6th graders), early adolescents (7th and 8th graders), mid-adolescents (9th and 10th graders), and late adolescents (11th and 12th graders). There were 13 boys and 13 girls in each age group with the exception of the late adolescent group, which consisted of 12 boys and 12 girls. All came from two-parent families, and both parents also participated in the research. (A separate sample of 32 single-parent families with children in the 6th through 11th grades was also obtained but results for this group are not discussed in this chapter.) The subjects were primarily Caucasian, middle- to upper-middle class, and well-educated. Mothers were, on average, 41 years old, and fathers were, on average, 43. Families were recruited with the cooperation of a suburban school district near Rochester, New York. They participated in one 2.5 to 3 hour session at the University, which consisted of lengthy individual interviews and a videotaped family interaction task (which will be discussed in a later publication).

There were three sections to the interview. In the *Hypothetical Authority Interview* section, family members' judgments and justifications regarding the legitimacy of parental authority in the moral, conventional, and personal domains were assessed. In the *Conflict Interview* section, family members were interviewed about rules, authority, and relationships with parents (or adolescents) in general and then about self-generated issues of conflict. To assess conflict on the issues deemed salient by each participant, conflict was first operationally defined as follows:

Most children (parents) have told us that even when they generally get along well with their parents (children), there may be times when they don't get along or have conflicts or disagreements. These may be about major issues or decisions, or they may be about everyday responsibilities, like feeding the pets or doing the chores. We would like to talk about the kinds of things that come up in your family. We are interested in all the issues that are really important and/or that seem to come up over and over again in your relationship with your parents (child). What kinds of conflicts or disagreements do you have with them (him/her)?

With the interviewer's probing, subjects generated exhaustive lists of the disagreements and conflicts they had with parents (or children). Participants were then interviewed extensively about each issue to obtain their reasoning and quantitative ratings of these conflicts, as described in more detail later.

Adolescents' developmental level of social-conventional reasoning was assessed in the semi-structured, clinical *Social-Conventional Interview* section. Children were administered two hypothetical stories used in previous research (Turiel, 1978, 1983), one focusing on the use of titles (e.g., the appropriate way to address a teacher in school) and the other on appropriate dress. Responses to each story were scored as a single level of reasoning, if only one level was evident, or as a mixture of more than one level, with the more dominant level (e.g., in percentage of responses) obtaining a major code and the less dominant level obtaining a minor code. These scores were then weighted to reflect the percentage of pure or mixed scores for each story and averaged to obtain an average social-conventional reasoning score.

The results of the Hypothetical Authority Interview are considered first, as they provide a context in which to consider parents' and adolescents' descriptions of their relationships.

Hypothetical Judgments of Parental Authority

In the Hypothetical Authority Interview, children's and parents' evaluations of the legitimacy of parental authority were examined for acts in different conceptual domains. Both conceptual and methodological concerns led to the development of this task. Observational studies of dominance patterns have indicated shifts in influence and authority between parents and children during early adolescence (Hill, this volume; Hill & Holmbeck, in press; Steinberg, 1981; Steinberg & Hill, 1978). Similarly, interview studies have shown that children view parental authority as declining during adolescence (Hunter & Youniss, 1982) or that they reconceptualize parental authority during adolescence (Damon, 1977; Selman, 1980). However, adolescents' conceptions of parental authority have not been examined in relation to the domain in which authority is exerted.

Because the Conflict Interview focused on self-generated issues of conflict, the number and type of cross-domain comparisons potentially varied by subject.

By employing standardized stimuli, as was done in the Hypothetical Authority Interview, judgments in different domains could be systematically compared. Thus, the Hypothetical Authority Interview was employed to identify the domains in which actual parental authority might be contested. The methods employed were similar to those used in other studies examining distinctions between the domains with two exceptions. Parents' judgments and justifications were also assessed and compared to their children's responses, and the items selected as exemplars of the domains were contextualized within the family rather than presented more abstractly.

In previous research, Nucci (1981) has defined the personal domain to include acts that are judged by subjects as having consequences for the actor, although they might violate rules or norms. Although children may view such acts as under their personal jurisdiction, it was hypothesized that parents probably would not. Therefore, distinctions were made between acts that might be seen to affect only the actor but that potentially violated parental rules and norms, and those that appeared only to affect the actor. The former are referred to as multifaceted events; the latter are referred to as personal events.

Family members were each presented with descriptions of 15 hypothetical acts, 4 moral, 4 conventional, 4 multifaceted, and 3 personal.[1] Subjects' judgments regarding the legitimacy of parental rule making ("Would it be OK for parents to make a rule?"), subjects' reasoning, or their justifications for the wrongness or permissibility of the acts ("Why is the act wrong [or permissible]?"), and their judgments of the independence or contingency of the act on parental authority were obtained. Contingency was assessed by asking subjects to sort each item as moral ("Wrong whether or not parents say so"), conventional ("Wrong only if parents say so"), or personal ("Up to the individual—not an issue of right or wrong"). Reasoning was scored in 17 justification categories expanded from previous research (Davidson et al., 1983; Nucci, 1981; Smetana, 1985, 1986) on the basis of pilot testing and analysis of a subset of responses. The justification categories are defined in Table 4.2.

For purposes of analysis, justifications were collapsed within domains. Appeals to fairness, others' welfare, and obligation all have been associated with morality in previous research (Davidson et al., 1983; Smetana, 1985, 1986) and thus were combined to form the moral category. Justifications pertaining to social coordination, customs and norms, politeness, appeals to authority, responsibility, appeals to punishment, and social noncomformity have all been associ-

---

[1]The moral items were lying to parents, stealing pocket money from parents, not sharing (communal property) with brothers and sisters, and hitting brothers and sisters. The conventional items were not keeping parents informed of activities, not doing the chores, not cleaning up after a party, and calling parents by their first names. The multifaceted items were not going on a picnic with the family, wearing punk clothes, not cleaning one's room, and hanging out with friends that parents don't like. The personal items were sleeping late on weekends, watching MTV, and talking on the telephone (when no one else wants to use it).

TABLE 4.2
Justification Categories

Category	Description
Others' welfare	Appeal to the interests of persons other than the adolescent
Obligation	References to feelings of obligation, including personal conscience, trust, and duty
Appeal to fairness	References to maintaining a balance of rights between persons
Appeal to authority	Appeal to the approval of specific authority figures or to the existence of rules or laws
Social nonconformity	References to the negative personal-social consequences of acting contrary to group norms
Social coordination	Appeal to the need for social organization or for maintaining a system of shared expectations between persons, including appropriate role relationships or status differences
Custom or norm	Appeal to personal, family, and peer group customs, as well as to social customs and traditions
Politeness	References to politeness, manners, consideration, or courtesy
Punishment avoidance	References to negative reactions of other persons toward the child, including social condemnation as well as explicit punishment
Interpersonal	Appeal to friendship, interpersonal relationships, affective bonds, or to the effects of acts on interpersonal relationships
Psychological-dispositional	Appeal to the child's psychological development, or to traits, behavioral styles, and dispositional characteristics
Autonomy/Individuation	References to rebellious behavior, autonomy-seeking, psychological separation from family, or identity exploration
Developmental Appropriateness*	Appeal to the developmental appropriateness, lack of appropriateness, or need for age-appropriate behavior
Responsibility	Appeal to the need for the actor to be responsible for his/her own behavior or to the importance of developing a sense of responsibility
Personal Choice	Appeal to the child's preferences or prerogatives and/or general permissibility of the act
Egoistic*	Appeal to personal preferences or prerogatives with recognition that act is wrong or behavior ought to be regulated
Prudential reasons	References to nonsocial negative consequences to the child, such as personal comfort or health
Pragmatic	References to practical needs and consequences
Unintentional*	Behavior is seen as unintentionally or unconsciously performed, forgotten, or not meant to cause offense
Don't know*	
Unscorable**	

*Used only in scoring Conflict Interviews
**Used only in scoring Hypothetical Parental Authority Interviews

ated with conventionality and were collapsed to form the conventional category. Psychological or dispositional reasons, autonomy, and interpersonal reasons were all considered aspects of the psychological domain. Personal choice, also an aspect of the psychological domain, was examined separately because it was so frequently used.

The analyses are described in detail elsewhere (Smetana, in press). To summarize, parents and children did not differ in their judgments of the legitimacy of parental authority regarding unambiguously moral or conventional events; all strongly agreed that parents ought to retain authority over these issues. However, both moral and conventional events were judged to be more legitimately subject to parental jurisdiction than were multifaceted and personal events. These results are depicted graphically in Fig. 4.1.

Parents' and children's conceptions of hypothetical personal and multifaceted issues consistently differed. Children were more likely to reason about and sort both personal and multifaceted items as under their personal jurisdiction than were parents, whereas parents were more likely to view them within a normative framework than were children. Parents reasoned conventionally about these items and sorted them as contingent on parental authority. For example, parents were more likely to sort "cleaning one's room" (a multifaceted item) as contingent on parental authority and to reason about it as an issue of social coordination than were adolescents, whereas adolescents were more likely to reason about and sort the same item as an issue of personal choice than were parents.

The findings also indicated that the boundaries of legitimate parental authority regarding these issues shift as children move into adolescence. Personal and multifaceted events were viewed as more legitimately subject to parental authori-

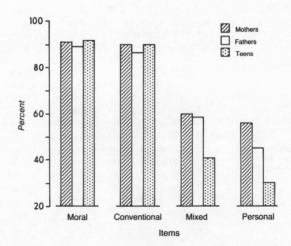

FIG. 4.1. Legitimacy of parental authority.

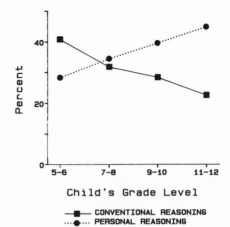

FIG. 4.2. Conventional and personal reasoning about multifaceted items.

Child's Grade Level

—■— CONVENTIONAL REASONING
···◆··· PERSONAL REASONING

ty by families with preadolescents (Grades 5 and 6) than by families with adolescents (Grades 7–12), but there were no corresponding age differences in judgments of moral and conventional items. As children moved through adolescence, parents were seen to retain their authority to legislate hypothetical moral and conventional issues, based on moral (for moral items) or conventional concerns (for conventional items). This did not vary according to family member, grade level, or sex. There was, however, a linear decrease from preadolescence to late adolescence in family members' conventional reasoning about the multifaceted and personal items and their sorting of these items as contingent on parental authority. Correspondingly, there was a linear increase from preadolescence to late adolescence in their personal reasoning and sorting of the multifaceted events as issues of personal jurisdiction. These age trends are illustrated in Fig. 4.2. Interestingly, from preadolescence to mid-adolescence, children became increasingly likely to reason about the personal items in terms of personal choice, but parents of children at these ages did not demonstrate similar changes (see Fig. 4.3). These findings differ from Nucci (1981), who found no age differences in children's and adolescents' judgments and justifications about personal events.

In addition, mothers and children, though not fathers and children, were found to differ in their judgments of the legitimacy of parental authority regarding personal and multifaceted issues (but not regarding moral or conventional issues). Since adolescents have been found to have more conflicts with their mothers than with their fathers (Montemayor, 1982), these findings were not surprising, but the pervasiveness of these differences was. Children consistently judged events to be less legitimately subject to parental authority than did moth-

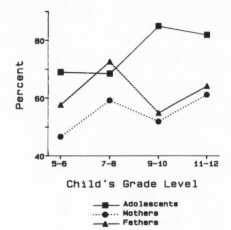

Child's Grade Level

FIG. 4.3. Personal justifications
for personal items.

—■— Adolescents
···●··· Mothers
—▲— Fathers

ers; mother-child differences in judgments regarding personal issues were evident among even the preadolescent group and were not reconciled until late
adolescence. Mother-child differences in judgments of the legitimacy of parental
rule-making regarding multifaceted issues were initiated in early adolescence
(Grades 7 and 8) and persisted throughout adolescence.

To summarize, parents and preadolescents differed in their interpretations of
personal and multifaceted events. Over the adolescent years, these events were
increasingly reconceptualized as falling under adolescents' personal jurisdiction.
It is important to note that children from preadolescence throughout adolescence
and their parents not only agreed on the legitimacy of parental authority regarding unambiguously moral or conventional issues, but viewed them as legitimately subject to parental authority. Others have reported that parental authority
decreases in adolescence (Hunter & Youniss, 1982). These findings suggest that
parental authority decreases only for certain types of issues (e.g., multifaceted
and personal) and is retained over other types of issues (e.g., unambiguously
moral or conventional).

Does the same pattern of results emerge when we consider the more emotional
sphere of actual parent-child conflict? To address this question, we turn now to
the data on actual family conflicts obtained in the Conflict Interview. To place
the discussion of parent-child conflict in perspective, parents' and children's
ratings of the extent, severity, frequency, and issues of conflict are presented
first. Participants' interpretations of these issues are presented next, followed by
data on the development of social-conventional reasoning and its relation to
disagreements in the family.

Conflict and its Vicissitudes

The general picture that emerged from responses to the Conflict Interview was consistent with previous research: adolescents and their parents generally view their relationships as harmonious. Conflicts occurring over everyday details of family life were ubiquitous but not very serious: conflicts occurring, on the average, nearly once or twice a week over an average of 3.68 issues. Finally, although the conflicts were viewed as relatively mild, the issues causing conflict were seen as fairly important.

Parents' and children's interpretations of their relationship, as obtained through their ratings of conflict, differed significantly. First, children and adolescents reported a greater number of ongoing conflicts with parents (an average of 4.32 issues) than mothers and fathers reported having with their adolescents (an average of 3.62 and 3.09 issues, respectively). Furthermore, parents reported getting along better with their adolescents than did adolescents with their parents. When asked to rate their agreement with the other's perspective on particular conflicts, however, adolescents agreed more with their parents' perspectives than parents did with adolescents' perspectives.

As has been found elsewhere (Montemayor, 1982), and consistent with the results of the legitimacy of rule-making task in the Hypothetical Authority Interview, both children and parents viewed mother-child relationships as more difficult than father-child relationships, perhaps because mothers are more involved in regulating the everyday details of family life. When asked to identify which parent their conflicts were with, children reported that 52% of their conflicts were with both parents, 35% of their conflicts were with mothers alone, and only 14% of their conflicts were with fathers alone. Children's ratings of how well they got along with their mothers and fathers did not differ significantly, but both boys and girls rated conflicts with mothers as significantly more serious than conflicts with fathers. Further, fathers saw themselves as getting along better with their children than did mothers, and mothers rated conflicts with their children as more serious than did fathers. Conflicts with fathers were reported as more frequent among families with preadolescents than among all other families.

Others have reported that conflict between mothers and daughters is more common than conflict between mothers and sons (Montemayor, 1982). Girls in this sample generated a greater number of conflicts in general, reported a greater proportion of their conflicts to be with their mothers, and reported getting along worse with their mothers than did boys. Furthermore, mothers and their daughters reported more frequent conflicts than did fathers of daughters.

Conflicts also did not decline significantly in frequency until late adolescence. Early adolescence has been considered a particularly difficult time for mother-daughter relations (Hill & Holmbeck, in press; Larson, Livingston, & Tron, 1985; Peterson, 1986). Mothers in this sample reported poorer relations with 7th-

and 8th-grade daughters than with 11th- and 12th-grade daughters and with 7th- and 8th-grade daughters than with 7th- and 8th-grade sons. Although conflicts with fathers were reported to be more frequent in preadolescence than in adolescence, fathers, in contrast to mothers, reported getting along better with preadolescent daughters than with adolescent daughters and with preadolescent sons than daughters.

To summarize, conflicts, though recurrent and frequent, were not seen as serious or as fundamentally undermining the quality of the relationships. Disagreements were viewed more as everyday irritants, although both parents and children, when asked to rate their importance, considered the issues underlying conflicts as relatively important. Nevertheless, parents' and adolescents' interpretations of their relationships differed, with adolescents reporting a greater number of ongoing conflicts than did parents and with parents viewing relationships as more harmonious than did adolescents. Furthermore, both parents and adolescents viewed mother-child relationships as more difficult than father-child relationships, with mother-daughter relationships, particularly in early adolescence, seen as more difficult than mother-son relationships.

Issues Causing Conflict

The types of issues that caused conflict were coded into the ten content categories defined in Table 4.3. The percent frequency of each is presented in Fig. 4.4 with responses collapsed across family member and child's grade level. The types of issues that were reported as eliciting adolescent-parent disagreement closely resemble findings from previous investigations; they entail the everyday details of family life. Overall, doing chores, getting along with others, regulating activities, and the adolescent's personality characteristics were the most frequent conflicts cited, accounting for 18%, 17%, 12% and 12% of the conflicts, respectively. Family members' descriptions of family conflict were congruent with four exceptions: regulating activities, regulating interpersonal relationships, adolescents' personality characteristics, and health and hygiene issues. Both parents mentioned conflicts over adolescents' behavioral style and mothers mentioned conflicts over health and the adolescent's activities more often than did adolescents, whereas adolescents mentioned conflicts over parental regulation of their interpersonal relationships more often than did parents. Furthermore, families with girls experienced more conflict over the child's appearance than did families with boys; families with boys experienced more conflicts over interpersonal relations (getting along) than did families with girls.

With the exception of chores and achievement, the types of issues causing conflict did not vary in frequency from preadolescence to late adolescence. Conflicts over chores were more frequent in mid-adolescence and beyond than in preadolescence. This is consistent with reports that children gain increasing responsibilities in the household as they grow older. Conflicts over homework

TABLE 4.3
Content Categories

Category	Description
Chores	Maintaining family duties and responsibilities, such as doing the dishes, cleaning, walking the dog, setting the table, or shoveling snow
Appearance	Concerns regarding acceptable standards of dress and appearance including hair, make-up use, or condition or style of clothing
Personality/Behavioral Style	Concerns regarding consistent, irritating personality traits or behavioral styles, such as being very excitable, hyperactive, stubborn, playful, or overtalkative
Homework & Academic Achievement	Concerns regarding doing homework or doing homework when expected, not obtaining acceptable grades or not maintaining one's academic average
Interpersonal Relations	Concerns regarding getting along with others, such as fighting with siblings or friends, hitting, quarreling, arguing, teasing, or hurting
Regulation of Interpersonal Activities	Regulation of one's choice of friends, decisions regarding when to see friends, participation in social activities, such as parties or clubs, or other interaction with people.
Bedtime & Curfew	Concerns regarding appropriate times to be home after school or in the evening or when to go to bed
Health & Hygiene	Concerns regarding diet, health, hygiene, or substance abuse
Regulation of Activities	Concerns regarding choice or timing of activities, such as amount of time spent on the phone or watching TV, not practicing the piano, engaging in sports after school, or going shopping
Finance	Concerns regarding the spending habits, pocket money, earning money, budgeting and being responsible with money, and acquisitive behavior
Other	

and achievement peaked in early adolescence, coinciding with the transition from elementary to middle school. This is consistent with the view that this transition is a stressful life event (Hamburg, 1974; Peterson, 1986) and with evidence that school grades decline in the seventh and eighth grades (Peterson, 1986; Simmons, Blyth, Van Cleave, & Bush, 1979). In sum, the increased conflict over homework and achievement among parents and seventh and eighth graders, as compared to preadolescent or mid-adolescent families, may have

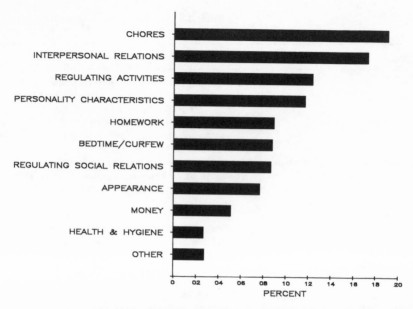

FIG. 4.4.   Issues of conflict.

been due both to difficulties in adapting to a new school setting and to declining grades.

Thus, like others, conflicts were found to occur primarily over "hair, garbage, dishes, and galoshes" (Hill & Holmbeck, in press, p. 216). For the most part, children and their parents did not differ in their perception of the issues that cause disagreements. The focal point of our analysis, however, is not the types of issues that cause conflict, but rather family members' interpretations of those issues, as examined by social-cognitive domain.

The Interpretation of Conflict

Two types of interpretations were obtained. First, family members reasoned about, or justified, the wrongness or permissibility of an event from their own perspective. Then, they reasoned about the issue from the other's perspective. The former are referred to as justifications, and the latter are referred to as counterarguments. Both were scored in the justification categories described in Table 4.2. As was done for responses to hypothetical issues, justifications were collapsed into domains for the purpose of analysis. As described in Table 4.2, three categories were added to score actual conflicts: Unintentional, Egoistic, and Don't Know (for counterarguments only).

Justifications.   The frequency of parents' and children's use of different justifications is presented graphically in Fig. 4.5. The results mirrored those from the Hypothetical Authority Task and the quantitative ratings of conflicts in indicating that parents' and children's interpretations of conflicts differed markedly, with parent-child differences occurring most frequently over conventional and personal justifications. Mothers reasoned about 42% of the issues causing conflict and fathers reasoned about 37% of these issues from a social-conventional perspective, whereas children and adolescents took a conventional perspective on only 11% of conflicts. Thus, parents (but not children) most frequently viewed the issues causing conflicts as of a conventional nature. In contrast, children most frequently saw conflicts to occur over issues of exercising or maintaining personal jurisdiction; nearly half (49%) of children's justifications regarding issues of conflict entailed appeals to personal choice. Not surprisingly, parents very rarely treated conflictual issues as matters of the child's personal jurisdiction.

Parents and adolescents differed in their interpretations of nearly all other issues as well. Parents were more likely to view issues causing conflicts in prudential and pragmatic terms, fathers were more likely to view issues as moral matters, and mothers were more likely to view issues causing conflicts in psychological terms than were children. Children, in contrast, were more likely to justify their behavior as unintentional or to reason egoistically than were parents. (Justifications were scored as personal only when the acts were considered to be

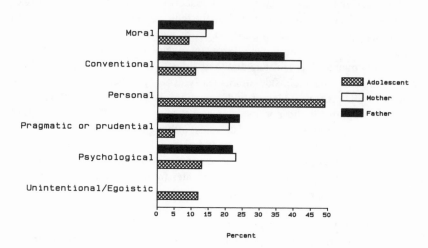

FIG. 4.5.   Conflict justifications.

permissible. Justifications were scored as egoistic when subjects acknowledged the wrongness of the acts, despite their intention or desire to perform them.)

Overall, with only a few exceptions, reasoning was consistent across grade level. Families with preadolescents were more likely to treat issues as matters of moral concern than were families with early and late adolescents. Reflecting a concern over issues such as driving and alcohol, fathers of late adolescent boys were also more likely to reason about issues causing conflicts in terms of prudential concerns than were fathers of late-adolescent girls. Mothers of preadolescent girls were more likely to view conflictual issues from a conventional perspective than were fathers of same-aged girls or than preadolescents themselves.

Counterarguments. Family members' counterarguments are presented graphically in Fig. 4.6. As can be seen, the results for counterarguments mirror the findings for justifications. Parent-child differences were pervasive and occurred for each type of counterargument. When asked to take their parents' perspective regarding the disagreement under consideration, 38% of adolescents' counterarguments were conventional in nature. Thus, although adolescents rejected conventional interpretations of the issues when asked to justify the issue from their own perspective, they understood and articulated a conventional orientation when asked to take their parents' perspective on the dispute. Similarly, when asked to take their child's perspective, parents understood and articulated adolescents' personal orientation, although they themselves never viewed the issues as ones of the child's personal choice. Reflecting this, adolescents never treated their parents' perspectives as personal in their counterarguments.

Adolescents also rearticulated their parents' prudential, pragmatic, and moral concerns and their fathers' interpersonal concerns. Parents, in contrast, provided psychological attributions, reasoned about their adolescent's professed lack of culpability for conflict-inducing behaviors, or viewed their adolescent's reasoning as egoistic. Reflecting fathers' lesser involvement in the issues, fathers were more likely than mothers to state that they did not know how their child reasoned about the issue under consideration; nearly 10% of fathers' counterarguments reflected their professed lack of understanding of their child's thinking.

Counterarguments did not vary much according to adolescents' grade level. Pragmatic orientations to conflictual issues, although generally infrequent, were greater among seventh- and eighth-grade families than among all other families. As conflicts over homework and achievement were primarily treated as pragmatic concerns, this appeared to reflect the greater frequency of conflicts regarding these issues during early adolescence.

Figure 4.7 depicts the interaction obtained between family member, grade level, and sex for conventional counterarguments. When reasoning from their parents' perspective, boys' conventional reasoning increased between early and late adolescence; 11th- and 12th-grade boys evidenced more conventional reasoning than boys in the 5th through 8th grades. Thus, the findings for boys

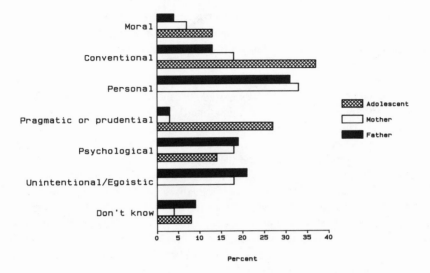

FIG. 4.6. Conflict counterarguments.

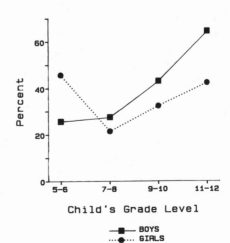

FIG. 4.7. Adolescents' conventional counterarguments.

suggest an increasing ability with age to take their parents' perspective and view conflicts within the framework of the social system of the family. For girls, however, there was a significant drop in early adolescence, compared to both preadolescence and late adolescence, in their ability or willingness to take their parents' conventional perspectives on conflictual issues. This decrease in girls' conventional perspective-taking in early adolescence may be related to the often-reported finding of increased parent-daughter conflict in early adolescence (Hill, this volume; Hill & Holmbeck, in press). Indeed, the frequency of girls' conventional counterarguments was found to be significantly correlated with their agreement with parents' perspectives on the issues ($r = .37$, $p < .01$).

Thus, although preadolescents and adolescents agreed with their parents over the types of issues that lead to conflict, they disagreed in their interpretations of these issues and constructed them in conceptually different domains. Preadolescents and adolescents understood but rejected, or subordinated, their parents' conventional interpretations of conflictual issues and reinterpreted them as issues of personal jurisdiction. Parents similarly understood but rejected, or subordinated, their adolescents' claim to personal jurisdiction, restating the issues instead in conventional terms.

Types of Conflict and their Interpretation.   The kinds of parent-child differences in interpretation that emerged in the Conflict Interviews were strongly suggestive of the differences that emerged regarding hypothetical multifaceted and personal issues (but not regarding moral and conventional issues) in the Hypothetical Authority Interview. However, parents' reasoning about actual conflicts was not entirely conventional, nor was children's reasoning entirely personal. Although these orientations predominated, parents and children both reasoned in a variety of ways about the issues causing conflicts, and it is not clear whether certain types of issues were more likely to elicit this tension between the social system of the family, as reflected in conventional reasoning, and adolescents' claim for personal jurisdiction. Certain types of issues causing conflicts may have elicited greater agreement in domain than others. To answer this question, children's and parents' reasoning (e.g., their justifications) about actual conflicts was examined in relation to the content coding of conflicts.

Although the content categories used to code actual issues of conflict do not correspond directly to the hypothetical items in the Hypothetical Authority Task, some of the categories are close enough to invite comparisons. For instance, as defined in Table 4.3, interpersonal relations (getting along) roughly corresponds to the hypothetical moral issues of hitting and not sharing with siblings (although interpersonal relations is a broader category in that it may also include acts that have no moral significance). There were no significant differences in parents' and children's reasoning about interpersonal conflicts. They were seen as moral by 40% of children and by 30% and 32% of mothers and fathers, respectively, and as interpersonal by 24% of children and by 27% and 36% of mothers and fathers, respectively. Further, as was found for hypothetical issues, the frequency of moral or interpersonal justifications did not vary according to the child's grade level. Thirty-seven percent of mothers, 27% of fathers, 15% of children viewed these issues as conventional, roughly corresponding to the cases that pertained to conventionally inappropriate behavior, such as poor manners, impoliteness, rudeness, and so on.

Two aspects of these findings deserve note. First, although personal reasoning was pervasive among adolescents, it was used infrequently for interpersonal conflicts (10%). Thus, adolescents did not claim personal jurisdiction over all types of issues. Those that resembled moral conflicts in that the child's actions were seen to affect others were not seen by adolescents to be personal. Also, not all conflicts entailed conceptual differences in interpretation (e.g., conflicts in domain). Conflicts also occurred when children and parents justified the issue using different reasons within the same domain. A frequently occurring example was fighting with siblings. Parents often worried about the physical safety of their children (a moral concern with welfare), whereas children often saw fighting as justified to rectify some inequity in the sibling relationship (a moral concern with fairness).

Presented hypothetically, doing assigned chores was treated as conventional by both parents and children. With regard to real-life conflicts coded as chore-related, parents' reasoning was primarily (75%) conventional (usually pertaining to social coordination), whereas adolescents' reasoning was primarily personal (38%) and less often egoistic (20%), moral (16%), conventional (9%), and unintentional (i.e., forgetful, 9%). Two factors accounted for the discrepancy between reasoning in hypothetical and actual contexts. First, conflicts over chores most frequently pertained to cleaning the child's room, which adolescents viewed as a personal issue when presented hypothetically. Also, for parents, the crux of chore-related conflicts was whether the child did her chores, whereas for adolescents, conflicts entailed moral concerns pertaining to fair distribution in the assignment of chores and personal concerns regarding their jurisdiction in deciding when and how the chores were to be done.

Items such as appearance (dressing punk) and regulating activities, which were seen as multifaceted and entailing conventional and personal components when presented hypothetically, were also multifaceted in actual conflict situations. Conflicts over appearance were unambiguously conventional for parents. Eighty-two percent of mothers' and 84% of fathers' justifications were scored as conventional; they reasoned primarily about customs and social norms and about social nonconformity. Adolescents reasoned about their appearance as an issue of personal jurisdiction (51%), but they also reasoned in significant frequencies about conventions (35%), rejecting parental standards and affirming those of their peer group. Furthermore, adolescents' conventional reasoning about appearance was found to decline significantly from early adolescence to mid- and late adolescence, whereas their personal reasoning was found to increase significantly over this same developmental period. However, the frequency of their parents' conventional reasoning did not change as their children grew older.

Reasoning about regulating activities in real-life contexts was also multi-faceted, although complexly so. For children, parental regulation of their activities was primarily seen as a violation of their personal jurisdiction (68%). For mothers and fathers, these conflicts were sometimes conventional (23% and 29%, respectively), but often prudential (16% and 18%, respectively), pragmatic (18% and 32%, respectively), moral (21% and 11%, respectively), and disposi-tional (e.g., psychological, 13% and 4%, respectively).

The issue most consistently treated as personal by all family members in the Hypothetical Authority Task was sleeping late on weekends. This issue rarely arose as a conflict in the real-life context, most likely because it was treated as an issue of personal choice and therefore not contested. Conflicts over bedtimes and curfews did arise. Like sleeping late, bedtime and curfew issues were treated as outside of the realm of conventional regulation and moral concern. Parents argued primarily on the basis of prudence (52% and 68% for mothers and fathers, respectively), and less often on the basis of convention (22% and 26%, respec-tively), whereas children reasoned primarily on the basis of personal choice (60%) and less often on the basis of convention (8%), prudence (4%), morality (8%), pragmatics (6%), and egoistic desires (8%). Similarly, issues pertaining to finances and health and hygiene were seen by parents as governed by prudential and pragmatic concerns in real-life contexts, whereas they were seen by children to entail personal jurisdiction. Thus, these issues, too, were seen by parents as outside the boundaries of familial convention.

These results suggest that there is some consistency between reasoning about hypothetical transgressions and actual family conflicts. Differences occurred because when issues became contextualized in real-life settings, different com-ponents, and sometimes a wider range of concerns, emerged. Occasionally, family members' reasoning was conceptually similar but took opposing posi-tions. For instance, conflicts over appearance were often conceptualized as con-ventional by both parents and adolescents, but they disagreed as to whose con-ventions (parents' or adolescents') took precedence. More frequently, parents and adolescents interpreted the issues in conceptually different ways. Thus, the issues themselves were transformed, and when conflicts occurred, parents and adolescents were arguing over fundamentally different issues.

Conventional Reasoning about Hypothetical and Actual Issues

The results thus far provide support for the hypothesis that family conflict occurs over adolescents' and parents' different interpretations of conflict issues. It was also hypothesized that conflict would be related to adolescents' developmental level of conventional reasoning. The distribution of social-conventional reasoning levels in this sample is presented in Table 4.4. As can be seen, adolescents ranged from the second to the sixth developmental level of social-conventional reasoning (see Table 4.1 for a description of the levels), with most children falling between the third and sixth levels. Only these four developmental levels were included in analyses.

Children and adolescents at each developmental level exhibited characteristic modes of conventional reasoning that were evident in both responses to the hypothetical stories and actual family conflicts. Adolescents' conventional reasoning about conflicts was not scored for developmental level as the Conflict Interviews were not constructed for this purpose and therefore did not consistently yield scorable data. (Adolescents did not reason conventionally about each issue, and when they did, more detailed probing of their reasoning would have been necessary.) Nevertheless, continuities in adolescents' construction of the hypothetical stories and real-life family squabbles were evident. These continuities are illustrated qualitatively below for the four developmental levels represented in this sample. These descriptions are followed by a section detailing the results of quantitative analyses of the relationship between conventional reasoning and adolescent-parent conflict.

At the third level, social conventions are treated as arbitrary, and there is no intrinsic basis for maintaining conventions. Conventional acts are evaluated in relation to the rules and authoritative expectations of the social system, concretely conceptualized. Social relations are viewed as governed by a system in which individuals hold positions of authority, and authority is derived from the power of individuals in these positions. For instance, when interviewed about a hypothetical story character named Peter, who addresses his new teacher by her first name, the following sixth-grade subject responds:

I think he was wrong. WHY? Well, it's probably ok to call his parents by their first names, but like at school, the teachers aren't his parents, and they want to be addressed formally, and I think they should be. WHY IS IT NECESSARY TO ADDRESS THEM FORMALLY? Because it treats them with respect. WHY IS IT

TABLE 4.4
Adolescents' Social-Conventional Reasoning (in %) by Grade Level

	Grades			
	5th–6th	7th–8th	9th–10th	11th–12th
Social Conventional Levels:				
2	8	0	0	0
3	65	32	8	4
4	27	48	8	8
5	0	20	52	33
6	0	0	32	54

IMPORTANT TO SHOW RESPECT? If they want to be called Mr. or Mrs., then they should be, but if they don't mind, it's all right. WHY IS IT IMPORTANT TO CALL THEM WHAT THEY WANT TO BE CALLED? Because they're like— their power is above you. WHY IS CALLING THEM BY THEIR TITLES A SIGN OF RESPECT? They're [above you] . . they can do anything. . . DO YOU THINK PEOPLE SHOULD BE CALLED BY THEIR TITLES? Yes. WHY? Because they're older and they know more.

This subject considers the use of titles to be arbitrary and subject to the whims of those in authority. Rudimentary notions of social system are evident, but they are concretely conceptualized in terms of the power relationship between teacher and student. Now consider this same subject's reasoning about a family conflict pertaining to cleaning the bathroom.

WHY DO YOU THINK IT'S OK NOT TO [CLEAN THE BATHROOM?] Because like Mom's there during the day when I'm in school, so she can do it. I don't think that it is important. WHY IS IT ALRIGHT FOR YOUR MOM TO DO IT? Because she does most of the housework. WHY IS IT ALRIGHT FOR HER TO DO MOST OF THE HOUSEWORK? Because that's usually what moms are for. WHY DOES SHE WANT YOU TO [CLEAN THE BATHROOM]? . . . Because she told me to do it. DO YOU AGREE WITH YOUR MOTHER? Mm hmm. WHY? Because she's right. She was a child too, and she knows.

Since there is no intrinsic basis for performing the desired chore, this subject views her mother's expectations as arbitrary. She evaluates the maternal role concretely; her mother is seen to hold a position of familial authority that demands obedience. The family social system is maintained by her conformity to her mother's authoritative expectations.

Another child, reasoning at the same level about the same conflict, puts it this way:

She [has the right to get mad] because she told me that I am supposed to do the bathroom, and if I am supposed to do it, then I am supposed to do it, and if I don't do it, she has the right to say no [to certain privileges] because I haven't been doing my duties around the house. WHY IS THAT IMPORTANT? Again, if you live in the house, you have to participate in doing jobs around the house. It is definitely my fault, and I should do it and say "I am really sorry."

For this subject, the rightness of the expectation is seen to derive from the mother's role as an authority figure. Although the expectation is seen as arbitrary, it should be obeyed.

At the fourth level, as at the previous level, conventional acts are seen as arbitrary, but the evaluation of an act is now coordinated with the evaluation of the rule or expectation to which the act pertains. Since conventional acts are viewed as arbitrary, rules or expectations about such acts are rejected as invalid.

For instance, the ability to communicate with others is seen as important, but the use of titles in the hypothetical story is regarded as arbitrary. Names are seen as ways of identifying people, and it is assumed that communication can be achieved using either first names or titles. Individuals have the right to make their own decisions, and therefore conventions are seen as "nothing but" the expectations of others. This is illustrated in the following 10th-grade subject's reasoning about using titles and about family conflicts.

DO YOU THINK PETER WAS RIGHT OR WRONG TO CONTINUE CALLING HIS TEACHERS BY THEIR FIRST NAMES? I think he was right. WHY? Because that was what he was taught to do; he believes that you should call everybody by their first names. IS IT IMPORTANT TO CALL TEACHERS BY THEIR TITLES OF MR. AND MRS.? I don't think it's important, but the schools do, and so do parents. WHY? I guess you're supposed to show respect for your teachers. HOW IS USING THEIR TITLE SHOWING RESPECT? Well, usually if you call someone Mr. or Mrs., that means that you're on a more formal relationship with them. They're usually people who are above you . . . in status. YOU SAID THAT IT WASN'T IMPORTANT [TO USE TITLES]. WHY NOT? I think that the relationship between teachers and students should be less formal. That maybe students could learn a little better, I don't know, I just—it isn't important to me.
LET'S TALK ABOUT DOING STUFF AROUND THE HOUSE. I don't know, I just think he [the father] envisions things the way they were when he was younger. All the kids were really good and they obeyed their parents and stuff like that, you know, before dishwashers and things like that. WHEN CLEANING YOUR ROOM COMES UP, IS IT THAT YOU DON'T WANT TO CLEAN YOUR ROOM? I don't care about whether I clean it up or not, it's just that, its a big issue with my mother, she gets really upset about it. WHY? It's just that way, because I'll go, "I don't care," and she says, "Well, I do," and it keeps going. WHY DO YOU THINK SHE MAKES YOU CLEAN IT THEN? I don't know. I'M ASKING YOU TO THINK ABOUT WHAT SHE THINKS . . . I don't know, she keeps saying "All little kids have to clean their room." WHAT DO YOU THINK ABOUT THAT? She's probably right, but I don't think I should have to, I don't think I should have to like make sure there's nothing gross in there . . . and have to clean up an entire room.

For this subject, conventions about cleanliness are seen as arbitrary, and therefore expectations about cleaning the room are rejected as invalid. Conventions become an issue of personal choice.

Systematic concepts of social organization are formed at the fifth level. At this level, subjects develop notions about the role of individuals within social units or collective systems that are defined as systems of individuals interconnected in an organization with a hierarchical order. Conventions are defined as shared behavior mediated by concepts of society; such behavior is seen as necessary because of the function served by uniformity in the social system. Therefore, convention is viewed as normative regulation in a system with uniformity, fixed roles, and hierarchical organization. The following 12th-grade subject articulates these notions in the Social-Conventional Interview and again when talking about actual conflicts over doing the chores:

DO YOU THINK PETER WAS RIGHT OR WRONG TO CONTINUE CALLING HIS TEACHERS BY THEIR FIRST NAMES? Wrong. WHY? Because that's the rule that they've had in school, and if teachers want to be called by their formal titles, then he should call them by their formal titles. WHY IS IT IMPORTANT TO FOLLOW THE RULES? Because this way he's on the same level as the rest of the kids, and they don't feel that he's being in any way privileged and above them. It's a rule, and he should learn how to follow rules. WHY IS IT IMPORTANT FOR HIM TO LEARN TO FOLLOW RULES? Because there are rules in society. So, if he has to call people by their formal titles, then he has to call people by their formal titles. . . WHY? Because they're the ones who are instructing the kids, and you can't really instruct the kids if they argue with you all the time . . . You have to be on a higher level. Otherwise they won't respect you as much. WHY IS CALLING THEM BY THEIR TITLES A SIGN OF RESPECT? It's just more formal and less familiar . . . You can't have a good teacher/student relationship if the student doesn't respect the teacher.

WHY DO YOU THINK IT'S OK NOT TO DO THE CHORES? Usually I'm curled up in a corner reading a good book, and they call me right out of it. WHY DO YOU THINK IT'S IMPORTANT TO DO IT, THEN? Just so I take part in the job. WHY IS THAT IMPORTANT? Because I live in the house, too, and if I live in it, I should take care of it, too. WHAT DO YOUR PARENTS WANT YOU TO DO? They want me not to argue when they tell me to do them. They don't usually tell me, they'll ask me. So they ask me with the expectation that I will happily do it. WHY DO YOU THINK YOUR PARENTS THINK IT'S WRONG IF YOU DON'T DO IT AT THE TIME THEY ASK YOU? Because they feel that they work really hard, and I live there, and they give me clothes and food and a bed, and the least I could do is help out a little around the house. WHAT DO YOU THINK OF THAT? They're right.

Unlike the previous subject, this subject affirms the validity of her parents' expectations. Her reasoning illustrates that this affirmation is based on an understanding of social systems as consisting of fixed roles and hierarchical structures. When reasoning about titles, this entails the reciprocal roles of teacher and student; when reasoning about her family, this entails the reciprocal obligations that parents and children, by virtue of their roles, engender. In fact, she views conflict as built into her role by parental expectation:

SO WHEN YOU DISAGREE WITH THEM, WHAT HAPPENS? I'll get up and do it. YOU DO GET UP? Well, I have to give a little token resistance. They wouldn't think I'm normal if I didn't.

Conflicts still occur because the expectations are poorly timed or because they conflict with her desires, but she continues to affirm her parents' conventional expectation that she share in the household labor.

Subjects in transition between developmental levels expressed confusion in both their hypothetical conventional reasoning and their reasoning about actual family conflicts. The following subject is in transition between the fourth and fifth level and vacillates between them; although he demonstrates a developing understanding of level 5 concepts, he also shows some negation characteristic of level 4.

DO YOU THINK PETER WAS RIGHT OR WRONG TO CONTINUE CALLING TEACHERS BY THEIR FIRST NAMES? Wrong. WHY? Well, you've gotta respect teachers as being like, above your level of knowledge or something. So you should like, treat them the way they want to be treated. So you should call them by their formal names. WHY DO YOU HAVE TO RESPECT THEM? Well, because if you want to learn from them, they've gotta respect you and you've gotta respect them, but it's gotta be like, equal respect for each other. But sometimes, they think they're on a different level, and you speak to them like you're definitely inferior. IS IT IMPORTANT TO MAINTAIN THAT . . . DIFFERENCE IN LEVELS? Yeah. Oh, for the teachers, yeah. It's important because they're trying to teach, and a lot of times, they don't want to get too close to the student, for some reason. Sometimes they're afraid of like a whole bunch of students. It's kind of like, the students are a threat, that's what some teachers think. So they just like to maintain that they're above the students and like to be respected. DO YOU AGREE WITH THAT? Oh yeah, I guess so. If they want. It doesn't really matter that much to me. WHY NOT? Because you don't want to get too friendly with teachers, because it doesn't seem right. I've always liked to call people by their last names . . . Because when you start talking with informal names, nicknames, or just regular first names, it's more like a friendship relationship. And these teacher relationships aren't always friendships.

In reasoning hypothetically about using titles, this subject simultaneously negates the convention as being unimportant and providing barriers between student and teacher and affirms the use of titles as maintaining appropriate teacher-student roles. His reasoning about family conflicts is characterized more by affirmation than negation, but in an unusual way. In applying his developing notions of social structure, he overextends his understanding of hierarchical organization and confuses role relationships, affirming the social structure in such a way as to cause conflict with his parents:

Well, my parents don't like me to yell at [my brother] or anything for doing stuff . . . I think that I should be able too—like if he does anything wrong, like totally and obviously wrong, like leaving stuff out in the yard or something, I should be able to tell him. Whatever you say, it's like "I don't want to do it."

Like, sometimes he does it afterwards, but that's only after coaxing. SO YOU
THINK YOU SHOULD BE ABLE TO DISCIPLINE HIM. I think so. To some
extent. Not like major spanking or anything like that. BUT TELLING HIM WHAT
TO DO, YELLING ONCE IN A WHILE, THINGS LIKE THAT? Yeah. WHY?
Well, because my parents aren't always around, and he's got to learn to respect
everyone. Because it might get to the point where he's just like—you know, he
won't pay any attention to my sister, who's older than him, or [to me]. AND
YOUR PARENTS—See, this is what I don't understand. They think that they've
got to like, show him, they've gotta do it themselves. Because they're afraid that I
might get too hostile or something. He's my brother and I might beat him up . . .
WHY DO YOU THINK IT'S OK FOR YOU TO DISCIPLINE MICHAEL? Well,
because I know all the rules by now.

Confused by the hierarchical organization of the family and his position in it
as both subordinate to parents and superordinate to his brother (because he is
older), this subject attempts to replicate the parent-child role in his relationship to
his brother. Yet he recognizes the inappropriateness of his behavior in acknowl-
edging his parents' concern that in doing so he might behave more like a sibling
(and beat up his brother).

The social system concepts at the fifth level are rejected at the sixth level,
when conventions are viewed as "nothing but" societal expectations. Conventions are still regarded as part of the social system in that they are defined as
codified societal standards that provide uniformity within the group; at the sixth
level, however, uniformity, per se, is no longer regarded as necessary for the
social system to function adequately. Individual diversity or variation is seen as
compatible within a social system. Since uniformity is not required, conventions
are regarded as arbitrary dictates and are no longer seen to serve societal functions. Therefore, it is assumed that conventions exist because they have become
habitual and are maintained by tradition. The following 12th grader expresses it
in this way:

DO YOU THINK PETER WAS RIGHT OR WRONG TO CONTINUE CALLING
HIS TEACHERS BY THEIR FIRST NAMES? I think he was wrong, just because
people have to respect other people's wishes, especially if they are dealing with
them . . . WHY DO YOU THINK IT IS SO IMPORTANT FOR THE TEACH-
ERS IN PETER'S SCHOOL TO BE CALLED BY THEIR TITLES. I don't think it
is. WHY DO YOU THINK THEY INSIST THAT PETER CALL THEM BY
THEIR TITLES? The only thing I can think of is that it has been like that. I mean
that is the way it has been, and there isn't an obvious reason to change it so we are
just keeping it up. IS IT IMPORTANT TO KEEP IT UP? I don't think so. In other
countries students call their teachers by their first names.

This rejection of uniformity as embodied in convention as "nothing but"
societal expectation and an accompanying affirmation of individuality was a
consistent theme in level 6 adolescents' reasoning about family conflicts. Indeed,

more than at any other level, the negation of convention at the sixth level gave voice to a rebelliousness that was echoed over and over again in subjects' responses. For the aforementioned subject, conflicts with his parents arose out of his rejection of various parental conventions.

WHAT DO YOU THINK OF YOUR PARENTS' ARGUMENT THAT YOU SHOULD DATE [A GIRL OF THE SAME RELIGION]. I think it depends. People have done it [dated others of the same religion], but for me, it's not significant enough to make a difference. You know it's not important to me right now. WHY DON'T YOU WANT TO WEAR WHAT YOUR PARENTS WANT? I don't think it's necessary . . . WHY DO YOU THINK YOUR PARENTS EX-PECT YOU TO WEAR CERTAIN TYPES OF CLOTHES? I think it's the way they were raised, what they were exposed to. I think it's not really valid, their expectations. When I first got it done [had his ear pierced], they were very, very annoyed. But my dad was only upset . . . that his son wears an earring. . . . They don't like the earring, but I do. SO WHY DO YOU WANT TO WEAR THIS EARRING? I just like it, I think it's kind of cool. WHY DON'T THEY LIKE IT? I think they're just conservative. Boys or men don't wear earrings. SO WHY DO YOU THINK IT'S OK TO WEAR THE EARRING EVEN THOUGH YOUR PARENTS DON'T LIKE IT? Whether I wear an earring or not, it doesn't matter. If I like it, fine. If people like plaid, they can wear plaid.

Adolescents at the sixth level also characteristically "conventionalized" is-sues that were usually not treated as conventional issues by adolescents at other developmental levels. For instance, the following 11th-grade subject treats con-flicts over homework as conventional, rejecting her parents' conventions and defining herself through negation.

WHY DO YOU THINK SHE HAS THIS EXPECTATION [THAT YOU DO YOUR HOMEWORK?] Um, genetics, maybe. I don't know. I know it comes from her childhood, also. Her parents wanted her to be a good student, and she was a good student herself. She wanted to be a good student, and she wants me to be a good student. But she doesn't realize that I don't want to be a good student, or I don't want to be the head of the class, because she usually was the head of the class.

Although the themes of individual expression, rebellion against societal con-ventions, and rejection of parental conventions were prevalent among adoles-cents at the sixth level, not all adolescents wanted to define themselves through negation. As the following ninth-grade boy says:

WHY DO YOU THINK IT'S OK TO HAVE YOUR HAIR THE LENGTH YOU HAVE IT? It's just something that doesn't matter that much to me. It's just a little social thing, which I really don't care for. It doesn't really matter to me. I'm not trying to be different.

The Development of Conventional Concepts and Adolescent—Parent Conflict

The second hypothesis of this study was that conflict would be related to adolescents' developmental level of conventional reasoning. This hypothesis was based on the premise that conflict occurs over issues in the social-conventional domain. The results presented thus far, however, indicate that in thinking about conflictual issues, children and adolescents often subordinated conventional considerations to personal jurisdiction. Therefore. the developmental hypothesis needs to be restated. The development of social-conventional concepts would be expected to be related to conventional reasoning about conflictual family issues, but not to conflicts containing no conventional components. This is based on the assertion that because the domains are distinct, self-regulating systems, reasoning in one domain would not be expected to predict or guide behavior in another. Said differently, relationships between judgments and action would be expected within, but not across, social-cognitive domains (see Turiel & Davidson, 1986, or Turiel & Smetana, 1984, for an elaboration of this view).

Justifications and Counterarguments. Justifications and counterarguments regarding conflictual issues were examined as a function of developmental level of conventional reasoning. As expected, only conventional reasoning about actual conflicts varied according to adolescents' developmental level of reasoning. Significant differences in adolescents' conventional counterarguments were found according to their developmental level of conventional reasoning. As can be seen in Fig. 4.8, adolescents who had constructed systematic concepts of social systems at the fifth level were more likely to view their parents' reasoning in conventional terms than were children and adolescents at the two previous developmental levels. Thus, an understanding of conventions as integrated aspects of hierarchical social systems appears to facilitate adolescents' appreciation of their parents' perspective. As Fig. 4.8 also illustrates, the pattern of results obtained for mothers partially supports the developmental hypothesis of this study. Mothers of daughters who affirmed the importance of social conventions in structuring social interactions (e.g., at levels 3 and 5) were more likely to reason conventionally when taking their daughter's perspective than were mothers of daughters who negated conventions (e.g., at levels 4 and 6). These findings are especially interesting, since girls' justifications did not conform to this pattern. Perhaps mothers of daughters at affirmation phases in the development of conventional concepts overgeneralized their daughters' affirmation of conven-

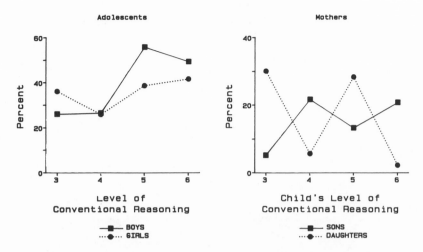

FIG. 4.8. Conventional counterarguments by conventional reasoning level.

tions and perceived more congruence between their and their daughters' reasoning than actually existed.

Intrapersonal Consistency in Justifications and Counterarguments. The analyses thus far compared different family members' justifications and counterarguments, but they did not directly assess the perceived consistency between parents' and adolescents' justifications, or the extent to which adolescents viewed their reasoning to be conceptually similar to their parents (and vice versa). Accordingly, justifications and counterarguments were examined for within-domain consistency. The results are presented in Fig. 4.9. As can be seen, adolescents generally saw their parents' justifications as conceptually dissimilar to their own; only 16% of their justifications and counterarguments matched conceptually. Parents also saw their and their adolescents' reasoning as differing conceptually; 18% of mothers' and 13% of fathers' justifications and counterarguments matched conceptually. Mothers of adolescents who had attained a social-systemic view of conventions (at the fifth level) saw more conceptual similarity between their and their adolescents' reasoning than mothers of children and adolescents at the two prior developmental levels. Since the results for counterarguments indicate that adolescents at the fifth level are more likely to take their parents' (conventional) perspectives than adolescents at the previous developmental phases, these results suggest that mothers of adolescents at this level are accurately perceiving increases in similarity between their own and their adolescents' thinking. However, contrary to expectation, adolescents saw greater

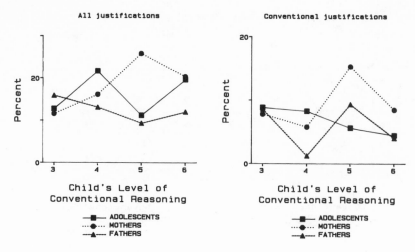

FIG. 4.9. Perceived consistency between self and other's justifications.

conceptual similarity between their own and their parents' reasoning when they were in negation phases in the development of conventional concepts than when they were in affirmation phases. Although the meaning of this finding is not entirely clear, it suggests that within-domain conflicts increase during negation phases in the development of conventional concepts.

The latter findings prompted a reexamination of the data in terms of only those instances in which justifications and counterarguments were both viewed as conventional. These results are also presented in Fig. 4.9. As can be seen, these constituted a smaller proportion of the conflicts that occurred over issues in the same domain. The proportion of conflicts that adolescents viewed to be conventional, both from their own and their parents' perspective, declined significantly from early to late adolescence. Thus, adolescents were less likely to perceive a conceptual match between their own and their parents' conventional thinking as they moved through adolescence. Nevertheless, mothers of adolescents who affirmed conventions at the fifth level still perceived more consistency between their own and their children's perspectives than mothers of adolescents at other developmental levels. Furthermore, fathers of adolescents who affirmed conventions at the third and fifth levels perceived greater conceptual similarity between themselves and their children than fathers of adolescents who negated conventions (at levels 4 and 6).

Age Versus Development.   As Table 4.4. suggests, grade and developmental level, as well as age and developmental level, were strongly related (r's = .76, .70, respectively, $p < .0001$), raising questions as to whether these findings are merely an artifact of grade level. To explore this hypothesis, regression analyses were conducted separately to determine whether grade level or developmental level accounted for more of the variance in the frequency of conventional counterarguments.[2] The differences were small and nonsignificant (R^2 = .28. .24 for developmental level and grade level, respectively), but in the expected direction, lending some support to a developmental interpretation of the findings. They suggest that the development of conventional concepts may be related to the extent to which children and adolescents recognize and articulate the conventional components of multifaceted events but not to children's justifications or counterarguments in other domains.

The extent or severity of conflicts was also reexamined as a function of developmental level of conventional reasoning.[3] Families with children who negated social conventions at the sixth level treated issues as less important and conflict as less frequent than all other families. Adolescents who negated conventions as nothing but social expectations (level 4), however, treated the issues underlying conflicts as more important than adolescents who rejected conventions as nothing but habitual societal standards (level 6). Regression analyses indicated that the proportion of variance accounted for by either developmental level or grade level was very small, although developmental level was as predictive or predicted more of the variance than grade level (R^2 = .04 vs. .009 for importance; R^2 = .10, .094 for frequency, respectively). None of these differences achieved statistical significance, however.

Sex differences also emerged. The pattern for boys was consistent with the hypothesis that conflict is related to negation phases in the development of conventional concepts. As was initially hypothesized, boys who negated conventions at the fourth level rated conflict as more frequent than did boys who negated conventions at the sixth level. Further (although not quite statistically significant), families with boys who negated convention at the fourth level generated a greater number of conflicts than families with boys at all other levels, with conflicts declining from the sixth negation level to the two affirmation levels (3 and 5), respectively (M's = 3.97, 3.70, 3.67, 3.15, respectively). Boys at the sixth negation level also reported significantly poorer relations, in general, with their mothers than boys at all other levels (M's = 2.27, 1.88, 1.64, 1.58 for levels 6, 4, 3, 5, respectively, where 1 = very positive relations and 5 = very poor relations). Boys who had acquired a systematic conception of convention at the fifth level reported the most positive relations with their mothers.

---

[2]Some (e.g., Wohlwill, 1973) have argued that developmental variables should always be used in preference to age, since age is not a developmental variable and indexes other biological, social, and cognitive developmental processes.

[3]These analyses could not be restricted to ratings of conventional justifications or counterarguments, since the resulting cell frequencies were too small and there were too many empty cells. Therefore, exploratory analyses were run on all conflict ratings.

The pattern for girls differed from that of boys. Families with girls who affirmed conventions as normative regulation within social systems and as arbitrary conventions (levels 5 and 3) reported a significantly greater number of conflicts than families with girls who negated conventions at the fourth level (M's = 4.13, 4.00, 2.87, respectively), and girls who negated conventions at the fourth level also reported getting along significantly better with their mothers than all other girls. Girls at the sixth level also reported the least positive relations with their mothers (M's = 1.54, 2.15, 2.18, 2.20 for levels 4, 3, 5, 6, respectively, where 1 = very positive relations and 5 = very poor relations). Developmental level of conventional reasoning accounted for more of the variance in boys' ratings of their relations with mothers than did grade level (R^2 = .14 versus .08, respectively), whereas grade level accounted for more of the variance in girls' ratings of how well they got along with their mothers than did developmental level (R^2 = .08, .03, respectively). Again, however, neither grade level nor developmental level accounted for much of the variance.

It is not clear why the patterns differed for boys and girls. It is possible that the biological changes of puberty, which are more dramatic for girls than boys in early adolescence, are more important to mothers' and girls' changing perceptions of their relationship than shifts in social-cognitive structures. This hypothesis is consistent with reports on the mental health of children, which indicate that girls have more difficulties with adjustment in adolescence than do boys (Rutter, 1980). Two findings argue against this interpretation, however. First, not all effects of developmental level of conventional concepts on parent-child relationships were sex-differentiated, and those that were not sex-differentiated were more robust than those that were, as assessed by the proportion of variance accounted for (.30's versus .02—.13). Also, previously reported findings on the effects of pubertal status (Hill & Holmbeck, 1985) suggest that this variable does not account for more of the variance in conflict than does social-cognitive development.

DISCUSSION AND CONCLUSIONS

Early Adolescence as a Developmental Transition

Hamburg (1974, 1985), as well as others (Lipsitz, 1977; Peterson, 1986), have proposed that early adolescence is a critical developmental transition due to the interactive effects of the biological changes of puberty, transitions in schooling, and entry into a new role status, and because development prior to this phase is disjunctive with later development. Echoing this theme, Thornburg (1986) has called for a model of adolescence that is not too closely tied to childhood, asserting that comprehensive theories do not account adequately for the nature of the transition from childhood to adolescence.

With regard to cognitive and affective realignments in parent-child relations, our results indicate that early adolescence is both continuous and disjunctive with the prior developmental phase. Although much attention has been paid to parent-child conflict in early adolescence, little research has focused on the extent to which this conflict is continuous with childhood conflicts. Our investigation suggests that parent-child conflict, as assessed by verbal report, does not shift dramatically from preadolescence to adolescence. This is consistent with the finding that parents' ratings on the Child Behavior Checklist of children's disobedience at home shows little change between the ages of 10 and 16, although disobedience is less frequent in adolescence than in childhood (Achenbach & Edelbrock, 1981).

Further evidence of continuity between childhood and early adolescence was found in the different ways adolescents and parents conceptualized actual conflicts and hypothetical issues. Domain differences were evident in preadolescence and persisted throughout adolescence. Age-related declines in the frequency of conventional reasoning and judgments about hypothetical items and increases in conventional perspectives on actual conflicts (counterarguments) were linear rather than disjunctive. Increases with age in the extent to which events were judged as personal were also linear rather than disjunctive.

With regard to children's developing conceptions of social conventions and social systems, early adolescence is disjunctive with preadolescence, just as mid- and late adolescence are disjunctive with early adolescence and with each other. Children develop qualitatively different modes of thinking about social conventions that are reorganized with age. (The development of conventional concepts are, at the same time, also continuous in that each level represents advances in thinking that are constructed out of the previous mode of thought.) Four different modes of thinking, roughly corresponding to preadolescence, early adolescence, mid-adolescence, and late adolescence, chronologically defined, were represented in children's thinking in this sample. They represent a dialectic of affirmations and negations of the importance of conventions in regulating social life. These different modes of thinking were also found to structure children's and adolescents' thinking about family conflicts. Despite the continuity in the way children at each level structured conflicts, conflicts were evident at each development level.

Developmental shifts in children's concepts of convention and social systems were related, although complexly, to the quality of adolescent-parent relationships. The development of systematic and integrated conceptions of social systems in mid-adolescence appears to represent a developmental hallmark in adolescent-parent relationships. Adolescents at this developmental level were better able to take their parents' conventional perspectives in conflict situations, and mothers and fathers were significantly more likely to see conceptual similarities in their and their children's justifications (although this did not preclude parent-child differences as to whose conventions were affirmed). Boys at this level generated fewer conflicts and reported more positive relations with their mothers than boys at other developmental levels. Thus, particularly for boys, these findings suggest that the emergence of a social-systemic perspective distinguishes mid-adolescence from earlier developmental phases.

For girls, the results are more consistent with the prevailing notion that early adolescence is a period of particular disruption in parent-child relations (Hamburg, 1985; Hill, this volume; Hill & Holmbeck, in press; Hill et. al., 1985; Montemayor, 1986; Petersen, 1986; Steinberg, 1981). Girls' conventional counterarguments decreased in frequency in early adolescence, as compared to earlier and later developmental periods. This drop was consistent with mothers' reports that their relationships with their daughters declined in quality in early adolescence, as compared to late adolescence. These affective patterns differed for boys and girls, as did the extent to which developmental shifts in conventional reasoning were related to affective realignments in parent-child relationships. For boys, the findings were consistent with the initial developmental hypothesis of this study, but for girls, chronological age appeared to predict the quality of parent-child relationships as well as or better than developmental level.

Conflict and Individuation During Adolescence

The results from both the Hypothetical Authority Interview and the Conflict Interview indicated that adolescents' personal reasoning (about hypothetical issues and some types of actual conflicts) increased as adolescents grew older. These findings suggest that the inclusion of actions in the personal domain represents an important aspect of the adolescent's developing autonomy or distinctiveness from others (Nucci, 1981). Descriptions of the development of autonomy have focused primarily on its affective components, either within the individual or in family relationships (Cooper et al., 1983; Erikson, 1968; Grotevant & Cooper, 1986; Steinberg & Silverberg, 1986; White, Speisman, & Costos, 1983). The increases in personal reasoning obtained here also suggest that individuation during adolescence may contain a social-cognitive component entailing the increasing subordination of familial convention to personal jurisdiction.

It must be underscored that adolescents did not subordinate all types of issues to personal jurisdiction; claims of moral significance, for instance, were never rejected in favor of maintaining or exerting their personal jurisdiction. It is also important to note that concepts of personal jurisdiction do not arise de novo in adolescence. Even for preschool children, there are a set of issues that are categorized as personal (Smetana, 1986a) and a set of criteria that are used consistently by children across a broad age range to distinguish personal events from moral or conventional ones (Killen, 1986; Nucci, 1977, 1981; Smetana, Bridgeman, & Turiel, 1983).

Furthermore, the finding that adolescents' but not parents' personal reasoning increases during adolescence suggests that parents must also face a developmental task in separating from their children and that this task is not accomplished during their child's adolescence. Although there may be little disagreement between parents and children during middle childhood on the conventionality of a variety of family issues, children view themselves as becoming increasingly emancipated from their parents' conventional perspectives during adolescence. Torn between the necessity of maintaining the family social system and allowing their child increasing jurisdiction over her own behavior, parents may encounter difficulty in relinquishing their authority. Thus, parents' conventional perspective, which may be functional during their child's early years, may become increasingly maladaptive or inappropriate as adolescents move into young adulthood.

Conflict and Adaptation

In considering these findings, it is necessary to consider the relationship of conflict to development. In an attempt to clarify the meaning of conflict in adolescence, Roll (1980) distinguished between different dimensions of adolescent-parent conflict. She proposed that conflict may be either intrapsychic or external (between parents and children), self-defined (whether or not it is perceived to be a conflict with others) or other-defined (in that it is perceived by others, whether or not the adolescent is aware of it), and episodic or continuous. Although psychoanalytic theory promulgated the view of adolescence as a period of intrapsychic conflict (Blos, 1979; A. Freud, 1973/1958), most researchers today focus on externally defined conflict. Although researchers have varied somewhat in the extent to which they have operationalized conflict as self- or other-defined, most have focused on conflicts entailing mutual engagement and negotiation. Montemayor and Hanson's (1985) telephone survey of 10th graders is useful in this respect. They note that 47% of conflicts with parents are resolved by walking away, and only 15% are marked by negotiation. These data indicate that self-defined conflicts may constitute a much greater proportion of parent-child conflicts in adolescence than actual contentious interchanges. Yet most researchers have focused on the more limited sphere of contentious interchanges and actual encounters in early adolescence.

By asking family members in our investigation to generate conflicts for discussion, our investigation appears to have tapped a broader spectrum of conflicts than is typically assessed (which may have served to minimize the relationships observed). We assessed both self-defined and other-defined conflicts (for instance, parents' descriptions of adolescents' obnoxious personality characteristics), as well as contentious interchanges. Our data on conflict resolution strategies are also consistent with Montemayor and Hanson (1985). Family members were also asked how each conflict typically was resolved. Responses were coded into two sets of categories. One pertained to the process of conflict resolution, and the other pertained to conflict solutions, including two types of unilateral solutions (parent concedes or child concedes—actively or passively, by walking away) and two types of bilateral solutions (compromise or no resolution—again, either actively agreeing that resolution cannot be reached or passively, by walking away). Parents and children did not differ significantly in their report that adolescents acceded to parental demands in 56% of all conflicts, whereas parents acceded to child demands in only 18% of conflicts. Similar to Montemayor and Hanson (1985), joint discussion accounted for only 13% of all conflict resolutions.

Hill and Holmbeck (in press) have written insightfully on the functions of conflict for adaptation. They assert that conflict can be seen as adaptive to the extent that perturbations in parent-child relationships change the power balance of the family. Our data indicate that families' modes of conflict resolution varied as a function of the adolescent's developmental level of conventional concepts. Both parents and adolescents reported that parents were more likely to accede to adolescents who negated conventions at the sixth level than to adolescents at the two previous developmental levels. Conversely, adolescents who negated conventions at this level were less likely to give in to parents than were adolescents at the three lower developmental levels studied here. Thus it appears that adolescents become increasingly adept at putting theory into action. Their understanding of the family social system and their role and status within it (characteristic of the fifth level), combined with the rejection of convention characteristic of the subsequent developmental level, forms a mode of reasoning that persuasively subverts their parents' authority. That is, adolescents' social-cognitive development appears to affect not only family affective relationships, but behavioral interactions as well. It is indeed ironical that a full appreciation of the role of conventional uniformities as functional for maintaining social systems, attained in young adulthood, does not emerge until adolescents in our culture have separated from their families. This newly obtained knowledge may be necessary for young adults to see the wisdom of the parental conventions and expectations that they so vigorously rejected in adolescence.

ACKNOWLEDGMENTS

I am very grateful to the many families who participated in this research, to the administrators and teachers in the Brighton School District for their help in recruiting families, and to Beth Arcuri, Jenny Chan, Lisa Elliot, David Farrokh, Mario Kelly, Jeff Laminiaux, Cindy Rohrbeck, and Rubina Saigol for their assistance with data collection. I am also grateful to Jenny Chan, David Farrokh, and Mario Kelly for their able assistance with coding and data entry, Maria Nucci for her coding of the Social-Conventional Interviews, and Craig Barclay and Judy Braeges for their helpful comments on an earlier draft of the manuscript. This research was supported by NIMH Grant #R01-MH39142.

REFERENCES

Achenbach, T. M. & Edelbrock, C. S. (1981). Behavioral problems and competencies reported by parents of normal and disturbed children aged four through sixteen. *Monographs of the Society for Research in Child Development*, Serial 188, *46*, 1–82.

Blos, P. (1979). *The adolescent passage*. New York: International Universities Press.

Coleman, J. C. (1974). *Relationships in adolescence*. London: Routledge & Kegan Paul.

Collins, W. A. (1985, April). *Cognition, affect, and the development of parent-child relationships*. Paper presented at the biennial meetings of the Society for Research in Child Development, Toronto, Ontario.

Cooper, C. R., Grotevant, H. D., & Condon, S. M. (1983). Individuality and connectedness in the family as a context for adolescent identity formation and role-taking skill. In H. D. Grotevant, & C. R. Cooper (Eds.), *New directions for child development: Adolescent development in the family* (pp. 45–60). San Francisco: Jossey-Bass.

Csikszentmihalyi, M., & Larsen, R. (1984). *Being adolescent: Conflict and growth in the teenage years*. New York: Basic Books.

Damon, W. (1977). *The social world of the child*. San Francisco: Jossey-Bass.

Davidson, P., Turiel, E., & Black, A. (1983). The effect of stimulus familiarity on the use of criteria and justifications in children's social reasoning. *British Journal of Developmental Psychology, 1*, 49–65.

Dix, T. (1984, August). *Social-cognitive processes during parent-child disciplinary episodes*. Paper presented at the annual convention of the American Psychological Association, Toronto, Ontario.

Douvan, E., & Adelson, J. (1966). *The adolescent experience*. New York: Wiley.

Dworkin, R. (1978). *Taking rights seriously*. Cambridge, MA: Harvard University Press.

Erikson, E. (1968). *Identity: Youth and crisis*. New York: Norton.

Feldman, D. H. (1980). *Beyond universals in cognitive development*. Norwood, NJ: Ablex.

Freud, A. (1958). *The ego and the mechanisms of defense*. London, England: Hogarth Press. (original work published 1937)

Gewirth, A. (1978). *Reason and morality*. Chicago: University of Chicago Press.

Grotevant, H. D., & Cooper, C. R. (1986). Individuation in family relationships: A perspective on individual differences in the development of identity and role-taking skills in adolescence. *Human Development, 29*, 82–100.

Hall, G. S. (1904). *Adolescence: Its psychology and its relations to physiology, anthropology, sociology, sex, crime, religion, and education* (Vols. 1 and 2). New York: Appleton.

Hamburg, B. A. (1974). Early adolescence: A specific and stressful stage of the life cycle. In G. V. Coelho, D. A. Hamburg, & J. A. Adams (Eds.), *Coping and adaptation* (pp. 101–124). New York: Basic Books.

Hamburg, B. A. (1985). Early adolescence: A time of transition and stress. *Early Adolescence, 78*, 158–167.

Hill, J. P. (1980). The family. In M. Johnson (Ed.), *Toward adolescence: The middle school years. The seventy-ninth yearbook of the National Society for the Study of Education* (pp. 32–55). Chicago: University of Chicago Press.

Hill, J. P., & Holmbeck, G. N. (1985, April). *Familial adaptations to pubertal change: The role of conflict*. Paper presented at the Biennial Meetings of the Society for Research in Child Development, Toronto, Ontario.

Hill, J. P., & Holmbeck, G. N. (in press). Familial adaptation to biological change during adolescence. To appear in R. M. Lerner & T. Foch (Eds.), *Biological-psychosocial interactions in early adolescence: A life-span perspective*. Hillsdale, NJ: Lawrence Erlbaum Associates.

Hill, J. P., Holmbeck, G. N., Marlow, L., Green, T. M., & Lynch, M. E. (1985). Menarcheal status and parent-child relations in families of seventh grade girls. *Journal of Youth and Adolescence, 14*, 301–316.

Hunter, F., & Youniss, J. (1982). Changes in functions of three relations during adolescence. *Developmental Psychology, 18,* 806–811.

Inhelder, B., & Piaget, J. (1958). *The growth of logical thinking from childhood to adolescence.* New York: Basic Books.

Keil, F. (1986). On the structure dependent nature of stages of cognitive development. In I. Levin (Ed.), *Stage and structure: Reopening the debate.* (pp. 144–163). Norwood, NJ: Ablex.

Killen, M. (1986). *Morality in context: Children's coordination of moral and social contexts.* Unpublished manuscript, Wesleyan University.

Kohlberg, L. (1971). From is to ought: How to commit the naturalistic fallacy and get away with it in the study of moral development. In T. Mischel (Ed.), *Cognitive development and epistemology* (pp. 151–235). New York: Academic Press.

Larsen, J., Livingston, J., & Tron, R. (1985, April). *Mothers and adolescent daughters: Personal issues of conflict and congruency.* Paper presented at the Biennial Meetings of the Society for Research in Child Development, Toronto, Ontario.

Lipsitz, J. (1977). *Growing up fourteen.* Lexington, MA: D. C. Heath.

Mill, J. S. (1963). *Utilitarianism.* New York: Washington Square Press. (original work published 1863)

Montemayor, R. (1982). The relationship between parent-adolescent conflict and the amount of time adolescents spend alone and with parents and peers. *Child Development, 53,* 1512–1519.

Montemayor, R. (1983). Parents and adolescents in conflict: All families some of the time and some families most of the time. *Journal of Early Adolescence, 3,* 83–103.

Montemayor, R. (1986). Family variation in parent-adolescent storm and stress. *Journal of Adolescent Research, 1,* 15–31.

Montemayor, R., & Hanson, E. A. (1985). A naturalistic view of conflict between adolescents and their parents and siblings. *Journal of Early Adolescence, 3,* 83–103.

Nucci, L. (1977). *Social development: Personal, conventional, and moral concepts.* Unpublished doctoral dissertation, University of California, Santa Cruz.

Nucci, L. (1981). The development of personal concepts: A domain distinct from moral or societal concepts. *Child Development, 52,* 114–121.

Nucci, L. (1984). Evaluating teachers as social agents: Students' ratings of domain-appropriate and domain-inappropriate teacher responses to transgressions. *American Education Research Journal, 21,* 367–378.

Offer, D. (1969). *The psychological world of the teenager.* New York: Basic Books.

Offer, D., & Offer, J. (1975). *From teenage to young manhood.* New York: Basic Books.

Paikoff, R. L., Collins, W. A., & Laursen, B. (1986, March). *Perceptions of parental influence techniques in middle childhood and early adolescence.* Paper presented at the first Biennial Meeting of the Society for Research on Adolescence, Madison, WI.

Peterson, A. C. (1986, April). *Early adolescence: A critical developmental transition?* Paper presented at the annual meetings of the American Educational Research Association, San Francisco.

Rawls, J. (1971). *A theory of justice.* Cambridge, MA: Cambridge University Press.

Remmers, H. H., & Radler, D. H. (1962). *The American teenager.* Indianapolis, IN: Bobbs-Merrill.

Rest, J. (1983). Morality. In J. H. Flavell & E. M. Markman (Eds.), *Handbook of child psychology: Vol. 3. Cognitive development* (pp. 556–629). New York: Wiley.

Roll, E. J. (1980). Psychologists' conflicts about the inevitability of conflict during adolescence: An attempt at reconciliation. *Adolescence, 59,* 661–670.

Rutter, M. (1980). Emotional development. In M. Rutter (Ed.), *Scientific foundations of developmental psychiatry* (pp. 306–321). London, England: Heinemann Medical.

Selman, R. L. (1980). *The growth of interpersonal understanding.* New York: Academic Press.

Shantz, C. U. (1983). Social cognition. In J. H. Flavell & E. M. Markman (Eds.), *Handbook of child psychology: Vol. 3. Cognitive development* (pp. 495–555). New York: Wiley.

Shweder, R. A., Turiel, E., & Much, N. (1981). The moral intuitions of the child. In J. H. Flavell & L. Ross (Ed.), *Social-cognitive development: Frontiers and possible futures* (pp. 288–305). Cambridge, England: Cambridge University Press.

Simmons, R., Blyth, D., Van Cleave, E. F., & Bush, D. M. (1979). Entry into early adolescence: The impact of school structure, puberty, and early dating on self-esteem. *American Sociological Review, 44,* 948–967.

Smetana, J. G. (1981a). Preschool children's conceptions of moral and social rules. *Child Development, 52,* 1333–1336.

Smetana, J. G. (1981b). Reasoning in the personal and moral domains: Adolescent and young adult women's decision-making regarding abortion. *Journal of Applied Developmental Psychology, 2,* 211–226.

Smetana, J. G. (1982). *Concepts of self and morality: Women's reasoning about abortion.* New York: Praeger.

Smetana, J. G. (1983). Social-cognitive development: Domain distinctions and coordinations. *Developmental Review, 3,* 131–147.

Smetana, J. G. (1985). Preschool children's conceptions of transgressions: The effects of varying moral and conventional domain-related attributes. *Developmental Psychology, 21,* 18–29.

Smetana, J. G. (1986). Preschool children's conceptions of sex-role transgressions. *Child Development, 57,* 862–871.

Smetana, J. G. (in press). Adolescents' and parents' conceptions of parental authority. *Child Development.*

Smetana, J. G., Bridgeman, D., & Turiel, E. (1983). Social cognition: Differentiation of domains and prosocial reasoning. In D. Bridgeman (Ed.), *The nature of prosocial development: Interdisciplinary theories and strategies* (pp. 163–183). New York: Academic Press.

Steinberg, L. (1981). Transformations in family relations at puberty. *Developmental Psychology, 17,* 833–840.

Steinberg, L. D. (1985, April). *The ABC's of transformations in the family at adolescence: Changes in affect, behavior, and cognition.* Paper presented at the Biennial Meetings of the Society for Research in Child Development, Toronto, Ontario.

Steinberg, L., & Hill, J. (1978). Patterns of family interaction as a function of age, the onset of puberty, and formal thinking. *Developmental Psychology, 14,* 983–684.

Steinberg, L., & Silverberg, S. B. (1986). The vicissitudes of autonomy in early adolescence. *Child Development, 57,* 841–851.

Thornburg, H. (1986, March). *Toward a theory of human performance.* Presidential address delivered at the First Biennial Meetings of the Society for Research on Adolescence, Madison, WI.

Turiel, E. (1975). The development of social concepts: Mores, customs, and conventions. In D. J. Palma & J. M. Foley (Eds.), *Moral development: Current theory and research* (pp. 7–38). Hillsdale, NJ: Lawrence Erlbaum Associates.

Turiel, E. (1978). The development of concepts of social structure: Social convention. In J. Glick & A. Clarke-Stewart (Eds.), *The development of social understanding* (pp. 25–108). New York: Gardner Press.

Turiel, E. (1979). Distinct conceptual and developmental domains: Social convention and morality. In C. B. Keasey (Ed.), *1977 Nebraska Symposium on Motivation* (pp. 77–116). Lincoln: University of Nebraska Press.

Turiel, E. (1983). *The development of social knowledge: Morality and convention.* Cambridge: Cambridge University Press.

Turiel, E., & Davidson, P. (1986). Heterogeneity, inconsistency, and asynchrony in the development of cognitive structures. In I. Levin (Ed.), *Stage and structure: Reopening the debate* (pp. 106–143). Norwood, NJ: Ablex.

Turiel, E., & Smetana, J. G. (1984). Social knowledge and action: The coordination of domains. In J. L. Gewirtz & W. M. Kurtines (Eds.), *Morality, moral development, and moral behavior* (pp. 261–282). New York: Wiley.

Weston, D., & Turiel, E. (1980). Act-rule relations: Children's concepts of social rules. *Developmental Psychology, 16,* 417–424.

White, K. M., Spiesman, J. C., & Costos, D. (1983). Young adults and their parents: Individuation to mutuality. In H. D. Grotevant & C. R. Cooper (Eds.), *New directions for child development: Adolescent development in the family* (pp. 61–76). San Francisco: Jossey-Bass.

Wohlwill, J. F. (1973). *The study of behavioral development.* New York: Academic Press.

Youniss, J. & Smollar, J. (1985). *Adolescent relations with mothers, fathers, and friends.* Chicago: University of Chicago Press.

5 Cumulative Change at Entry to Adolescence

Roberta G. Simmons
Richard Burgeson
Mary Jo Reef
University of Minnesota

The transition from childhood to adolescence is a period marked by many changes. Adolescents experience extensive alteration in their peer networks, role expectations, relationships with adults and members of the opposite sex, along with the physical changes associated with puberty. Many of these changes are the normal, scheduled, and inevitable life-event transitions of adolescence, whereas others are unplanned and experienced by a minority of individuals. Coping with all of these changes, even the normative ones, necessarily involves some degree of discomfort. Since adolescence is inevitably a period of transition, we feel the vital issue to be addressed is the timing and spacing among the various life changes. The purpose of this investigation is to examine the impact of experiencing several major life transitions simultaneously in early adolescence. We predict that youngsters will be able to cope more effectively with major life transitions if they occur separately rather than simultaneously. We propose that experiencing several important life changes at once will cause difficulty.

For many children, entry into adolescence is accompanied by a major shift in school environment. Our prior work has shown that students making the transition from a small elementary school into a large, impersonal junior high school in seventh grade are at a disadvantage compared to students who remain in an intimate elementary school setting until Grade 9 (Blyth, Simmons, & Carlton-Ford, 1983; Simmons & Blyth, 1987; Simmons, Blyth, Van Cleave, & Bush, 1979).[1] We believe the disadvantage arises (1) because Grade 7 may be too early

---

[1]For other discussions of the difficulty of the large junior high, see Hamburg (1974) and Lipsitz (1977). There is some evidence outside of our work of negative effects of the junior high compared to the elementary school. See the large-scale study by Eccles' group: Eccles, Midgley, and Adler

for this transition into a large, impersonal organizational setting (or context) and (2) because many youngsters are forced to cope with this fundamental shift in organizational context at the same time they are undergoing dramatic biological changes and social redefinitions.

A primary question for this chapter, then, is whether the change into a new type of organizational environment is more difficult if it occurs simultaneously with other aspects of the changes from childhood into adolescence. Relevant to this issue is the research on life events (see reviews of this approach and its controversies by Dohrenwend & Pearlin, 1981; Johnson, 1982; Kessler, 1979; Kessler, Price & Wortman, 1985; Newcomb, Huba, & Bentler, 1981; Pearlin, Lieberman, Menaghan, & Mullan, 1981; Tausig, 1982; Thoits, 1983; Zautra & Reich, 1983). The focus of the life-event literature, however, is somewhat different from our own. That is, relatively few studies in the life-event area have dealt with normal adolescents (see Gad & Johnson, 1980; Gersten, Langner, Eisenberg, & Orzeck, 1974; Gersten, Langner, Eisenberg, & Simcha-Fagan, 1977; Johnson & McCutcheon, 1980; Newcomb et al., 1981; Padilla, Rohsenow, & Bergman, 1976; Swearingen & Cohen, 1985a, 1985b), and those few that have, by and large, have not focused on the normal, scheduled life-event changes of adolescence—movement into junior high, pubertal development, onset of dating and so on (see Padilla's cross-sectional study of boys, 1976, for an exception).[2] Like Elder and Rockwell (1979), we think life events have to be considered in the context of normative transitions in the life course; it is in this context that we investigated the consequences of concurrently experiencing multiple life changes.

In previous related analyses we have attempted to test Coleman's (1974) "focal theory" of change (Simmons & Blyth, 1987; Simmons, Burgeson, Carlton-Ford, & Blyth, 1987a).[3] The focal model argues that in adolescence gradual adjustment to one major life change prior to confrontation with another will be beneficial. Being able to focus on each of these changes sequentially rather than simultaneously should reduce the difficulty of the transitional process.

In specific, we posited that it would be difficult for children to make the transition into junior high school while they were also experiencing other major scheduled (normative) changes—in particular, the onset of puberty and the ini-

---

(1984), Reuman (1984), and studies by Katz and Zigler (1967) and Haladyna and Thomas (1979). Also see Levine (1966), Levine, Wesolowski, and Corbett (1966), Felner, Primavera, and Cauce (1981), and Felner, Ginter, and Primavera (1982) for evidence that school and residential changes produce negative results, especially in terms of academic achievement. However, comparisons of K–8 to junior high schools do not always favor the K–8 school. (See McCaig, 1967, for a study based in the suburbs rather than a large city).

[2]Most studies of adolescence do include a change of schools as a life event but do not distinguish between the normative scheduled change into junior high and atypical changes.

[3]Also see Rutter (1979, 1980), Thoits (1983), Hetherington (1979), and Wells and Stryker (1988) for development of similar propositions.

tiation of dating relations—or when they were subjected to important non-normative changes. In our studies, we have investigated the effects of a nonnormative change in residence and of disruption in parents' marital status.[4] Children who experienced several important life changes simultaneously were expected to be at greater risk than were those who had time to adjust to one change before the next change was encountered.

Our previous work demonstrated the negative effects of multiple transitions upon white students' self-esteem, grade point average, and their level of participation in extracurricular activities (Simmons et al., 1987a). This present chapter reviews earlier results and then extends the analysis to include (1) an examination of the impact of the number of transitions upon problem behavior in school; (2) a comparison of the effects of multiple changes upon socially advantaged and disadvantaged students (including white versus black students); and (3) the effects of a constant, stable peer group at entry to junior high school as a possible buffer against the negative consequences of multiple transitions.

METHODS

Sample

The data for the present study were collected within the Milwaukee Public Schools between 1974 and 1979. Eighteen schools of different types were sampled, using basically a stratified random sample design (see Simmons & Blyth, 1987). We sampled three main populations of schools: (1) kindergarten through Grade 8 schools (K–8) which did not involve a transition of schools for the student in seventh grade, (2) kindergarten through Grade 6 schools (K–6) that involved a change into junior high school at Grade 7 and which possessed social characteristics similar to the K–8 schools—in particular, they were predominately white schools, and (3) the remaining kindergarten through Grade 6 schools (K–6), which were primarily black.[5]

Within the schools sampled, all sixth-grade students were invited to participate, which gave every student within each stratum an equal probability of being included. Parental permission was secured from 85% of those invited. If the students remained in the Milwaukee public school system we attempted to follow

---

[4]See Gad and Johnson (1980) and Padilla et al. (1976) for a list of other possible non-normative life events. This study was initiated prior to the publication of the life-events literature and measured only these limited, but important, non-normative events.

[5]The data show that the sample K–8 and comparable K–6 schools are very similar on a wide variety of social characteristics that include median family income, achievement scores, teachers' background, mean percentage of children who move in and out of the school, mean percentage of teachers with only a B.A. degree, mean percentage of teachers with only one year of experience (Blyth, 1977; Simmons et al., 1979; Simmons & Blyth, 1987).

them in Grades 7, 9, and 10. Survey interviews were conducted then in Grades 6, 7, 9, and 10. (See Simmons & Blyth, 1987, for more detail.)

Additionally, each student was examined several times by a registered nurse who measured the student's level of physical development. When all variables to be used in this analysis are considered together, complete data on 447 white youths are available.[6] Although the data for black boys are not yet readily available for analysis,[7] the data for black girls ($N = 79$) have been analyzed. In this chapter we describe the results for the transition from Grade 6 to Grade 7.

Measurement

As a measure of recent cumulative change at the point of entry into adolescence, the following types of changes were considered:

1. School change—movement into junior high school (JH) in Grade 7 versus remaining in an intimate kindergarten through eighth grade (K–8) school at the same age.

2. Pubertal change—recency of major pubertal change to the time of the Grade 7 interview. For girls, recent pubertal change was defined as onset of menstruation within 6 months prior to or up to 3 months after the seventh-grade interview. Among boys, recent pubertal change was defined as peak height growth prior to the Grade 7 interview (see Simmons & Blyth, 1987).

3. Early dating defined as going on dates with a member of the opposite sex alone or going steady versus dating in groups or having no dating experience.[8]

---

[6]Some sample loss for this analysis was due to children leaving the Milwaukee school system, to their entering an unusual school transition sequence in Grade 7 (rather than moving from K–6 to junior high or staying in K–8 as expected), or to missing data on some of these variables—primarily on the puberty variables.

[7]We are not able to include black males from our sample in this analysis since we are in the process of calculating the pubertal timing variable for these students. Although the determination of pubertal timing for girls is relatively simple (based on menarche), calculation for males is more difficult depending on both height growth curves and secondary sex characteristics. (See measurement section and Simmons & Blyth, 1987).

[8]One caveat should be noted. One could question whether the causal ordering between dating and our dependent variables is recursive. In our prior analysis (Simmons & Blyth, 1987; Simmons, Carlton-Ford, & Blyth, 1987b), we did investigate the causal relationships over time between these dependent variables and opposite sex popularity for boys (opposite sex popularity as a construct included dating behavior among its indicators). Parameters were estimated, with a LISREL model that included these variables both in Grade 6 and Grade 7. Although there was an indirect causal effect of opposite sex popularity (of borderline significance) upon later self-esteem, there was no causal effect of prior self-esteem, prior GPA, or prior extracurricular participation upon subsequent opposite sex popularity. In any case, our emphasis here is upon the effects of the synchronicity of life changes; the adoption of the new roles involved in dating relationships certainly involves the individual in a meaningful life change.

4. Geographic mobility defined as moving to a new neighborhood in Grades 6 or 7 or to a new school in Grade 6 (when most children did not make these changes).

5. Major family disruption defined as major parental change since age 9, including death, divorce, or remarriage of a parent.[9] (There were too few cases to examine the impact of divorce, parental death, and remarriage separately.)

Because there are not enough cases to examine the effects of the specific combinations of changes, the data were examined simply according to the cumulative number of these transitions each student experienced.[10] The scores could range from 0 to 5 changes, but due to few cases experiencing the maximum number of changes, categories have been collapsed, as necessary, in the various subgroups (see figures below).

Some children make the transition from elementary to junior high school along with a large group of peers; that is, their elementary school "feeds into" one particular junior high. Other youngsters are unaccompanied by large numbers of peers. In order to investigate whether this factor affects the impact of transition upon adjustment, youngsters were characterized according to the number of students from their Grade 6 class who made the Grade 7 transition to the same junior high school. This information was secured from the school system. This "cohort movement" variable ranged from 0 to 69 and in some analyses was dichotomized as 29 or fewer moving together and 30 or more fellow students moving together.

Our four dependent variables included self-esteem, grade point average (GPA), extracurricular participation in school, and school problem behavior. (See Simmons & Blyth, 1987, for more extensive descriptions of these variables.) Self-esteem refers to the overall positive or negative feeling a person holds about him- or herself and was measured by the Rosenberg-Simmons scale. (See Rosenberg & Simmons, 1972; Simmons & Blyth, 1987; Simmons, Rosenberg, & Rosenberg, 1973, for a discussion of validity and reliability.) GPA was used as an indicator of academic achievement and was secured from school records for core academic courses (e.g., math and social studies, but not gym and basket weaving). Extracurricular activities in school included membership in school clubs as well as participation in sports, as reported by the students. The

---

[9]It is assumed that short-term adjustment to such changes may take several years (Hetherington, Cox, & Cox, 1982). In addition, if we used a more recent cut-off, we would not have enough cases of family disruption to analyze.

[10]For more information on the impact of school and of pubertal change considered separately and in conjunction with individual resources, see Simmons and Blyth (1987). It should be noted that in life-event studies, a simple summation of positive and negative life events has yielded as high correlations with outcome variables as more complex attempts to weight the events according to perceived life change or impact (Johnson, 1982).

school problem behavior variable was created by scoring instances of self-reported misbehavior, including:

> Do you get into . . a lot of trouble at school, a little trouble at school or do you never get into trouble at school?

> How much trouble do your teachers feel you get into at school? Would your teachers say you get into . . . a lot of trouble, a little trouble or no trouble at school?

> Since the end of school last year, how many times have you been sent to the principal's office because you had done something wrong? Have you . . . never done this, done it only 1 or 2 times, done it 3 or 4 times, 5 to 10 times, or more than 10 times?

> Since the end of school last year, how many times have you been placed on school probation or suspended from school? Have you . . . never done this, done it only 1 or 2 times, done it 3 or 4 times, 5 to 10 times, or more than 10 times?

> (Score ranged from 4 to 12. Cronbach's Alpha of .71.)

It should be noted that for self-esteem, GPA, and extracurricular participation, low values have negative connotations and high values are considered positive. For school problem behavior the reverse is true; higher scores indicate more negative behavior. (Social class was also used in several analyses; the head of household's occupation was measured and scored according to Hollingshead & Redlich, 1958).

Analysis

The goal of this analysis was to investigate the impact of the number of transitions experienced by the student on adjustment in Grade 7. As noted above, the dimensions of adjustment at issue are self-esteem, GPA, extracurricular participation, and school problem behavior in Grade 7. Information about the transitions facing the child were determined from data gathered in both Grade 6 and Grade 7. For each dependent variable, the number of transitions was entered into a regression equation, and then it and its square were entered into a second regression equation. In this way, it was possible to investigate the effects of number of transitions (cumulative change) upon each measure of adjustment. In fact, this procedure allowed both the linear and quadratic components of cumulative change to be examined. If either component demonstrated significant negative effects, then the child experiencing multiple changes could be considered at risk.

A significant negative linear relationship between number of changes and self-esteem, GPA, or activity participation thus would indicate that the simple cumulation of events has placed the child in jeopardy. A significant positive linear relationship to problem behavior would lead to the same conclusion. In this situation, each transition would have independent, though perhaps small, unfavorable consequences. Taken together, these unfavorable consequences would cumulate and the student who experienced many transitions would be at a disadvantage compared to children who faced fewer changes.

In this analysis, we also looked for one type of significant curvilinear relationship. We have predicted that the slope of the curve would become significantly steeper at some point after one transition. That is, whatever happens between no change and one change, the negative effects would become sharper once there were two or more changes facing the student. Such an outcome would suggest that the occurrence of multiple transitions produces negative effects above and beyond the independent consequence of each individual change: having to cope with several transitions simultaneously has more serious implications than would be expected due to a simple additive effect.

All analyses were run separately for the various groups: white males, white females, and black females. Additionally, controls were instituted to help rule out the effects of initial differences among subjects. For example, in an equation with Grade 7 self-esteem as the dependent variable, Grade 6 self-esteem and social class were entered into the equation to ensure that differences observed in Grade 7 were not due simply to students' prior levels of self-esteem or to their social class.

It should be noted that some of the types of transition being measured occur more frequently at this age than do other types of transition. The "normative" changes—transition into junior high school, pubertal change, and onset of dating behavior—were the most common events experienced by the students, and were also the most likely to occur in combination with each other. The "non-normative" changes—recent family disruption and recent geographic mobility—occurred less frequently, and not very frequently together in this sample.[11] Although it would be ideal to examine the effects of all separate combinations and permutations of transitions, the number of cases did not permit such an analysis. This was the reason we opted to investigate simply the effects of number of changes. However, as discussed later, special analyses have been performed to make certain that no single transition variable, either alone or in combination, was responsible for what appeared to be the consequences of cumulative change.[12]

---

[11]See Simmons et al. (1987a) for a breakdown of the frequency of the various transition variables, both alone and in combination with others, and also for information on the bivariate effects of each type of transition upon self-esteem, GPA, and extracurricular participation for white students. See below for similar analyses for black girls, and for white students involving school problem behavior.

[12]In order to avoid Type II error, we utilize a generous significance level ($p < .10$). However, in all cases, significance levels are reported for the reader who wishes to impose a stricter standard.

RESULTS

Effects on Self-Esteem, GPA, and Extracurricular Participation (White Students)

In our earlier work involving only white students, we demonstrated substantial negative effects of multiple change upon self-esteem, GPA, and extracurricular participation (Simmons & Blyth, 1987; Simmons et al., 1987a). We review these findings briefly and then turn attention to the effects of change on problem behavior for white students as well as to an investigation of the consequences for the black girls in the sample, and to an analysis of factors that may modify the effects of cumulative change.

White Males.   For white males, as shown in Table 5.1 and Fig. 5.1, number of life changes has significant negative linear effects on extracurricular participation and upon academic grade point average but not on self-esteem. There were no significant curvilinear relationships. As the number of transitions increases, extracurricular participation and GPA decrease. Although we have no evidence that coping with one change complicates adjustment to another, it does appear that boys who experience more changes within a short period of time are at greater risk.

For school grades, we are talking about a difference of .89 GPA points, which is the equivalent of almost one entire letter grade—e.g., the difference between a $B-$ and a $C-$. For extracurricular participation, we are talking about a difference of one activity. Because the average child belongs to less than one activity, this difference is meaningful.

White Females.   For white girls, we found that as the number of changes increased, self-esteem, GPA, and extracurricular participation decreased significantly (Table 5.1, Figs. 5.2, 5.3). The significant effects of these combined changes on self-esteem and participation were in the linear component (Table 5.1). The more changes the girl has recently experienced, the lower her self-esteem and participation in activities.

For GPA, the effect was not only significant, but curvilinear as well. Thus, for academic achievement the effects represent more than a simple process of additive negative impact. For this variable, the experience of several changes appears to make additional ones more difficult (see Fig. 5.3). For one change to interfere with the adjustment to a second change, the child obviously has to have experienced more than one change. We predicted that whatever the slope between no changes and one change, we would see a steeper descent with the negative effects becoming sharper once there were two or more changes. In fact, for both GPA (Fig. 5.3) and self-esteem (Fig. 5.2A) we observed such a pattern, although only in the case of GPA was the curvilinear effect significant. In

TABLE 5.1
Effects of Multiple Transitions on Self-Esteem, GPA, and Participation for Grade 7 White Students

	A. Males (N = 246)				B. Females (N = 201)			
	Bivariate Linear Regression		Quadratic Controlling for Linear		Bivariate Linear Regression		Quadratic Controlling for Linear	
	b (S.E.)	Beta	b (S.E.)	Beta	b (S.E.)	Beta	b (S.E.)	Beta
Self-Esteem	.0495 (.101)	.0315	.053 (.082)	.127	-.333*** (.135)	-.173	-.165 (.136)	-.268
Extracurricular Participation	-.166** (.079)	-.134	.033 (.064)	.099	-.293**** (.085)	-.238	.024 (.086)	.062
GPA	-.197**** (.051)	-.241	.011 (.042)	.052	-.238**** (.059)	-.275	-.152*** (.059)	-.594

One-tailed test:
****$p \leq .001$; ***$p \leq .01$; **$p \leq .05$

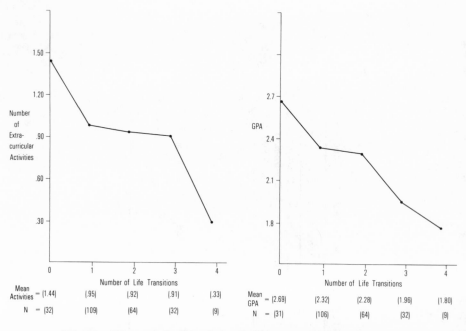

FIG. 5.1.   Effects of number of life transitions for grade 7 white males.

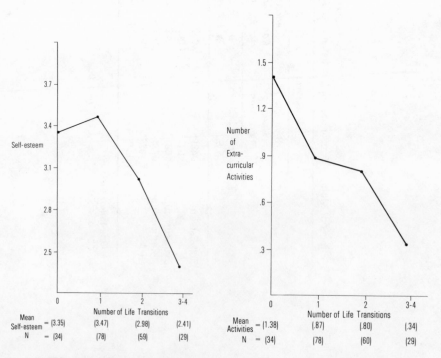

FIG. 5.2.   Effects of number of life transitions for Grade 7 white females.

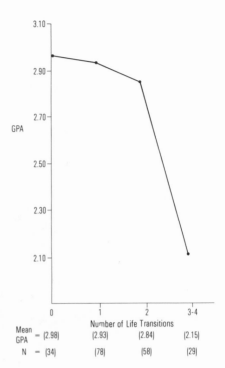

FIG. 5.3.   Effects of number of life transitions on GPA for Grade 7 white females (N = 199).

	0	1	2	3-4
		Number of Life Transitions		
Mean GPA =	(2.98)	(2.93)	(2.84)	(2.15)
N =	(34)	(78)	(58)	(29)

addition, the magnitude of the effects was sizable: about one half of a standard deviation unit of self-esteem, more than one extracurricular activity (when the average number of activities is less than one), and .83 GPA units (or the difference between a B and a C).

For both boys and girls, we entered social class background and the initial Grade 6 score on the relevant dependent variable into the equations as control factors to make sure the observed differences were not due to these factors. All conclusions remain the same. Steps were also taken to guard against the possibility that any single life change alone or in combination could have produced these results. All regression models were replicated controlling for each transition variable in turn, to determine whether the negative relationship between the number of changes and the outcome variables was retained. That is, the analyses were rerun within the K–8 cohort and within the junior high cohort, for recent pubertal developers and for non-recent developers, for early and for non-early daters. There were not enough cases to repeat the analysis for youngsters who had experienced parental marital disruption or residential change; however, the analyses were replicated for students who had not faced parental marital change and for those adolescents who had not changed residences.

By and large the coefficients that were significant and negative in the full model remained so in each of these submodels (see Table 5.2). In general, the more changes experienced, the lower the self-esteem (for girls), the more un-

TABLE 5.2
The Effect of Number of Transitions: Comparison of Significant Effects in Full Model with Models for Subgroups
COMPARATIVE REGRESSION STATISTICS FROM SUBGROUP MODELS
(Slope Coefficients and Standard Errors)

Significant Effects in Full Model	Junior High	K-8	Pubertal	Non-Pubertal	Dating	Non-Dating	No Family Disruption[a]	No Geographic Movement[a]
Boys								
Extracurricular participation:								
Linear	.047	-.023	-.052	-.205**	-.444***	-.426****	-.131*	-.128*
	(.102)	(.168)	(.119)	(.125)	(.151)	(.106)	(.095)	(.095)
GPA:								
Linear	-.166***	-.180*	-.294***	-.258****	-.126*	-.177**	-.158***	-.226****
	(.067)	(.116)	(.107)	(.072)	(.092)	(.081)	(.060)	(.059)
Problem behavior:								
Linear	.513****	.530***	.630****	.325**	.011	.031	.285***	.315***
	(.151)	(.226)	(.180)	(.171)	(.201)	(.164)	(.129)	(.129)

Girls								
Self-esteem:								
Linear	-.411**	-.095	-.939***	-.126	-.650**	-.275*	-.345***	-.404***
	(.212)	(.277)	(.348)	(.167)	(.319)	(.185)	(.154)	(.157)
Extracurricular participation:								
Linear	-.062	-.140	-.651****	-.272***	-.671***	-.411****	-.304****	-.269***
	(.114)	(.160)	(.184)	(.111)	(.230)	(.105)	(.098)	(.102)
GPA:								
Linear	-.325****	-.197**	-.444****	-.248****	-.474****	-.106*	-.204****	-.188***
	(.091)	(.106)	(.139)	(.075)	(.148)	(.078)	(.066)	(.068)
Quadratic	-.309**	-.151*	-.284****	-.144**	-.198	-.086	-.143*	-.133*
	(.142)	(.109)	(.201)	(.073)	(.224)	(.079)	(.065)	(.026)
Problem behavior:								
Linear	.495****	.228	.545**	.080	.429*	-.193*	.173*	.151
	(.157)	(.180)	(.256)	(.133)	(.271)	(.131)	(.121)	(.121)
Quadratic	.472**	.146	.448	.296***	-.502	.316***	.306***	.346***
	(.247)	(.192)	(.367)	(.129)	(.405)	(.131)	(.119)	(.118)

aThere are not enough cases with family disruption or geographic mobility to examine as a separate subgroup. One-tailed test: ****$p \leq .001$; ***$p \leq .01$; **$p \leq .05$; *$p \leq .10$

favorable the GPA (both sexes), and the lower the level of participation in activities (both sexes). The negative curvilinear trend involving GPA for girls remains intact in all cases.

Effects on School Problem Behavior (White Students)

White Males.   Once it was found that a greater number of concurrent changes was detrimental for adolescent boys' GPA and extracurricular participation, the question arose whether misbehavior was similarly affected. Given the extent of the increase in deviant behavior in adolescence in the general population (Greenberg, 1981), this question appears an important one. Before looking at the effects of cumulative change on boys' school problem behavior, we investigated the effects of each transition by itself on this behavior. For boys, school problem behavior was not affected by school change, pubertal status, or geographical mobility when each bivariate effect was examined in isolation. School problem behavior was significantly related to onset of dating, $F (1, 279) = 32.14$, $p < .001$, with early daters being more involved in problem behavior than boys who had not begun dating, and family disruption, $F (1, 290) = 12.88, p < .001$, with boys who have experienced family disruption being more likely to exhibit problem behavior than boys from intact families.[13]

The regression analysis (Table 5.3, Fig. 5.4) demonstrated that problem behavior rose significantly with an increase in number of life transitions. As evident in Table 5.3, the effect was linear rather than curvilinear. Figure 5.4 illustrates the increase in problem behavior as the number of life changes becomes greater. In fact, the difference in mean problem behavior for boys experiencing no changes and those experiencing four transitions represents more than one half of a standard deviation in the distribution of boys' problem behavior (0.6 s.d. units).

As in the previous analysis, the initial Grade 6 score in problem behavior and social-class background were controlled. When these controls were instituted, a positive curvilinear effect became significant.[14] Therefore, not only does problem behavior rise with the number of transitions, but there is some evidence that the effect is multiplicative. Also as before, we investigated whether the findings persisted when each individual transition variable was controlled in turn. In general, the findings remained the same, except when dating behavior was controlled. For boys who dated early, the relationship between number of changes and problem behavior disappeared; whereas for non-daters, the relationship was significant, positive, and curvilinear.

---

[13]Throughout the chapter, all bivariate analyses have a greater number of cases than the regression models due to recovery of several missing cases that were lost in constructing the multiple change variable.

[14]With these controls, problem behavior decreases as one moves from 0 to 1 and 2 changes, but increases sharply as one moves to 3 changes and then 4 changes. (Quadratic affect controlling for linear effect: $b = .148.$ $s.e. = .076, p < .05.$)

TABLE 5.3
Effects of Multiple Transitions on Problem Behavior for Grade 7 White Students

| | A. Males (N = 244) | | | | B. Females (N = 200) | | | |
| | Bivariate Linear Regression | | Quadratic Controlling for Linear | | Bivariate Linear Regression | | Quadratic Controlling for Linear | |
	b (S.E.)	Beta	b (S.E.)	Beta	b (S.E.)	Beta	b (S.E.)	Beta
Problem Behavior	.322*** (.111)	.184	.080 (.090)	.172	.190** (.105)	.127	.317**** (.104)	.666

One-tailed test:
****$p \leq .001$; ***$p \leq .01$; **$p \leq .05$

137

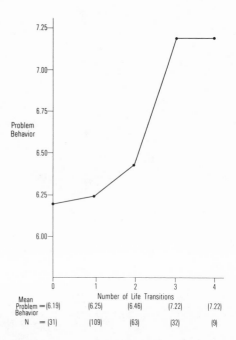

FIG. 5.4. Effects of number of life transitions on problem behavior for grade 7 white males (N = 244).

White Females.   Before presenting the results of cumulative change and school problem behavior for girls, we report the bivariate effects of each transition on this behavior. For white females, school problem behavior has significant bivariate associations with school change, dating behavior, and geographical mobility. As would be expected, early dating girls exhibit more problem behavior than non-daters, $F (1, 249) = 27.09$, $p < .001$, and those who have recently moved score higher than those with residential stability, $F (1, 256) = 3.44$, $p < .10$. However, it should be noted that girls who recently made the transition into junior high school scored significantly lower in problem behavior than those who remained in K–8 schools, $F (1, 238) = 3.18$, $p < .10$. Problem behavior was unaffected by pubertal status and family disruptions.

In terms of cumulative change, problem behavior for girls was influenced by the number of transitions experienced. As can be seen in Table 5.3, the effect for girls was significant for both the linear and quadratic models, and in the predicted direction (Fig. 5.5). Thus, not only does problem behavior increase as the number of transitions rises, but the rate of increase becomes sharper as transitions accumulate (see Fig. 5.5). The difference between girls who have experienced one transition and those who have undergone three to four changes represents three fourths of a standard deviation unit in problem behavior.

As with boys, controls were instituted for Grade 6 score and social class, and the findings remain unaltered. Also, when each of the individual transition variables was controlled in turn, all conclusions held. For some subgroups only

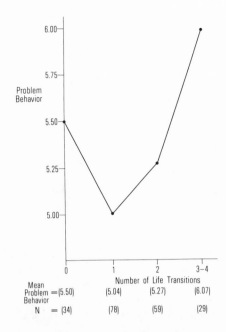

FIG. 5.5. Effects of number of life transitions on problem behavior for Grade 7 white females (*N* = 200).

	0	1	2	3-4

Number of Life Transitions

Mean Problem Behavior	= (5.50)	(5.04)	(5.27)	(6.07)
N	= (34)	(78)	(59)	(29)

the linear component retained statistical significance (recent pubertal developers and early daters), and in some cases the quadratic element was significant (non-recent pubertal developers and those with residential stability). For only one subgroup, the K–8 school cohort, was neither effect significant. However, the results were in the predicted direction.

Effects Within Social Class Groups (White Students)

Since research indicates that social-class background may modify the effects of stressors (Dohrenwend, 1973; Gad & Johnson, 1980; Meyers, Lindenthal, & Pepper, 1974; Pearlin et al., 1981; Rutter, 1979), we questioned whether students who were relatively socially disadvantaged might react to multiple life transitions differently than those who were relatively advantaged. It might be expected that a less advantaged social-class background would act as an additional stressor for the early adolescent, exacerbating the effects of life-event changes. Therefore, we repeated the analyses separately for students from working-class families and those from middle-class backgrounds.

White Males. For boys, the negative impact of multiple changes upon extracurricular participation, GPA, and problem behavior was evident for both social-class groups. With only one exception, the regression coefficients for the linear components were statistically significant and in the predicted direction. The one exception involved working-class boys and extracurricular participation, in which case the relationship remained negative but did not reach statistical significance. There were no significant curvilinear effects.

For both extracurricular participation and GPA there was a significant interaction between social class and the number of transitions ($p < .10$ for participation and $p < .05$ for GPA). This was due to the fact that for both of these dependent variables, white-collar boys fared better than their blue-collar counterparts when they experienced few transitions (0, 1, or 2), but they dropped below blue-collar boys when they faced many transitions (3 or 4) (see Figs. 5.6 and 5.7). That is, the effects of multiple change were more severe for white-collar boys as reflected in the regression coefficients. For extracurricular participation the unstandardized regression coefficient for white-collar boys was $-.246$ compared to only $-.041$ for blue-collar boys. For GPA the respective coefficients were $-.260$ and $-.114$.

White Girls.   For girls, the relations between multiple transitions and the four dependent variables observed in the full models was significant for both the working-class and white-collar subgroups with two exceptions. The two exceptions were for white-collar girls. For them the curvilinear effect for GPA and the linear coefficient for problem behavior were not significant, but were in the same direction as for the total sample. In the case of girls there were no significant interactions between social class and number of life transitions.

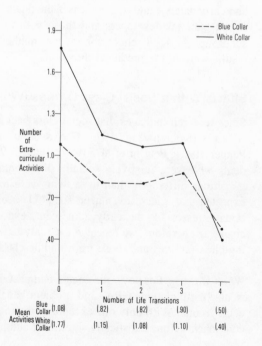

FIG. 5.6.   Effects of number of life transitions for Grade 7 males from white-collar versus blue-collar families on extracurricular participation.

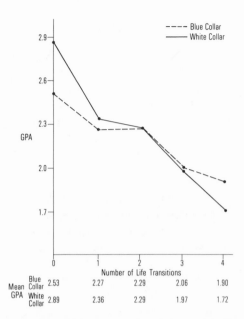

FIG. 5.7. Effects of number of life transitions for Grade 7 males from white-collar versus blue-collar families on GPA.

| Mean GPA | Blue Collar | 2.53 | 2.27 | 2.29 | 2.06 | 1.90 |
| | White Collar | 2.89 | 2.36 | 2.29 | 1.97 | 1.72 |

In general, then, the negative effects of multiple change observed in earlier sections of this chapter were maintained for both social-class groups. In fact for boys, the detrimental effects of change were more pronounced for the socially advantaged youngsters than for those from working-class backgrounds. These latter findings are contrary to the hypotheses suggested originally.

Effects for Black Females

Within the black subgroup we focus our attention on black girls because we do not yet have puberty measures calculated for black boys and therefore cannot include them in this analysis. Furthermore, although the range of transitions extends from 0 to 5, we have combined those girls experiencing 0 to 1 and 3 to 5 changes due to the small numbers of cases in certain categories; that is, we trichotomized the number of transitions—0–1, 2, and 3–5. The reason for the small number of cases in some categories is that virtually all black girls made the junior high school transition rather than remaining in a K–8 school, and very few had begun dating.

When the bivariate effects of each transition were examined, very few significant relationships were found. For self-esteem, only geographic mobility produced a significant relation, $F (1, 81) = 3.76$. $p < .10$, with black girls who had not moved exhibiting higher self-esteem. The other significant association involved problem behavior and was contrary to prediction; black girls who had recently gone through puberty were less involved in problem behavior than black girls who had not experienced recent pubertal development, F (1, 80) = 2.96, p < .10.

Black girls reacted somewhat differently than white students to multiple transitions. For black girls the effects of experiencing multiple transitions were not widespread. There were no significant, predicted effects on extracurricular participation, academic achievement, or problem behavior. However, number of transitions did have a significant and negative impact upon self-esteem. The significant effect was linear rather than curvilinear (b = −.559, $s.e.$ = .263, p < .05, one-tailed test).[15] In terms of size of the effect, the difference between girls experiencing few and many changes represents six tenths of a standard deviation.

When controls for Grade 6 score and social class were added, all results for black girls remained identical to the original findings. When each of the individual transitions was controlled in turn, the negative effect upon self-esteem was retained, but in one instance was no longer statistically significant—i.e., for girls who had not recently experienced family disruption.[16]

In summary, although life transitions did not have as pervasive effects for black as for white girls, those black girls experiencing more of such changes did show lower self-esteem.

Stability of the Junior High School Cohort as a Possible Buffer

In preceding sections of this chapter evidence has been given supporting the notion that experiencing several life changes simultaneously in early adolescence presents difficulty. At the onset, the transition into junior high school was identified as a key, normative life event for young adolescents. Since the negative consequences associated with multiple change appear significant, it would be valuable to determine whether there are aspects of the school transition process that may modify the negative outcomes. Rutter, Maughan, Mortimore, Ouston,

---

[15]In light of these findings, it is interesting to note that black girls maintain higher self-esteem for each level of change encountered. Therefore, in terms of self-esteem, although the negative consequences of cumulative change are similar for black and white girls, black girls demonstrate an overall advantage. Our prior work (see Rosenberg & Simmons, 1972; Simmons, Brown, Bush, & Blyth, 1978; and that of other investigators (e.g., Powell & Fuller, 1970) show that in large, representative samples, black children do not score lower in self-esteem than white children. In fact, in our two urban samples, black children score higher. For discussion of the reasons for these findings and a review of the literature, see Rosenberg and Simmons, 1972, and Simmons, 1978.

[16]There are not enough cases to separately analyze black girls who did not change schools, who had begun early dating relations, had recently changed residence, had recently experienced family disruption, or had recently experienced menarche. However, we did separate analyses for those who changed into junior high, those who have not begun dating, those who have not changed residences, and those who have not recently experienced menarcheal (pubertal) change as well as those without family disruption.

and Smith (1979) report that students who remain with a stable group of peers over the school years are less likely than others to exhibit deviant behavior. One might expect that the transition into junior high school would be less disruptive if a large group of familiar peers made the transition together from elementary to junior high school. Conversely, more difficulty might be predicted if there were few familiar classmates in the new school. The object of the next analysis was to investigate whether the presence of such a stable cohort can lessen or buffer the negative effects of multiple transitions for junior high students.

White Junior High Students. There was little indication that changing schools with several students from one's elementary school softens the impact of numerous changes. For neither white boys nor white girls did cohort movement alone relate significantly to any of the dependent variables. Furthermore, the presence of a large number of familiar peers at the junior high transition did not significantly decrease the negative effects of multiple changes on those dependent variables for which significant effects were reported above. Finally, there were no significant interactions between cohort stability and number of transitions for those dependent variables.

Black Female Junior High Students. It should be reiterated that nearly all black girls in our sample made the change into junior high at Grade 7. Unlike their white peers, black girls did appear significantly affected by cohort movement. To begin with, there was a significant relation between self-esteem and size of cohort for black girls. Girls who made the change with 30 or more students maintained higher self-esteem scores ($M = 4.23$) than did those who moved with fewer classmates ($M = 3.09$), $F (1, 69) = 7.07, p < .01$. Also, in this case, like Rutter and his colleagues (1979), we found that the presence of a stable group of peers over the years was associated with a lower level of problem behavior. Black girls who moved into junior high school with 30 or more peers exhibited a significantly lower mean problem behavior score ($M = 5.95$) than did those who moved with 29 or fewer peers ($M = 6.84$), $F (1, 68) = 3.65, p < .10$.

However, there were no significant interactions between cohort movement and number of life transitions with regard to any of the dependent variables. In fact, the tendency for lower self-esteem to be associated with a greater number of recent life changes persisted both for children who moved with a smaller and those who moved with a larger number of peers (Fig. 5.8).

SUMMARY AND CONCLUSION

In this chapter we have examined the reactions of early adolescents to the cumulation of life transitions during an important developmental period. The longitudinal study at issue involved a random sample of adolescents in Grades 6

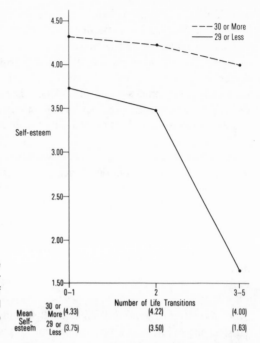

FIG. 5.8. Effects of number of life transitions on self-esteem for Grade 7 black females by size of cohort that moves with the child from Grade 6 elementary school to junior high school.

and 7. Overall, there was considerable evidence that having to cope with several important life transitions in early adolescence is problematic. For both white boys and white girls, GPA and extra curricular participation decreased and problem behavior increased under these circumstances. For white girls, self-esteem also declined. Black girls demonstrated fewer effects, but self-esteem also declined for them when more transitions were experienced close to Grade 7. Most of these significant effects involve linear relations; however, there were a few significant curvilinear effects (primarily involving the impact of number of transitions upon white girls' GPA and level of problem behavior), an indication that the combination of multiple changes is especially difficult. The transitions at issue are scheduled movement into junior high school, recent major pubertal changes, onset of early dating, change of residences or schools at an unscheduled time, and recent major disruption of parents' marital status.

Although it was predicted that the effects might be stronger for disadvantaged youngsters, in fact where there were significant findings, they suggested the reverse. In general, the findings reported above persist for both working- and middle-class children; however, for white boys the effects of number of transitions were stronger in the middle class, with middle-class boys who experienced several transitions being at particular disadvantage. Similarly, whatever social disadvantage accrued in general for black students, number of transitions showed fewer, not more, negative effects for black than for white girls.[17]

Finally, we predicted that for those students who must change into junior high school in Grade 7, moving with a larger number of peers would help protect them from the negative effects of multiple transitions. Only for black girls are there significant effects due to the size of the cohort that moves with the child from Grade 6 to 7. Black girls who move with a larger, rather than smaller, number of peers show higher self-esteem and lower problem behavior. However, for neither black nor white students does the size of the cohort significantly alter the effects of multiple transitions reported earlier. It is important to note that Rutter and his colleagues (1979) in earlier research also demonstrated the power of a large number of familiar peers to reduce the likelihood of problem behavior.

Several questions are raised by this research. First of all, why should multiple transitions experienced close to one another in time cause difficulty for the early adolescent? Important to the interpretation of the data in this study are (1) a "developmental readiness" hypothesis—a hypothesis that transition into a new period can come too early for the individual (Simmons & Blyth, 1987); and (2) the "focal theory" of change (Coleman, 1974). The significant curvilinear effects especially lend support to the focal theory of change—that it is easier to cope with one change at a time. At this point, we would like to go a bit beyond our data and suggest that underlying both of these hypotheses is the idea of an "arena of comfort." If change comes too suddenly (that is, if there is too much discontinuity with prior experience) or if it is too early given children's cognitive and emotional status, or if it occurs in too many areas of life at once, then individuals will experience considerable discomfort. They will experience discomfort with self and discomfort with the world. Such children will not feel at one with themselves nor at home in their social environments. According to this interpretation, individuals do better both in terms of self-esteem and behavioral coping if there is some arena of comfort in their lives. Thus, more gradual change upon entry to the new life period of adolescence appears beneficial as do fewer simultaneous changes.

If the child is comfortable in some environments, life arenas, and role relationships, then one would predict that discomfort in another arena can be tolerated and mastered. Children appear less able to cope if at one and the same time they are uncomfortable with their bodies, due to physical changes; with family, due to changes in family constellation; with home, because of a move; with school, due to great discontinuity in the nature of the school environment; with peers, because of the emergence of opposite sex relationships and because of the

---

[17]There were too few cases in the black sample to examine these relationships separately for middle versus working/lower class blacks.

disruption of prior peer networks and the changes in peer expectations and peer evaluation criteria. We suggest that there needs to be some arena of life or some set of role relationships with which the individual can feel relaxed and comfortable, to which he or she can withdraw and become reinvigorated.

In all likelihood, successful coping with change has properties of the dialectic. A balance or synthesis of opposites is optimal. A balance between tension arousal and tension reduction, between over- and understimulation, between being challenged and being comfortable, between too many and too few demands, between growth and stability. We have discussed the discomfort that is the cost of challenge and change. On the other hand, too much comfort and stability clearly also has costs: i.e., the failure to grow to one's full potential and the acceptance of unnecessary restrictions and dependencies. For optimal self-esteem and coping in the long run, the individual cannot be totally comfortable; he or she has to leave the securities of childhood and to enter adolescence. In an urban context, the individual should learn to cope with large-scale organizational environments with all their opportunities as well as their impersonality. The child has to detach emotionally and physically from parents and accept expectations from peers and parents more suitable for this new period in the life course (Elder, 1968). Physical changes are inevitable, and most youth will have to deal with the new type of romantic/sexual relationships.

Coping with all of these ''normative'' changes will necessarily involve some degree of discomfort, even if non-normative and less desirable changes are absent. The issue that we have been emphasizing involves timing and pacing. Gradual rather than discontinuous changes, changes that are spread out and dealt with in turn rather than simultaneously, appear recommended.

A second question raised by our data involves the failure to confirm predictions concerning social class, i.e., number of transitions is not more strongly related to adjustment in the less advantaged or working class. In actuality, one aspect of the findings does fit our expectations: the fact that among boys, the youngsters who are at greatest advantage are those in the middle class who do not have to experience any of these transitions close to Grade 7. Both their class status and the absence of fundamental change at the time of entry into adolescence appear to protect them.

The puzzling question is why, among boys who have experienced multiple changes, middle-class students fare slightly worse than their counterparts in the working class rather than better. The issue may be a measurement one. We do not have enough cases to isolate the really deprived students whose families are beneath the poverty line. It is at this level that financial deprivation may intensify the impact of other life transitions (see Rutter, 1979). It is also possible, however, that the disadvantages entailed by working-class status act as a type of ''stress-inoculation'' (see Meichenbaum, 1977). Children who for most of their lives have had to adjust to some deprivations may be better able to cope with the challenges of life transitions in early adolescence. Additional research will be needed to replicate and untangle these relationships.

A final question raised by this study involves the failure of a large number of familiar peers to act as a buffer against the negative effects of multiple transitions. Perhaps, however, the issue is not whether one moves with a large number of peers from school to school but whether one moves with one's close friends (see Rutter, 1979). What is likely to matter is whether the peer network is disrupted or not. Unfortunately, we did not have measures of the peer network in Grades 6 and 7; thus exploration of these issues must await future research.

In future research it would also be advantageous to look at the effects of various combinations of specific changes and to include major life changes other than those measured here, as well as to test more extensively the hypotheses related to the idea of an "arena of comfort."

In conclusion, this study indicates that the experience of multiple life transitions within a relatively short time span places early adolescents at risk. The fact that the proportion of students who experience three or more simultaneous transitions is relatively small (about 15%) makes it both easier and more compelling for schools to provide extra support for such vulnerable youngsters. The data, at the very least, identify a group of early adolescents who are at risk due to the coincidence of scheduled (normative) transitions and non-normative transitions. The findings also have led us to suggest that in some cases children will benefit from an absence of stressors in at least one significant sphere. It should be easier to cope with major life changes if one still has "arenas of comfort" in which to obtain sanctuary.

ACKNOWLEDGMENTS

This work has been funded by NIMH grant R01 MH-30739 and a grant from the William T. Grant Foundation. The senior author is a 1986 Fellow at the Center for the Advanced Study of the Behavioral Sciences at Stanford, California where she was supported in part by the John D. and Catherine T. MacArthur Foundation. Segments of this chapter are reprinted by permission of Aldine de Gruyter, publisher of *Moving Into Adolescence* (see Simmons and Blyth, 1987— copyright © 1987 by Roberta G. Simmons and Dale A. Blyth), and by permission of the publisher of *Child Development* (Simmons et al., 1987a).

REFERENCES

Blyth, D. A. (1977). *Continuities and discontinuities during the transition into adolescence: A longitudinal comparison of two school structures.* Unpublished doctoral dissertation, University of Minnesota.

Blyth, D. A., Simmons, R. G., & Carlton-Ford, S. (1983). The adjustment of early adolescents to school transitions. *Journal of Early Adolescence, 3,* 105–120.

Coleman, J. C. (1974). *Relationships in adolescence.* Boston, MA: Routledge & Kegan Paul.

Dohrenwend, B. S. (1973). Social status and stressful life events. *Journal of Personality and Social Psychology, 28,* 225–235.

Dohrenwend, B. P., & Pearlin, L. I. (1981). Report of the Panel on Life Events from the Committee for Research on Stress in Health and Disease. Institute of Medicine, National Academy of Sciences, Washington, DC, 150–169.

Eccles (Parsons), J. Midgley, C., & Adler, T. F. (1984). Grade-related changes in the school environment: Effects on achievement motivation. In J. G. Nicholls (Ed.), *Advances in motivation and achievement* (Vol. 3, pp. 283–331). Greenwich, CT: JAI Press.

Elder, G. H. (1968). Adolescent socialization and development. In E. F. Borgatta & W. W. Lambert (Eds.), *Handbook of personality theory and research* (pp. 239–364). Chicago: Rand McNally.

Elder, G. H., & Rockwell, R. (1979). Economic depression and postwar opportunity in men's lives: A study of life patterns and health. In R. G. Simmons, (Ed.), *Research in community and mental health* (Vol. 1, pp. 249–303). Greenwich, CT: JAI Press.

Felner, R. D., Ginter, M., & Primavera, J. (1982). Primary prevention during school transitions: Social support and environmental structure. *American Journal of Community Psychology, 10,* 277–290.

Felner, R. D., Primavera, J., & Cauce, A. M. (1981). The impact of school transitions: A focus for preventive efforts. *American Journal of Community Psychology, 9,* 449–459.

Gad, M. T., & Johnson, J. H. (1980). Correlates of adolescent life stress as related to race, ses, and levels of perceived social support. *Journal of Clinical Child Psychology,* Spring, 13–16.

Gersten, J. C., Langner, T. S., Eisenberg, J. G., & Orzeck, L. (1974). Child behavior and life events: Undesirable change or change per se?. In B. S. Dohrenwend & B. P. Dohrenwend (Eds.), *Stressful life events: Their nature and effects* (pp. 159–170). New York: Wiley.

Gersten, J. C., Langner, T. S., Eisenberg, J. G., & Simcha-Fagan, O. (1977). An evaluation of the etiologic role of stressful life-change events in psychological disorders. *Journal of Health and Social Behavior, 18,* 228–244.

Greenberg, D. F. (1981). Delinquency and the age structure of society. In D. F. Greenberg (Ed.), *Crime and capitalism* (pp. 1181–1239). Palo Alto, CA: Mayfield.

Haladyna, T., & Thomas, G. (1979). The attitudes of elementary school children toward school and subject matters. *The Journal of Experimental Education, 48,* 18–23.

Hamburg, B. A. (1974). Early adolescence: A specific and stressful stage of the life cycle. In G. V. Coelho, D. A., Hamburg & J. E. Adams (Eds.), *Coping and adaptation* (pp. 101–124). New York: Basic Books.

Hetherington, E. M. (1979). Divorce: A child's perspective. *American Psychologist, 34,* 8551–8858.

Hetherington, E. M., Cox, M., & Cox, R. (1982). Effects of divorce on parents and children. In M. E. Lamb (Ed.), *Nontraditional families: Parenting and child development* (pp. 233–238). Hillsdale, NJ: Lawrence Erlbaum Associates.

Hollingshead, A. B., & Redlich, F. C. (1958). *Social class and mental illness.* New York: Wiley.

Johnson, J. H. (1982). Life events as stressors in childhood and adolescence. In B. B. Lahey & A. E. Kazdin (Eds.), *Advances in clinical child psychology* (Vol. 5, pp. 219–253). New York: Plenum.

Johnson, J. H., & McCutcheon, S. (1980). Assessing life events in older children and adolescents: Preliminary findings with the life events checklist. In I. G. Sarason & C. D. Spielberger (Eds.), *Stress and anxiety* (Vol. 7 pp 111–125). Washington, DC: Hemisphere.

Katz, P., & Zigler, E. (1967). Self-image disparity: A developmental approach. *Journal of Personality and Social Psychology, 5,* 186–195.

Kessler, R. C. (1979). A strategy for studying differential vulnerability to the psychological consequences of stress. *Journal of Health and Social Behavior, 20,* 100–108.
Kessler, R. C., Price, R. H., & Wortman, C. B. (1985). Social factors in psychopathology: Stress,
social support, and coping processes. *Annual Review of Psychology, 36,* 531–572.
Levine, M. (1966). Residential change and school adjustment. *Community Mental Health Journal,
2,* 61–69.
Levine, M., Wesolowski, J. C., & Corbett, F. J. (1966). Pupil turnover and academic performance
in an inner city elementary school. *Psychology in the Schools, 3,* 153–158.
Lipsitz, J. (1977). *Growing up forgotten.* Lexington, MA: Lexington Books.
McCaig, T. E. (1967). *The differential influence of the junior high school and elementary school
organizational patterns on academic achievement and social adjustment of seventh and eighth
grade students.* Unpublished doctoral dissertation, Loyola University.
Meichenbaum, D. (1977). *Cognitive-behavior modification: An integrative approach* (pp. 143–
182). New York: Plenum.
Meyers, J. K., Lindenthal, J. J., & Pepper, M. P. (1974). Social class, life events, and psychiatric
symptoms: A longitudinal study. In B. S. Dohrenwend & B. P. Dohrenwend (Eds.), *Stressful life
events: Their nature and effects* (pp. 191–205). New York: Wiley.
Newcomb, M. D., Huba, G. J., & Bentler, P. M. (1981). A multidimensional assessment of
stressful life events among adolescents: Derivation and correlates. *Journal of Health and Social
Behavior, 22,* 400–415.
Padilla, E. R., Rohsenow, D. J., & Bergman, A. B. (1976). Predicting accident frequency in
children. *Pediatrics, 58,* 223–226.
Pearlin, L. I., Lieberman, M. A., Menaghan, E. G., & Mullan, J. T. (1981). The stress process.
Journal of Health and Social Behavior, 22, 337–356.
Powell, G. J., & Fuller, M. (1970, March). *School desegregation and self-concept.* Paper presented
47th Annual Meeting of the American Orthopsychiatric Association in San Francisco, CA.
Reuman, D. (1984, April). *Consequences of the transition into junior high school on social com-
parisons of abilities and achievement motivation.* Paper presented at the annual meeting of the
American Educational Research Association, New Orleans, LA.
Rosenberg, M., & Simmons, R. G. (1972). *Black and white self-esteem: The urban school child.*
Washington, DC: American Sociological Association.
Rutter, M. (1979). Protective factors in children's responses to stress and disadvantage. In M. W.
Kent & J. E. Rolf (Eds.), *Primary prevention of psychopathology: Volume III. Social competence
in children* (pp. 49–74). Hanover, NH: University Press of New England.
Rutter, M. (1980). *Changing youth in a changing society: Patterns of adolescent development and
disorder.* Cambridge, MA: Harvard University Press.
Rutter, M., Maughan, B., Mortimore, P., & Ouston, J. with Smith, A. (1979). *Fifteen thousand
hours: Secondary schools and their effects on children.* Cambridge, MA: Harvard University
Press.
Simmons, R. G. (1978). Blacks and high self-esteem: A puzzle. *Social Psychology, 41,* 54–57.
Simmons, R. G., & Blyth, D. A. (1987). *Moving into adolescence: The impact of pubertal change
and school context.* Hawthorne, NY: Aldine de Gruyter.
Simmons, R. G., Blyth, D. A., Van Cleave, E. F., & Bush, D. M. (1979). Entry into early
adolescence: The impact of school structure, puberty, and early dating on self-esteem. *American
Sociological Review, 44,* 948–967.
Simmons, R. G., Brown, L., Bush, D., & Blyth, D. A. (1978). Self-esteem and achievement of
black and white early adolescents. *Social Problems, 26,* 86–96.
Simmons, R. G., Burgeson, R., Carlton-Ford, S., & Blyth, D. A. (1987a). The impact of
cumulative change in early adolescence. In H. Stevenson & D. R. Entwisle (Eds.), *Child
development, 58,* 1220–1234.
Simmons, R. G., Carlton-Ford, S. L., & Blyth, D. A. (1987b). Predicting how a child will cope

with the transition to junior high school. In R. M. Lerner & T. T. Foch (Eds.), *Biological-psychosocial interactions in early adolescence: A life-span perspective* (pp. 325–375). Hillsdale, NJ: Lawrence Erlbaum Associates.

Simmons, R. G., Rosenberg, M., & Rosenberg, F. (1973). Disturbance in the self-image at adolescence. *American Sociological Review, 39,* 553–568.

Swearingen, E. M., & Cohen, L. H. (1985a). Life events and psychological distress: A prospective study of young adolescents. *Developmental Psychology, 21,* 1045–1054.

Swearingen, E. M., & Cohen, L. H. (1985b). Measurement of adolescents' life events: The junior high life experiences survey. *American Journal of Community Psychology, 13,* 69–85.

Tausig, M. (1982). Measuring life events. *Journal of Health and Social Behavior, 23,* 52–64.

Thoits, P. A. (1983). Dimensions of life events that influence psychological distress: An evaluation and synthesis of the literature. In H. B. Kaplan (Ed.), *Psychosocial stress: Trends in theory and research.* New York: Academic Press.

Wells, L. E., & Stryker, S. (1988). Stability and change in self over the life course. In P. B. Baltes, R. M. Lerner, & D. L. Featherman (Eds.), *Life-span development and behavior* (Vol. 8, pp. 191–229). Hillsdale, NJ: Lawrence Erlbaum Associates.

Zautra, A. J., & Reich, J. W. (1983). Life events and perceptions of life quality: Developments in a two-factor approach. *Journal of Community Psychology, 11,* 121–132.

Adolescent Transitions in Developmental Perspective: Sociological and Historical Insights

6

Glen H. Elder, Jr.
University of North Carolina at Chapel Hill
Avshalom Caspi
Harvard University
Linda M. Burton
Pennsylvania State University

> *A study that does not come back to the problems of biography, of history, and of their intersection within society has not completed its intellectual journey.*
>
> —C. W. Mills, *The Sociological Imagination*

Over the past 25 years two lines of inquiry have converged in a perspective on the life course. One involves the study of lives and life-span development; the other, the study of social change and its dynamics. The convergence reflects an expanding and more profound appreciation of the link between changing lives and a changing society. This dual perspective relating life history and social history has important implications for the study of adolescents and their pathways to the adult years (Elder, 1980a; Elder, 1985; Elder & Caspi, in press). We explore two of these implications in this chapter by viewing the transition to adolescence and young adulthood in terms of history and the concept of interdependent lives.

Adolescence acquires specific meaning from its historical setting and from the experiences of significant others. For example, the difference between growing up in the depressed 1930s and in war-mobilized America of 1940–45 was literally a difference between two worlds of adolescence (Elder, 1981a). Such differences had much to do with the experiences of significant others, including parents, siblings, friends, and acquaintances. Hard times in the Great Depression influenced the lives of adolescents through the economic and job losses of parents, and also through its effects on the lives of grandparents who often moved in for a time. For young people during World War II, the distinctive features of adolescence included the war-related employment of parents from

151

sun-up to sun-down, the military service and war trauma of older brothers, and the mobilization of school children for civil defense and the war effort. To understand historical forces, then, we need a concept of lives lived interdependently, a notion that is fundamental to a life-course perspective.

Our objective in this chapter is to use sociological and historical insights to fashion an approach to the developmental study of transitions in adolescence and young adulthood. We begin with the premise that individual transitions are embedded in the life trajectories of other family members and kin. Intergenerational dependence ensures that events in one generation have consequences for the lives of both older and younger generations. Such interdependence represents a means by which historical change alters the life course and, as we shall see in greater detail, the dynamics of interdependence affect both the timing and content of social transitions to adolescence and young adulthood.

From the concept of interdependent lives, we move to the historical context of adolescence and especially to the task of linking social change to the transitions and experiences of adolescents. More studies than ever before are bringing historical facts to the study of adolescence and the life course, but they are doing so in ways that fail to increase our understanding of historical effects. We discuss this problem and explore alternative ways of linking social change to adolescent transitions.

The rationale for this essay is best illustrated by noting two classic studies of adolescence that fail to bring interdependent lives or the imprint of social history to the analysis: August Hollingshead's *Elmtown's Youth* (1949) and James Coleman's *The Adolescent Society* (1961). Hollingshead's study of adolescence in a midwestern community during World War II is largely blind to the historical realities of the 1930s and war years; it also fails to document the process by which the life course of parents influences the options of adolescents. Coleman's study of adolescents from the Chicago area examines the idea of an adolescent subculture cut off from parents and the adult community, but it does not interview parents or place the adolescents in historical context.

We begin, then, by reviewing these two studies. Next we explore the concept of interdependent lives in two provocative studies: a study of the reciprocal implications of adolescent childbearing for parents and the young mother, and a longitudinal study of the consequences of adolescent motherhood for both mother and child. Finally we build upon this discussion by viewing the dynamics of interdependent lives as a linking process between historical change and the adolescent experience.

TWO HISTORIC STUDIES AND A RATIONALE

Elmtown's Youth and *The Adolescent Society* portray different phases in the evolution of adolescence as a life stage in American society. The central theme of Hollingshead's Elmtown study is social class and life chances in the social world of adolescence in a small midwestern community, circa 1941–1942. Fifteen years later a rapidly expanding population of children and adolescents raised concern about the coercive peer group. Following the portrait of peer influence so vividly described by David Riesman in *The Lonely Crowd* (1950), James Coleman launched a survey of midwestern students to determine if adolescents were developing in a world apart from the adult community, possibly a subculture marked by the rejection of adult priorities such as school achievement.

Though differing in many ways, the two studies share a common neglect of intergenerational ties despite the relevance of these relationships for the issues at hand. Neither study surveyed parents in a systematic way. Equally striking is the blindness of the studies to historical context and processes. Both sets of limitations restrict the full potential of these pioneering inquiries.

Elmtown's Youth

Hollingshead and his research team came to Elmtown for a study of its young people during the early phase of homefront mobilization in World War II. The community had just begun to recover from nearly 10 years of hardship in the Great Depression. It was a time of concern for life chances—the chances lost and perhaps regained in the Depression decade, and the chances threatened by the military requirements of a global war. National statistics suggest that 7 out of 10 Elmtown boys who graduated from or left high school by 1941 were in uniform by the end of the war. Young women entered the work force in large numbers, especially in war-related industries. Instead of relating these developments to the life experience of youth, Hollingshead focused on the social structure of the town and its consequences for adolescents from the upper middle class to the lowest economic stratum of society.

Elmtown's Youth offers a vivid portrait of stratification in the social world of adolescents and documents the controlling functions of age and class in adolescent behavior. Four themes receive special attention: (a) the social ambiguity and status contradictions of this life stage, an "ill-defined no man's land"; (b) competition and conflicts among youth-training institutions; (c) age segregation as a social control mechanism; and (d) class variation in the transition to adult status. Field work in the Elmtown community disclosed few widely shared concepts regarding the lower or upper boundaries of adolescence, other than the span of years encompassed by secondary school and the assumption of adult roles. This definition varied markedly between social strata. Middle-class youth remained in school much longer than youth from the lower strata. With earlier school leaving, employment, and marriage, boys and girls from the lower classes followed an accelerated route to adult status.

Hollingshead found an elaborate system of age segregation in Elmtown that sought to ensure "proper" development by separating youth from the adult world of their parents. In anticipating concerns that became so prominent in the 1950s and 1960s, Hollingshead (1949) cites the self-defeating character of a system that turns young people toward themselves and away from the realities of adult life, "by trying to keep the maturing child ignorant of this world of conflict and contradictions, adults think they are keeping him 'pure' " (p. 108).

Hollingshead's account depends on a mechanism by which class position influences parents who in turn influence their children, but this interdependence is never explicitly assessed. With his eyes on Elmtown in 1941–42, Hollingshead did not see the Depression experience of parents and its consequences for children who became teenage members of his sample during the Second World War. Some of these consequences were expressed through the influence of father's unemployment and a severe income loss that led to adverse change in family roles and tensions. Income loss among men during the worst years of the Great Depression increased their irritability and general explosiveness, which in turn made family relationships less stable and supportive (Elder, Caspi, & Van Nguyen, 1986). Marital discord increased along with arbitrary and often punitive parental behavior. The Depression hit the working class especially hard, keeping a large percentage of families in a hard-pressed state until the 1940s. All of these changes had major implications for Hollingshead's thesis regarding the social classes and family behavior.

The neglect of lives lived interdependently is most striking when we consider the full implications of studying youth in the midst of a great war and its complex realities. Nearly 80% of the males with birth dates in the early 1920s were called to serve. Young women of these cohorts were drawn quickly into the work force of war industries, along with their mothers in many cases. Despite such developments and the activities of homefront mobilization, the Second World War does not appear in the index of *Elmtown's Youth* and to the best of our knowledge it is not even mentioned in the book. When combined with omission of the Depression decade, the study's disregard of the war could well mean that Hollingshead failed to appraise the most powerful determinants of the life opportunities of Elmtown's youth. In the book itself, Elmtown is described as if the Second World War had never occurred, as if no fathers and older brothers were called to serve. It is a community without propaganda and the pressures of home front mobilization—a community in the timeless realm of abstract sociological theory.

The Adolescent Society

Postwar change in America, partly expressed in schools of increasing size and specialization, gave greater emphasis to school and peer influences. This presumed transfer of control over socialization from the family set the stage for *The Adolescent Society*, James Coleman's (1961) study of the cleavage between the adult world and the isolated cultural setting of adolescents in high school. Across 10 high schools in the Chicago area, Coleman found that a sizable percentage of adolescents were more reluctant to break with a friend than to receive parental or teacher disapproval; that student leaders in the liberated climate of large high schools were more inclined than followers to side with peers (against the perceived wishes of parents) on issues involving social participation and club membership; that students placed greater emphasis on popularity, social leadership, and athletics than on academic excellence; and that the anti-intellectual climate of youth groups generally discouraged intellectual accomplishment. The overall impression seems to be one of stronger peer than parental influence and a cultural cleavage between the adolescent and adult communities.

The data that support these conclusions came from questionnaires completed by the adolescents. Parent interviews were not available to offer an alternative or differing view. Indeed, very little is learned about the parents and their life history, though various dates and events suggest that the majority were born between 1910 and 1925, the birth category of males that provided the largest proportion of men for the armed forces in the Second World War. This observation would have sensitized Coleman to factors that distinguished his particular adolescent sample in 1957 from neighboring cohorts, younger and older.

Most of the students in *The Adolescent Society* were born in the early 1940s and were thus exposed in large number to the deprivations of father-absence and the stress of family readjustments on fathers' return. Though socially accepted, the temporary absence of fathers (3 or more years) markedly altered family relations by placing mothers in a dominant, instrumental role, and by establishing fertile conditions for conflict when the returning veteran attempted to resume former family roles (Hill, 1949). Especially relevant to Coleman's generational theme are Stolz's (1954) empirical observations that sons born during the war experienced more stressful relations with fathers who served in the military than those born after the war to veterans. Even several years after the fathers' return to their families, their relations with war-born sons were characterized by greater emotional distance and strain.

No one knows whether such effects persisted into the high-school years, though Carlsmith's (1973) study of Harvard students is suggestive of this. Carlsmith compared students born during the war with a control group of men from homes in which the father was present and found that men who experienced father-absence during the war were more likely to describe their ideal self as more like mother. They also shared fewer interests with males in general, displayed a less masculine cognitive style, and projected a more delayed pattern of career establishment after college. Although father-absent students appeared well-adjusted to the college environment, Carlsmith concluded that "they feel somewhat less secure about their future roles as adult men" (p. 474). In combination, these studies are much too fragmentary to warrant generalizations regarding war-caused father-absence, but their findings obviously bear on the research concerns of Coleman. They also suggest the developmental implications of historical events for the lives of youth.

Our purpose in taking a brief look at two pioneering studies of adolescence, *Elmtown's Youth* and *The Adolescent Society*, is to suggest the potential benefit of research that brings the notion of interdependent lives and history to the experience of adolescents in place and time. Though both studies addressed questions that called for an understanding of interdependent lives and historical times, neither made effective use of such distinctions. These blind spots seem unbelievable from the vantage point of the 1980s and its life-course and historical concerns, but the advantage of hindsight is hardly remarkable. The important point is what these distinctions offer.

It is entirely possible to relate history to adolescent experience in ways that impede understanding, and we discuss some noteworthy examples of such work. For the most part, we are doing more research on historical factors in the lives of adolescents, but we are also learning less and less about them. There are good reasons for this unpromising trend. One reason is that we too often end up with historical effects that are not explained. The missing element in connecting social history to life history is a concept of the life course and its dynamic of interdependent lives. We turn now to this dynamic in select studies.

THE DYNAMICS OF INTERDEPENDENT LIVES

Research on the adolescent experience is finally giving attention to its precursors in childhood and to its consequences in early adulthood. Adolescence in the life course is now a widely held perspective, but there is still insensitivity to the life-stage experiences of significant others—parents, grandparents, other relatives, and adult friends—and their implications for adolescent development. Investigators frequently forget that most adolescents have parents with all of the stresses and options of their own life stage (Dragastin & Elder, 1975). Consider two 12-year-old children whose mothers are 50 and 32 years, respectively. The older mother is facing some of the physical changes of late middle age, whereas the younger mother has yet to enter the middle years. The older mother will be approaching retirement when the child reaches his or her 25th birthday. By comparison, the younger mother would be only 45 years old with nearly half of her expected life to live.

To bring out some of the valuable insights that come from the study of life-course interdependence, both across the life span and across the generations, we focus on two studies of adolescent parenthood: Burton's case-analytic study of three-generation black families in Los Angeles and Furstenberg's longitudinal study of black women from Baltimore. Burton's (1985) study clearly illustrates an intergenerational dynamic in which teenage pregnancy alters the status of multiple family members, thereby shaping the options and responses of the adolescent mother. A similar dynamic occurs when remarriage involves people of vastly different ages (Furstenberg, 1984). The Baltimore study (Furstenberg,

Brooks-Gunn, & Morgan, 1987) shows that the fate of the young child is bound to the life course of the mother and, specifically, to the patterning and timing of maternal events subsequent to adolescent childbirth.

Adolescent Childbearing and Interdependent Lives

Research on adolescent pregnancy has focused exclusively on the "insular dyad" of the adolescent mother and her child, an entity that often appears detached from other family members. But the lives of the young mother and her child are more often embedded in the lives of individuals beyond the dyad. An expanded view of interdependent lives and teenage parenting suggests that the consequences of accelerated or adolescent childbearing are not only experienced by the newly formed mother-child dyad, but in the lives of other family members as well. Moving beyond the insular dyad, we can begin to explore the broader reciprocal dimension of adolescent childbearing—one in which the lives of the teenage mother and her child are shown to influence and to be influenced by a web of interdependent lives.

Within this broader relational context, adolescent childbearing precipitates a series of premature role transitions: the teenage girl becomes a young mother, her mother becomes a young grandmother, and, in contemporary societies, a generation of great- and great-great-grandmothers is also formed. The consequences of accelerated childbearing thus spiral up the generational ladder, generating dramatic changes in the life-course trajectories of the entire lineage system.

The Burton (1985; Burton & Bengtson, 1985; Hagestad & Burton, 1986) study of adolescent parenting offers a unique perspective on the dynamics of accelerated childbearing and interdependent lives. She examines the "ripple" effects of teenage pregnancy in the context of multigenerational lineage units, tracing the consequences of adolescent childbearing for the entire lineage system. She is thus able to plot how an adolescent transition creates involuntary counter-transitions in the lives of other family members and produces alterations in their relationships with one another.

Burton interviewed members of 41 female lineages from urban multigenerational black families. Each lineage included the new mother, grandmother, and great-grandmother. Eighteen of these lineage units were classified as "early" transitions. The age ranges of respondents in these early lineages were 11–18 for the young mothers, 25–38 for the grandmothers, and 46–57 for the great-grandmothers. The remaining 23 lineage units were classified as "on-time" transitions. The age ranges for mothers, grandmothers, and great-grandmothers were 21–26, 42–57, and 60–73, respectively.

Evidence from this study suggests that role transitions in the on-time lineages were welcomed by the majority of new mothers, grandmothers, and great-grandmothers. In fact, childbirth heightened the lineage members' sensitivity to the connectedness of their lives and the timely flow of childbearing through generations. These lineage members were prepared for their transitions and thus moved systematically to their "generational stations," assuming their attendant responsibilities. One 22-year-old mother commented that she had become a mother at "the right time": "I was ready, my husband was ready, my mother was ready, my father was ready, my grandmother couldn't wait." A 46-year-old grandmother mentioned that her transition came at a time appropriate to her age status in life—at a time when she had expected it to happen. The great-grandmothers expressed similar sentiments.

In contrast, accelerated, early childbearing quickened a series of transitions and reactions that dramatically altered intergenerational role expectations, dependencies, and life trajectories. A brief profile of the dynamics manifested in the early lineage units is presented to show how the occurrence of teenage pregnancy, across two generations in most cases, altered the life trajectories of an entire lineage.

Young Mothers, Grandmothers, and Great-Grandmothers

Virtually all of the adolescent mothers *expected* their own mothers to assume an important role in the care of their child. This expectation never materialized for 83% of the young mothers. The vast majority of their mothers—their child's grandmothers—refused to assume an active grandparent role. One 15-year-old mother offered a representative statement concerning teenagers' expectations of their mothers as grandmothers:

> I thought my momma was just mad when she said that she was not going to be no grandmomma. I thought after the baby was born that she would do like her momma done by her . . . See, my momma had me when she was young and my grandmomma took care of me . . . But she wasn't lying . . . She came to the hospital to see me when David was born. She even bought me a few clothes for him. But she don't help me no other way. She don't ever feed him, give him a bath, or change his diaper. She never takes him to see her friends . . . I can't believe it! I just can't believe it! If it wasn't for my grandmomma's help I don't know what I would do.

When the adolescents' mothers refused involvement as grandparents, the teenagers were forced to redirect their performance expectation concerning parental responsibilities for their child. Forty-three percent of the teenagers whose mothers had rejected the grandparent role had no alternative but to assume primary care for their child. Fifty-seven percent, however, shifted the parental responsibilities for their child up the generational ladder to their grandmother, the new baby's great-grandmother.

The assumption of parental responsibility as it related to the roles of other family members shaped the teenage mothers' perceptions of their life trajectories. The young mothers who assumed primary care for their child recast their life course, excluding from the immediate future such activities as marriage, college, and a (professional) career. They were instead focused on getting through high school, maybe trade school, and providing for the child.

The aspirations of the teenage mothers whose grandmother (great-grandmother in the lineage) took care of their child were markedly different. The majority of these young mothers talked about enjoying life, having other children within two years, getting married and buying a house. One great-grandmother who heard her granddaughter express such plans during the interview commented: "This child is really young . . . She got high and mighty dreams at the expense of somebody else . . . That somebody else is ME!"

The catalyst for the role transformations experienced by the teen mother and her grandmother (the great-grandmother in the lineage) was the grandmother's rejection of her role. Her response to an early transition to grandmotherhood and her subsequent abdication of that role was a consequence, in part, of her own early childbearing history. Indeed, the early grandmothers, having been teenage mothers themselves, were collaborators in their own temporal dilemma. Through their daughters' decision to procreate, they were involuntarily propelled into a role that they did not expect or desire at that point in their lives:

> Being a grandmother is the one thing I can do without right now. I just wish that my daughter could have waited. I would have had more time to help her later. You see, being a teenage mother isn't easy. I should know. I was one myself . . . But now I got too many other things to do with my own life and raising another baby even if it is my own grandchild ain't one of them.

For the majority of early grandmothers the role of grandmotherhood conflicted with their own developmental agenda—an agenda that included a variety of "young adult" roles related to work, education, friendship and romantic involvement. For a few, that agenda also included childbearing. Three young grandmothers gave birth to children within a month of the birth of their grandchild. According to one of these grandmothers, her young-adult role-set was not consistent with the "old age role of grandmotherhood": "I can't be a young momma and grandmomma at the same time. Something seems funny about that, don't you think?"

In addition to the normal, expected activities of young adulthood, 33% of the young grandmothers seemed to be wrestling with unresolved issues from their own adolescence. Several of them noted that they had missed something in being a teenage mother that they had to "capture" before it was too late. For one 28-year-old grandmother "capturing" this missing element manifested itself in her efforts to dress like her daughter. For yet another, the experience included socializing with her daughter's friends. One teenager describes her mother's behavior accordingly: "Every time my friends come over, you always trying to hang out . . . trying to be young. You the one . . . always trying to act like you 15.''

The developmental overlap between adolescence and young adulthood was to some degree associated with a ''sibling-like'' relationship between 27% of the young grandmothers and their daughters. This relationship was a direct product of the grandmothers' own adolescent childbearing. As a result of her premature childbearing the age difference between the mothers and daughters was minimal—an average of 15 years. This small age distance between the two generations, coupled with the fact that in a number of instances both the daughter and her mother were raised together, further contributed to the collateral quality of their relationship. This quality was poignantly realized in observing their communication patterns. Virtually all of the adolescent mothers addressed their mothers by their first names.

These mothers (grandmothers in the lineage system) had experienced an acceleration of their life course, one that began with their own teenage childbearing. This event catapulted them into a limbo somewhere between adolescence and adulthood. Their early entry into grandmotherhood further accelerated the pace. A 32-year-old grandmother observed, ''It's all going too fast! I have to stop and catch my breath.'' Rejection of the grandmother status represented an attempt to slow the pace.

The desire of these young grandmothers to satisfy their immediate needs, whether those needs were related to young adult roles or were remnants of adolescence, was of great concern to the great-grandmothers in the lineage. The concern emerged in reaction to a ripple effect of their daughters' rejection of the grandmother role. When their daughters refused to assume the grandmother role, and in a number of cases the parental role to their teenage daughter, the responsibility of care for both generations was pushed up the generational ladder to the great-grandmother: ''I am very angry about this, but I am also very worried about my daughter. Will she ever know what being grown up is? Will she ever take her responsibilities seriously?''

Indeed, the impact of accelerated transitions, role expectations, and interdependent lives is most strongly realized among the great-grandmothers. The relinquishing of roles by two generations—the teenage mother and the young grandmother—resulted in 57% of the great-grandmothers being responsible for their grandchild and great-grandchild. As children or young people during the Great Depression, 42% of the great-grandmothers were responsible now for at least three generations, a duty that occurred in cases where the great-grandmother was the primary caregiver for her own aging mother or another elderly relative: ''I ain't got no time for myself. I takes care of babies, grown children, and old people. I work too . . . I get so tired I don't know if I'll ever get to do something for myself.'' Thus, meeting the obligations of kin interfered with attending to their own agenda. Some felt that they had to put their lives on hold until ''the older generation died or the three younger generations grew up.''

The theme of interdependent lives is exhibited at a variety of levels in this study. At the most basic level it is articulated through the use of the multigenerational family unit as the natural context for studying the impact of childbearing on the life course. This context represents a system of intricately woven lives where we find that a role transition for one family member creates an involuntary role transition for another. At a more complex, dynamic level, the theme of interdependent lives is demonstrated by a focus on the pacing of the contingent transitions as they relate to the normal, expectable life course (Hagestad & Neugarten, 1985; Hogan, 1981). Family members build shared expectations about how their newly acquired roles will complement each other. When transitions are temporally synchronized, role expectations and performances are more likely to be coordinated. However, accelerated transitions disrupt the lineage system by catching family members off-guard, without the opportunity of preparing for their new roles and redefining expectations for themselves (Hagestad & Burton, 1986). Moreover, when a sequence of off-time or premature role transitions is set in motion it often violates the life scripts that individual family members may have constructed for themselves. Because family members may not be in the appropriate "developmental frame of mind" to manage the unexpected transformation, their movement forward through the life course is constantly thwarted by a need to resolve unfinished pre-transition business.

The valuable insights offered by exploring the synchronic transition dimension of interdependent lives do not answer the question of how the life-course trajectories of each family member will proceed: What would happen if we were to draw out across time the intricate interdependencies suggested by Burton? How can off-time schedules and disrupted lineage systems be put back on track?

The Temporal Dynamics of Interdependent Lives

Some answers to these questions are provided in a Baltimore longitudinal study of adolescent mothers (Furstenberg et al., 1987). The data come from a sample of some 300 women from Baltimore who were first interviewed in the mid-1960s, shortly after they became pregnant. The initial phase of this research, carried out over a 4-year period, culminated in *Unplanned Parenthood* (1976), an assessment of life-course variations in the transition to adolescent motherhood. Seventeen years later, Furstenberg and his colleagues revisited these families. The children of the teenage mothers were then approaching adolescence.

The study first examines the processes linking teenage motherhood to outcomes later in adulthood. Under what conditions are the legacies of this disadvantage most likely to persist? Under what conditions can the life course be recast? The study also breaks fresh ground by exploring issues of continuity across generations in the life course of teenage mothers as well as their offspring.

It thus represents a unique blend of life course analysis and developmental psychology.

Contrary to what many observers might have predicted, a disadvantaged life course was not a certain outcome among teenage mothers. Furstenberg and his colleagues are able to explain some of the variability in outcomes at the 17-year follow-up by examining the occurrence, timing, and sequencing of multiple events in the mothers' life course subsequent to childbirth.

The most viable escape route from a disadvantaged life course involved education. Teen mothers who completed high school were half as likely to be receiving public assistance and twice as likely to be economically secure in adulthood. A second component of success can be traced to the young mothers' ability to restrict further child bearing. Women who did not have more children in the 5-year period after the birth of their first child were $3\frac{1}{2}$ times more likely to be economically secure in 1984. Fertility control not only improved a woman's chances of avoiding welfare, it also slightly improved her chances of marriage or remarriage. Indeed, a third important route to economic security was a stable marriage and independence from the family of origin.

By adapting to teenage motherhood in various ways, the teen mothers constructed life courses with varying prospects. Adolescent mothers can and do find a number of different routes for recovery and repair of damaged life chances. Nevertheless, adolescent mothers do not do as well in adulthood as women who postpone parenthood. Although many manage to offset the handicap of having children in their teens, adolescent mothers remain at a disadvantage in terms of economic stability and independence.

What is especially pioneering about this study is the attempt to connect the mothers' life course with their children's developmental trajectories. Indeed, the most startling findings from the follow-up study of teenage mothers are the consequences for their children. The teenage mothers' decisions and choices strongly influenced the environment in which their children were raised, and the costs of teenage parenthood were often felt by their offspring. In various domains, the children of teenage parents displayed more symptoms of maladjustment (acting out, social withdrawal, etc.) than did teenagers whose mothers were older when they had their first child. In addition, Furstenberg and his colleagues noted that variability in the children's outcomes could be explained, in part, by the timing and sequencing of maternal life events. For example, they found that high fertility in the years immediately following the birth of the first child was a negative predictor of academic success, suggesting that rapid subsequent fertility reduced time and resources spent on the first child. Powerful connections exist between the life courses of mothers and their children, and between decisions made by the mother subsequent to her off-time entry into motherhood and the fate of her child.

Both the Los Angeles and Baltimore studies provide reminders that in the transition to early parenthood the fates of adolescent mothers and their children are governed by a web of interdependencies, both within the dyadic unit and across the lineage system. However, generational status is not a reliable indicator of historical location, as shown in Fig. 6.1 on two lineages in the Burton study. In the on-time lineage, the bridging generation of grandmothers experienced childhood during the Great Depression, a time that has little in common with the historical experience of their daughters—the civil rights era of the 1950s and 1960s. By comparison, the early lineage relates three generations within a much shorter historical span. The great-grandmothers were born around the 1930s, their daughters immediately after the Second World War in the baby boom, and their great-granddaughters at the end of the 1960s through the mid-1970s.

The Baltimore data are also limited in relation to the historical record because they are based on a single cohort with a unique historical experience. The women in the Baltimore study came of age in the era of the Great Society and received a fairly generous amount of public support and services. They may have also been the last cohort of teenagers to believe that early marriage is a viable strategy for responding to premature parenthood. Their adaptations were clearly shaped by the resources and options of a particular historical period. If their daughters become pregnant as adolescents, they will in all likelihood respond differently, given institutional constraints and options that are continually reshaped by legis-

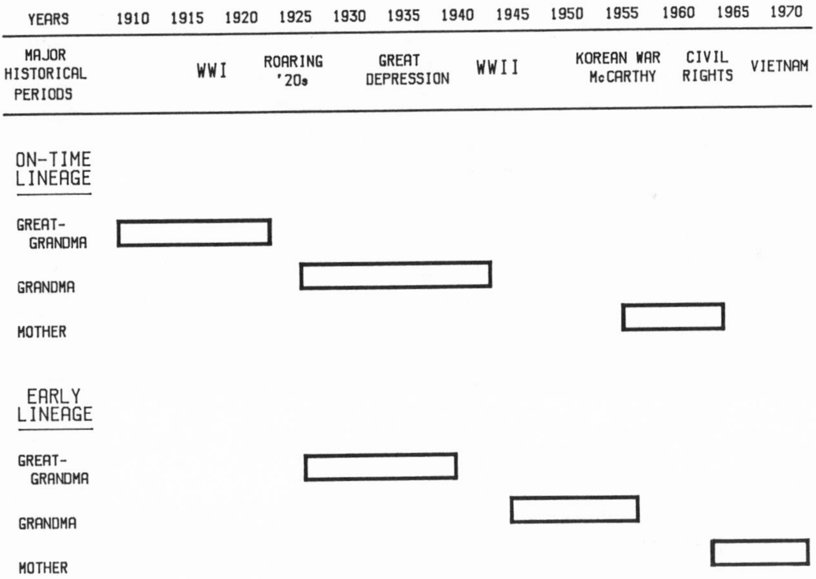

FIG. 6.1.   The Birth Years of Two Lineages of Black Females, On-Time and Early

lative actions. Whatever valuable insights we have gained about the timing, sequence, and synchronicity of transitions in the life course, these are still not informed by a sense of history.

LINKING ADOLESCENT EXPERIENCE
TO HISTORICAL CHANGE

How should history be brought to the study of adolescence and life-course transitions? Much thought has been given to questions of this sort, but the results have been disappointing. Historical variation in adolescent experience remains more of a problematic issue than a research option and line of advance. We briefly review some matters that relate to this appraisal, and conclude with studies that suggest a promising alternative in which the effects of social change are traced through the social dynamics of interdependent lives.

History as a Problematic Issue

Schaie (1984) claims that the life-span movement has shifted "the focus of concern from the search for purely developmental patterns of a normative nature to the context in which development occurs" (p. 1). Unfortunately, this does not apply to historical contexts. Oddly enough our neglect of historical context and influences is indebted to important essays that were intended to promote the study of historical effects. Ryder (1965) viewed the cohort as a concept for studying social change and Schaie (1965) proposed a general developmental model (see also Baltes, Cornelius, & Nesselroade, 1979).

Ryder's thoughtful essay linked age and time (such as birth years as historical time, chronological age as social time) in ways that produced greater understanding of the connections between historical and individual change. Since then cohort analysis has acquired greater prominence in studying life trajectories, as has the technical problem of disentangling three types of effects: cohort, period, and age (Glenn, 1983).

History is expressed as a cohort effect when social change or an event differentiates the life patterns of successive cohorts. Adolescents experienced the hardships of the Great Depression in different ways than did young children, and these differences are expressed across the life trajectories (Elder, 1979). History also takes the form of a period effect when the impact of a social change or secular trend is relatively uniform across successive cohorts. Some of the most noteworthy aspects of family patterns reflect period influences across the twentieth century. Examples include the scheduling of first marriages and first births, as well as divorce. A third type of effect occurs through a process of aging, as expressed in behavioral differences between people of different ages.

The type of analysis carried out by Ryder posed challenging problems for developmental psychologists. If social change places adjacent cohorts on different trajectories, then behavioral differences among people of different age could be attributed to both historical and life changes. The classic example of this ambiguity involved an assumed intellectual decline in old age. Schaie (1965) proposed a general developmental model and relevant design considerations that addressed the task of estimating cohort, period, and age effects relative to intellectual functioning, and his strategy continues to inform most other investigations of secular change and individual development. Efforts to partition the variance according to each effect have encountered little success, however. More important, this approach is not promising from the vantage point of historical understanding.

Two examples illustrate this observation. Nesselroade and Baltes (1974) carried out a longitudinal study of adolescent personality in four cohorts, as defined by birth years in 1955, 1956, 1957, and 1958. The basic question concerned normative patterns in personality development, not the influence of social change, but the results showed large cohort differences between the first and last two cohorts. The authors make some effort to explain these findings, but it is both too little and too late. Only one page in a 71-page monograph focused on historical effects and the cursory nature of the attempt merely underscores the inadequacy of the approach to understanding historical effects. In a critical review of the Nesselroade-Baltes study, Reese and McCluskey (1984) rightly conclude that it uses little more than speculation in explaining historical variations and that "speculation about probable causes without corroborating evidence is unlikely to be fruitful, unless it leads to theory-guided empirical questions" (p. 4).

This conclusion applies also to sociological studies of life transitions, such as entry into marriage—a critical marker of adult status. Rodgers and Thornton (1985) show that first marriage rates have varied dramatically from good to bad times in the United States. Using first marriage data on annual cohorts from 1900 to 1981, they found three empirical patterns. First, marriage rates changed dramatically with both World Wars and the Great Depression. Both wars preceded an upswing; a large valley occurred in 1930–33 during the Great Depression and another in 1943–44. Second, a long-term shift toward higher marriage rates occurred in the postwar era up to the 1970s, followed by a sharp decline after 1972. Third, changes in marriage rates were comparable for the most part by age, sex, and race, except for teenagers. They conclude that the big picture is one of overwhelming historical effects that influence all cohorts and subgroups in similar ways, but they offer no specification of the historical effects. Nor do they attempt to investigate the process by which such effects occur.

As shown in Panel A of Fig. 6.2, the Nesselroade-Baltes and Rodgers-Thornton studies attempt to link a particular outcome of interest to a host of distal and proximal events. The detection of historical effects is merely incidental in their research enterprise. Imagine, however, where we are likely to be on matters of

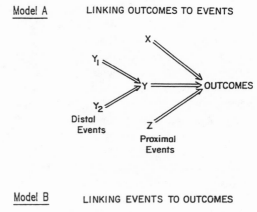

FIG. 6.2. Studying Social Change
in the Life Course: Two Models

theory if research continues to document large cohort and/or period effects that remain a "black box" of unknown contents. These effects are especially troublesome because they require understanding, and statistical strategies for partitioning variance will not provide it. History must enter the picture in problem formulation and model development in order to ensure a satisfactory analysis. As shown in Panel B of Fig. 6.2, the only viable strategy is to link historical variations to a system of outcome variables, and to do so in ways both useful and essential for the description and explanation of developmental change.

One application of this approach is illustrated by the Hamilton study, an intensive study of youth and their life paths to adulthood during industrialization in the city of Hamilton, Canada (Katz, 1975; Katz & Davey, 1978). This project brings history to the analysis of adolescence, but not the concept of interdependent lives and its social dynamics.

Industrialization and the Path to Adulthood

The time frame of the Hamilton study is uniquely suited for an examination of how the lives of youth were altered by events during the early stage of industrialization. Between 1851 and 1871 Hamilton was transformed from a small commercial center to an industrial-commercial center and its population nearly doubled. In this period the school system was modernized, segregating youth from children; local transportation and public services were improved; and the number of large firms increased threefold. To explore life-course changes among youth across this period, quantifiable data—especially on the configuration of residence, education, work, and marriage events—were obtained from census manuscripts, in 1851, 1861, and 1871.

Prior to industrialization, Katz (1975) notes a modal stage of semi-independence or partial autonomy in which young men and women worked and lived as members of a household other than that of their parents. Katz and Davey (1978) refer to this stage of semi-autonomy as the "lost phase" of the life course, for it was replaced in the course of industrialization by more prolonged residence in the parental home. For example, in 1851 a majority of Hamilton youth (ages 15–19) were living in nonparental residences; 20 years later this figure declined to one fourth of the males and one third of the females. In addition, the median age at leaving home increased for young men from 17 to 22; for women, from 17 to 20.

With the extension of family residence, we see also a pronounced decline in the prevalence of what might be called "idle" youth, those who were neither in school nor employed, a change that reflected increasing educational and economic opportunities. In 1851 nearly half of those aged 11 to 15 and one fourth of those aged 16 to 20 were neither enrolled in school nor working. Rising school enrollment markedly reduced this pool of youth during the first decade of educational expansion, followed by the impact of increasing job opportunities in a diversified and enlarged economic base. As shown in Fig. 6.3, among those aged 13 to 16 who were living at home, school and work recruited a larger proportion of boys in 1871 than in 1851; school attendance accounted for the major change in the status of girls.

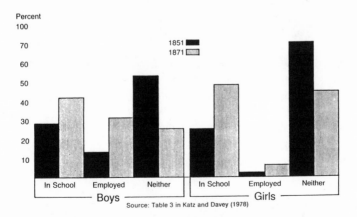

FIG. 6.3. Work and School Status Among 13–16 Year Olds Living at Home in Hamilton, Ontario 1851 and 1871

Rapid social change thus rearranged the timing and sequence of events in the transition to adult status. But industrialization had other consequences as well. With work place separated from the domestic unit and urban schools largely staffed by female teachers, prolonged family residence and education placed male youth in a socialization environment managed by women, an environment too sheltered, some believed, from male influence and real-world discipline. In turn, this climate of "masculine anxiety" converged with the perceived dangers of idle, unruly youth in the lower classes as a stimulus to middle-class support for adult-led organizations—Boys Clubs, YMCA, and Boy Scouts.

The Hamilton study is thus instructive in two respects. It shows (a) how sociohistorical changes are reflected in the way different cohorts age and (b) how the characteristics of different cohorts may bring about sociohistorical change. First, we see that industrialization is accompanied by alterations over time in age-appropriate norms and in practices of role allocation. The configuration of residential, educational, and work transitions after industrialization gave the adolescent an experience of a distinctly different pattern from that experienced before industrialization. Second, we see that as roles in society change, problems often ensue in the allocation of people to roles and in the proper socialization of individuals for these new roles. Indeed, the characteristics of cohorts after industrialization brought about new institutional forms, such as adult-sponsored youth organizations, that have continued to shape the experiences of subsequent cohorts.

A sense of historical depth notwithstanding, the Hamilton study produces demographic snapshots. Demographic records on events in adolescence and young adulthood describe the patterning of one segment of the life span at different times and places, but a precise understanding of such change and its developmental effects eludes our grasp with the available historical documents. Sequential strategies involving successions of longitudinal data are required to examine the interplay between historical change and life patterns.

Moreover, to understand the imprint of a historical event on the lives of children and adolescents we must first trace its effects on the family system as it is the family system that gives meaning to new conditions and trends. If developmental change qualifies as one of the most subtle and important consequences of social change, its understanding requires knowledge of the process by which these modes of change are linked, a process that involves family relationships (Elder, 1984). This is illustrated by Elder's Social Change Project, an ongoing study of the interplay between historical events and life experiences as mediated by the family.

Children of the Great Depression: The Interaction of History and Ontogeny

An interactional perspective on historical time and lifetime is rooted in Ryder's (1965) essay, "The Cohort as a Concept in the Study of Social Change." With its *life-stage principle,* the essay provides a point of departure toward greater understanding of the interplay of social change and life patterns: the influence of a historical event on the life course depends on the stage at which the change is experienced by individuals.

Consider two families in 1930: Family A has two children born around 1920, and family B has two children born in 1928–1930. On the basis of the life-stage principle, we would expect the meaning and significance of Depression hardship to vary significantly between the two sets of children. The older children were 9 to 16 years old during the height of the Depression, too young to leave school and face a dismal employment situation, and too old to be highly dependent on the family. By comparison, the younger children were 1 to 8 years old, ages when they would be most dependent on their families in the midst of the economic crisis and thus at the greatest risk of impaired development and life opportunities.

In addition to these differences, the historical experience of offspring in these two families may have varied according to the ages of the parents. The parents of family A were much older than those in family B. Because an economic decline makes a difference in families through the lives of parents, this age difference has powerful implications for children. The family is thus a meeting ground for members of different cohorts, a meeting ground for interdependent lives. With each person's actions a part of the others' social context, any change in one member's life constitutes a change in the lives and context of the other members. In view of such interdependence, we should think of the interaction between historical time and lifetime as a function of changes in the life courses of multiple family members.

Within a longitudinal perspective, we have examined the sociohistorical context of two cohorts who lived through the Great Depression: the Oakland Growth sample (birth dates, 1920–21) and the Berkeley Guidance sample (birth dates, 1928–29). With pre-Depression birth dates that differ by about 8 years, these cohorts seem to share historical conditions from the 1920s to the 1940s, but close examination of Table 6.1 shows noteworthy variations in developmental stage at points during which these cohorts encountered stressful times and prosperity, economic depressions and wars.

The 167 members of the Oakland cohort were children during the prosperous 1920s, a time of unparalleled economic growth in California, especially in the San Francisco Bay region. Thus, they entered the Depression after a relatively secure phase of early development. Later, they avoided the scars of joblessness after high school by virtue of wartime mobilization. By contrast, the 214 members of the Berkeley cohort encountered hard times in the vulnerable years of early childhood and the pressures of adolescence during the unsettled though prosperous years of World War II. Wartime pressures extended the Depression hardship for the Berkeley as compared to the Oakland cohort. Some Berkeley members endured economic hardship up to their departure from the family in the mid-1940s.

TABLE 6.1
Age of Oakland and Berkeley Cohort Members by Historical Events

Date	Event	Age of cohort members	
		Oakland	Berkeley
1880–1900	Birth years of OGS parents		
1890–1910	Birth years of GS parents		
1921–1922	Depression	Birth (1920–1921)	
1923	Great Berkeley Fire	2–3	
1923–1929	General economic boom; growth of "debt pattern" way of life; cultural change in sexual mores	1–9	Birth (1928–1929)
1929–1930	Onset of Great Depression	9–10	1–2
1932–1933	Depth of Great Depression	11–13	3–5
1933–1936	Partial recovery, increasing cost of living, labor strikes	12–16	4–8
1937–1938	Economic Slump	16–18	8–10
1939–1940	Incipient stage of wartime mobilization	18–20	10–12
1941–1943	Major growth of war industries (shipyards, munitions plants, etc.) and of military forces	20–23	12–15
1945	End of World War II	24–25	16–17
1946–1949	Postwar economic growth	25–29	17–21
1950–1953	Korean War and the McCarthy era	30–33	22–25
1954–1959	Civil Rights Era begins	34–39	26–31
1960–1973	Civil Rights mobilization, Urban Civil Strife, Vietnam War	40–53	32–45
1974–	End of Affluent Age in Postwar America: Energy Crisis, Rising Inflation	54–	46–

Variation in income loss serves as the point of departure for examining the effects of economic change on Oakland and Berkeley study members and their families. In Oakland, two deprivational groups within the middle and working classes of 1929 were identified according to income loss (1929–1933) relative to decline in cost of living (about 25% over this period). Families suffered asset losses with some frequency only when economic loss exceeded 40% of 1929 income. Therefore, deprived families were defined in terms of income losses above 35%; all other families were categorized as nondeprived. This division proved equally appropriate for the Berkeley sample. By this criterion, 36% of the Berkeley middle-class families were economically deprived, compared to 57% of the working-class families. Deprived families were more prevalent in both strata of the Oakland cohort (56% middle class versus 69% working class), than in the Berkeley cohort, a difference that partially reflects the more commercial-industrial character of Oakland's economy.

From the early 1930s to the end of the decade, three modes of change distinguished deprived families in both Oakland and Berkeley from relatively non-deprived families: changes in the family economy, in family relationships, and in the level of social and psychological stress (Fig. 6.4). In both cohorts income loss sharply increased: (a) indebtedness as savings diminished; (b) the curtailment and postponement of expenditures; (c) replacements of funds for services and goods with family labor; and (d) reliance on the earnings of women and older children. Changes in family relationships stemmed from fathers' loss of earnings, withdrawal from family roles, and adaptations in economic support. Economic loss increased the relative power and emotional significance of mother vis-à-vis father for boys and girls. Finally, economic deprivation heightened parental irritability, the likelihood of marital conflicts, arbitrary and inconsistent discipline with children, and the risk of fathers' behavioral impairment through heavy drinking, demoralization, and health disabilities (Elder, 1974; Elder, Liker, & Cross, 1984; Elder, Liker, & Jaworski, 1984; Liker & Elder, 1983). As we see below, the most adverse effects of these family patterns appear among the younger Berkeley boys and the older Oakland girls. Oakland boys and, to a lesser extent, Berkeley girls fared much better (see Elder, 1979; Elder, Caspi, & Van Nguyen, 1986).

Members of the Oakland cohort were beyond the critical early stage of development and dependency when the Great Depression hit; they left high school in the late 1930s during economic recovery and the initial phase of wartime mobilization. Unlike younger children, they were old enough to play important roles in the household economy and to confront future prospects within the context of Depression realities. In fact, our findings show that hard times lowered the social boundary of adulthood for youth from deprived families when compared to the life situation of youth from nondeprived homes. Deprived youth were more likely to be involved in adultlike tasks within the family economy, to aspire to grownup status, and to enter the adult roles of marriage and/or work at an early age. Self-image disturbances commonly observed in the course of adolescent development (e.g., self-consciousness, emotional vulnerability, desire for social acceptance) were more characteristic of boys and girls from deprived families,

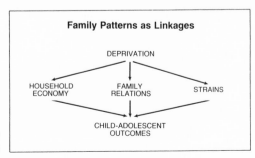

FIG. 6.4. Family Patterns as Linkages

but we find little evidence of an enduring social or psychological disadvantage by the end of the 1930s.

Males. Compared to the nondeprived, young men from hard-pressed families in Oakland entered adulthood with a more crystallized idea of their occupational goals and, despite some handicaps in formal education, managed to end up at midlife with a slightly higher occupational rank. These men not only valued work, they were also more inclined than the nondeprived to stress family activity, to consider children the most important aspects of marriage, to emphasize the responsibilities of parenthood, and to stress the value of dependability in children.

Members of the Berkeley cohort encountered the same historical event at a different point in their lives (see Table 6.1). Seven to 8 years younger than their Oakland counterparts, the Berkeley children experienced the crisis when they were more dependent on family nurturance and more vulnerable to family instability, emotional strain, and conflict (Rutter, 1979). Family hardship came early in their lives and entailed a more prolonged deprivation experience, from the economic trough to the war years and departure from home. Thus, in the Berkeley cohort, the causal link between economic deprivation in the early 1930s and adolescent behavior included a continuing pattern of socioeconomic instability, with its distorting influence on family life—the emotional strain of resource exhaustion, loss of an effective, nurturant father, and marital discord (Liker & Elder, 1983).

Our findings show that the Berkeley boys who grew up in deprived households were less likely to be hopeful, self-directed, and confident about their future than youth who were spared such hardship. This dysphoric outlook is one element of a "dependency" syndrome that emerged from personality ratings in adolescence—personal and social inadequacy, a passive mode of responding to life situations, feelings of victimization, withdrawal from adversity, and self-defeating behavior. Between adolescence and mid-life, deprived men achieved notable developmental gains in self-esteem and assertiveness, though not sufficient to erase completely the inadequacies of the early years.

In addition, boys from deprived families held lower aspirations during wartime adolescence than children from nondeprived families (no difference in IQ), and their scholastic performance turned sharply downward at this point, falling well below that of adolescents in nondeprived homes. The disadvantage of growing up deprived continued into the postwar years, limiting formal education among the sons of both middle- and working-class parents. Whereas deprivation among Oakland boys led to greater mobilization of effort and ambition for adult work and family security, the same historical conditions among the younger Berkeley boys fostered lower expectations and achievements.

The vulnerability of the younger Berkeley boys is in keeping with other findings showing that family stressors are most pathogenic for males in early childhood (e.g., Rutter & Madge, 1976). Indeed, economic loss often patterned the environments of Berkeley families in ways that exposed boys to the greatest risk of developmental impairment, an environment marked by an influential mother and weak father, and family disorganization. But why did the older Oakland boys fare so well in their transition to adolescence and young adulthood? Part of the answer centers on their family roles in economically deprived circumstances. The older Oakland boys were more likely to assume jobs outside the home in order to aid the financially troubled family. Family change of this sort enhanced their social and family independence and reduced their exposure to conflict and turmoil in the home.

But this is only part of the explanation. From a developmental standpoint, the wartime experiences of these cohorts are as consequential as their Depression experiences. Nearly all of the Oakland men were in uniform by the time of the invasion of Normandy in June, 1944 and few were discharged before a completed term of 3 years. The military experience of Oakland men in World War II provided opportunities and intiatives for altering the substance and course of their later lives (Elder, 1986; Elder & Bailey, in press). Military service removed the Oakland men from the immediate influence and setting of home and community. In this sense, the transition represented a passage from family dependence to independence and even personal autonomy. This family separation had noteworthy implications for men who came from mother-dominated and discordant families, as did a good many Oakland men from deprived households. The service also represented a moratorium relative to the age-graded career, a legitimate time-out from the commitment pressures that Erikson (1959) describes in the concept of role diffusion. This concept of service time appears in the recollections of a veteran who grew up in the Bay Area of California. "I didn't know what I wanted, though I probably wanted to get away from home and community. . . . I recall arguing with myself about maybe I'd grow up and settle down a bit if I got into the service" (Elder & Bailey, in press).

However, the most critical implication of military service for the Oakland men involved the educational and vocational benefits of military service, both during the period of active duty and after returning to civilian life. The postwar benefits were most tangibly linked to the benefits of the Servicemen's Readjustment Act of 1944, the G.I. Bill (Olson, 1974). For example, a term of 2 years in the army provided a man with college for a year under the first part of the bill and another 2 years under the second part. The act included a maximum of $500 per school year for all fees, tuition costs, books and supplies; as well as a monthly subsistence allowance ($50 for single, $75 for married veterans).

In various ways, all three of these implications of military service are at least partially rooted in the hardships of the Depression decade. Conditions that made leaving home especially urgent and compelling (e.g., family turmoil, maternal dominance) were products of unemployment and prolonged deprivation. A legitimate time-out from decision pressures in military service had particular value to youth who grew up in the unpromising and unstable era of the 1930s. Lastly, the political pressure to establish educational and housing benefits through a G.I. Bill was fueled by worrisome Depression memories of mass unemployment and unrest and their implications for postwar society upon the mass return of America's fighting men. Nearly half a million veterans took advantage of a college education who might not have done so without the G.I. Bill. Some of these men were members of the Oakland cohort. One can thus assume that wartime experiences and outcomes altered the Depression's legacy in the lives of Oakland males.

The homefront experience of Berkeley males provided an entirely different set of circumstances. They encountered World War II within the context of a family environment shaped by events of the depressed 1930s, and the return to better times through economic recovery during the late 1930s and war years did not always favor a more involved and effective role for deprived fathers in the lives of their sons. A good many of these fathers worked overtime in the late 1930s out of fear of job loss and economic need. Moreover, labor shortages during World War II extended this pattern and drew mothers into the labor force. Perhaps even more than the Depression era, civilian mobilization reduced the effective home presence of mother and father for Berkeley boys. Indeed, the far-reaching effects of their early deprivation cannot be understood from a developmental perspective apart from a life history that extends across the Depression decade to the war years.

Females.   Adolescence carried very different meanings for females in the two cohorts who grew up in deprived families. Whereas the earlier occurrence of economic loss in the Berkeley cohort took a heavier psychological toll on males, the later occurrence of deprivation in the Oakland cohort was somewhat more costly to females. During junior and senior high school, Oakland females from deprived families were socially disadvantaged relative to daughters of more affluent parents; the deprived were less well-dressed in school than the non-deprived and more often felt excluded from the groups and social activities of age mates. The deprived girls were also more self-conscious and experienced more hurt feelings and mood swings. A Depression adolescence was not a gratifying time for a good many of Oakland women; it typically represented a "worst stage of life" in adult memories of those who experienced economic deprivation.

Vulnerability of the Oakland girls is, in part, accounted for by their unique family experience in deprived households (Elder, Caspi, & Van Nguyen, 1986). In the scarcity economy of such households, the older Oakland girls were often called upon to assume major responsibilities as their mothers sought work. Family change of this sort meant greater exposure to discord and tension, especially from hard-pressed fathers, and involved them in adultlike responsibilities that assigned priority to a domestic career of marriage and parenthood.

Indeed, in their life course and values, the deprived Oakland females resemble most the "ultra-domestic" climate of the postwar years. During adolescence, these girls were more inclined to favor marriage and family over a career when compared to girls who were spared family hardship; they tended to marry at an earlier age; and they more frequently dropped out of the labor force after marriage or before the birth of their first child. At mid-life, family, children, and homemaking distinguished their priorities from those of the nondeprived, regardless of educational level or current social position.

A strikingly different impression of adolescence appears in the lives of the younger Berkeley females from deprived homes. They were not characterized in adolescence as less goal-oriented, competent, or assertive than the nondeprived. A deprived environment actually offered greater family security for the younger Berkeley girls, a difference that reflects the warmth of mother-daughter relations under conditions of extreme hardship (Elder, Downey, & Cross, 1986). This female bond stands out as the strongest intergenerational tie among families in the Great Depression, and represents a more general theme of family and kinship in situations where male support is precarious or absent.

But if such bonds generally develop under economic hardship, why don't we find similar family experiences among the Oakland and Berkeley girls? In fact, there are similarities. In both cohorts, girls from deprived families were more likely to experience marital discord, a growing prominence of mother as an authority and affectional figure, and a more peripheral status among fathers. The important difference involves the social-developmental status of the two groups of girls at the time of family hardship and the greater social involvement of the older girls with other girls and boys. Owing in large part to their family's precarious status, the Oakland girls were less equipped with clothes and a home life for social confidence and success. The younger Berkeley girls were too young to face the competitive, heterosexual pressures of secondary school. Considering the young age and university setting of the Berkeley mothers, their work and values may have established a broader concept of woman's sphere of activity in the upbringing of daughters, a concept that favors a resourceful, goal-oriented approach to a future with multiple options. This concept applies primarily to the better educated middle class at the time, and it is in this stratum that we find the strongest association between family deprivation and competence among girls.

In sum, although economic deprivation produced similar changes in the family environment of both cohorts (division of labor, altered family relationships, social strains), its developmental effects varied in ways that conform to differences in life stage relative to historical events. Historical conditions are variable at points in time and in how they are experienced by individuals of different ages. By encountering such times at different points in life, Oakland and Berkeley men and women have different stories to tell about their childhood, adolescence, and adulthood. It is the particular sequence of prosperity, Depression, and war—their variable timing in the life course and their variable meanings in the family—that distinguishes the developmental histories of the two cohorts.

CONCLUSION

Over the past half century of social science in the United States, adolescence has been viewed as a biological age of physical growth and maturation; as a social age of family, peer, and school experience; and as a historical age with meanings and circumstances specified by the times. Because each viewpoint is part of the picture, together they outline distinctive features of a life-course perspective— those of time, process, and context. In this chapter we have given particular attention to some contextual features of adolescence, both historical and social, and to a core element of social contexts, the interdependence of people and lives. Social interdependence forms a primary link between adolescents and their changing environment.

To bring out some implications of interdependent lives, we considered two studies that examined the social consequences of adolescent parenthood, the Los Angeles study of early childbearing across the generations and the Baltimore study of mothers and children who have been followed up to the mid-30s of the mothers. The Los Angeles study documents the way in which the off-timed nature of early births increases the likelihood that the mother will refuse to play the role of grandmother. In this case, the grandmother function is shifted up the generational ladder to the great-grandmother. Using longitudinal data, the Baltimore study of black mothers shows that the long-term effects of a teenage birth, whether negative or not, occurs primarily through the life course and fortunes of the mother herself. Mothers who managed to surmount the limitations of a teenage birth through employment and education were least likely to pass developmental disadvantages on to their children. Neither the Baltimore nor the Los Angeles study examined the influence of history, though both acknowledged the historical boundaries of the research.

Sensitivity to the historical boundaries of adolescence, from entry to exit, has increased over the past quarter century. We are far less likely today to conduct a community study of adolescents that remains impervious to its historical realities. Indeed, the emergence of life-span developmental psychology has focused attention on cohort, period, and life-stage effects, but this development has not given us greater understanding of social change in human lives. One explanation is that developmental studies are not actually concerned with social change as a causal factor of theoretical significance. Indeed, life transitions are typically studied without a sense of history, without recognition that they represent a point of articulation between the historical and ontogenetic process. And as Mills (1959:6) points out, our intellectual journey is incomplete, until we attend to "problems of biography, of history, and of their intersections within society".

This intersection is surely one of the most visible and problematic themes of life studies today.

ACKNOWLEDGMENTS

This chapter is based on a program of research on social change in the family and life course, supported by NIMH Grant MH-34172 and an NIMH Senior Research Scientist Award (MH00567) to Glen H. Elder, Jr. We are indebted to the Institute of Human Development, University of California, Berkeley, for permission to use archival data from the Oakland Growth Study and the Berkeley Guidance Study.

REFERENCES

Baltes, P. B., Cornelius, S. W., & Nesselroade, J. R. (1979). Cohort effects in developmental psychology. In J. R. Nesselroade & P. B. Baltes (Eds.), *Longitudinal research in the study of behavior and development* (pp. 1–39). New York: Academic Press.

Burton, L. M. (1985). *Early and on-time grandmotherhood in multigenerational black families.* Unpublished doctoral dissertation, University of Southern California.

Burton, L. M., & Bengtson, V. L. (1985). Black grandmothers: Issues of timing and continuity of roles. In V. L. Bengtson & J. F. Robertson (Eds.), *Grandparenthood* (pp. 61–77). Beverly Hills, CA: Sage.

Carlsmith, L. (1973). Some personality characteristics of boys separated from their fathers during World war II. *Ethos, 1,* 467–477.

Coleman, J. (1961). *The adolescent society.* New York: Free Press.

Dragastin, S. E., & Elder, G. H., Jr. (Eds.) (1975). *Adolescence in the life cycle.* Washington, DC: Hemisphere.

Elder, G. H., Jr. (1974). *Children of the Great Depression.* Chicago: University of Chicago Press.

Elder, G. H., Jr. (1979). Historical change in life patterns and personality. In P. B. Baltes & O. G. Brim, Jr. (Eds.), *Life-span development and behavior* (Vol. 2, pp. 117–159). New York: Academic Press.

Elder, G. H., Jr. (1980a). Adolescence in historical perspective. In J. Adelson (Ed.), *Handbook of adolescent psychology* (pp. 3–46). New York: Wiley.

Elder, G. H., Jr. (1980b). *Family structure and socialization.* New York: Arno Press.

Elder, G. H., Jr. (1981a). Social history and life experience. In D. H. Eichorn, J. M. Clausen, N. Haan, M. P. Honzik, & P. H. Mussen, Eds. *Present and past in middle life,* (pp. 3–31). New York: Academic Press.

Elder, G. H., Jr. (1981b). History and the life course. In D. Bertaux (Ed.), *Biography and society* (pp. 77–115). Beverly Hills, CA: Sage.

Elder, G. H., Jr. (1984). Families, kin, and the life course: A sociological perspective. In R. D. Parke (Ed.), *Review of child development research* (Vol. 7, pp. 80–136). Chicago: University of Chicago Press.

Elder, G. H., Jr. (Ed.). (1985). *Life course dynamics: Trajectories and transitions, 1968–1980.* Ithaca, NY: Cornell University Press.

Elder, G. H., Jr. (1986). Military timing and turning points in men's lives. *Developmental Psychology, 22(2),* 233–245.

Elder, G. H., Jr., & Bailey, S. (in press). The timing of military service in men's lives. In J. Aldous & D. Klein (Eds.), *Social stress and family development*. New York: Guilford.

Elder, G. H., Jr., & Caspi, A. (in press). Human development and social change: An emerging perspective on the life course. In N. Bolger, A. Caspi, G. Downey, & M. Moorehouse (Eds.), *Persons in context: Developmental processes* New York: Cambridge University Press.

Elder, G. H., Jr., Caspi, A., & Van Nguyen, T. (1986). Resourceful and vulnerable children: Family influences in hard times. In R. Silbereisen, H. Eyferth, & A. Rudinger (Eds.), *Development as action in context: Problem behavior and normal youth development* (pp. 167–186). New York: Springer.

Elder, G. H., Jr., Downey, G., & Cross, C. (1986). Family ties and life chances: Hard times and hard choices in women's lives since the Great Depression. In N. Datan (Ed.), *Life-span developmental psychology: Socialization and intergenerational relations* (pp. 151–183). Hillsdale, NJ: Lawrence Erlbaum Associates.

Elder, G. H., Jr., Liker, J. K., & Cross, C. (1984). Parent-child behavior in the Great Depression: Life course and intergenerational influences. In P. B. Baltes & O. G. Brim, Jr. (Eds.), *Life-span development and behavior* (Vol. 6, pp. 109–158). New York: Academic Press.

Elder, G. H., Jr., Liker, J. K., & Jaworski, B. (1984). Hardship in lives: Historical influences from the 1930s to old age in postwar America. In K. McCluskey & H. Reese (Eds.), *Life-span developmental psychology: History and cohort effects* (pp. 161–201). New York: Academic Press.

Elder, G. H., Jr., Van Nguyen, T., & Caspi, A. (1985). Linking family hardship to children's lives. *Child Development, 56*, 361–375.

Erikson, E. H. (1959). Identity and the life cycle. *Psychological Issues, 1*.

Furstenberg, F. F., Jr. (1976). *Unplanned parenthood*. New York: Free Press.

Furstenberg, F. F., Jr. (1981). Remarriage and intergenerational relations. In *Aging: Stability and change in the family* R. Fogel, E. Hatfield, S. Kiesler & D. March (Eds.) (pp. 115–141). New York: Academic Press.

Furstenberg, F. F., Jr., Brooks-Gunn, J., & Morgan, S. P. (1987). *Adolescent mothers in later life*. New York: Cambridge University Press.

Glenn, N. (1983). *Cohort analysis*. Beverly Hills, CA: Sage.

Hagestad, G. O., & Burton, L. M. (1986). Grandparenthood, life context, and family development. *American Behavioral Scientist, 29*, 471–484.

Hagestad, G. O., & Neugarten, B. L. (1985). Age and the life course. In R. H. Binstock & E. Shanas (Eds.), *Handbook of aging and the social sciences* (pp. 35–61). New York: Van Nostrand Reinhold.

Hill, R. (1949). *Families under stress*. New York: Harper & Brothers.

Hogan, D. P. (1981). *Transitions and social change*. New York: Academic Press.

Hollingshead, A. (1949). *Elmtown's youth*. New York: Wiley.

Katz, M. B. (1975). *The people of Hamilton, Canada West: Family and class in a mid-nineteenth century city*. Cambridge, MA: Harvard University Press.

Katz, M. B., & Davey, I. F. (1978). Youth and early industrialization in a Canadian city. *American Journal of Sociology, 84*, 81–119.

Liker, J. K., & Elder, G. H., Jr. (1983). Economic hardship and marital relations in the 1930s. *American Sociological Review, 48*, 343–359.

Mills, C. W. (1959). *The sociological imagination*. New York: Oxford University Press.

Nesselroade, J. R., & Baltes, P. B. (1974). Adolescent personality development and historical change: 1970–1972. *Monographs of the Society for Research in Child Development, 39*(1, Serial No. 154).

Olson, K. W. (1974). *The G.I. Bill, the veterans, and the colleges*. Lexington: University Press of Kentucky.

Reese, W. H., & McCluskey, K. A. (1984). Dimensions of historical constancy and change. In K.

A. McCluskey & H. W. Reese (Eds.), *Life-span developmental psychology: Historical and generational effects* (pp. 17–45). New York: Academic Press.

Riesman, D., Glazer, N., & Denney, R. (1950). *The lonely crowd.* New Haven, CT: Yale University Press.

Rodgers, W. L., & Thornton, A. (1985). Changing patterns of first marriage in the United States. *Demography, 22,* 265–279.

Rutter, M. (1979). Protective factors in children's responses to stress and disadvantage. In M. W. Kent & J. E. Rolf (Eds.), *Primary prevention of psychopathology: Vol. 3. Social competence in children* (pp. 69–76). Hanover, NH: University Press of New England.

Rutter, M., & Madge, N. (1976). *Cycles of disadvantage: A review of research.* London: Heinemann.

Ryder, N. (1965). The cohort as a concept in the study of social change. *American Sociological Review, 30,* 843–861.

Schaie, K. W. (1965). A general model for the study of developmental problems. *Psychological Bulletin, 64,* 94–107.

Schaie, K. W. (1984). Historical time and cohort effects. In K. A. McCluskey & H. W. Reese (Eds.), *Life-span developmental psychology: Historical and generational effects* (pp. 1–15). New York: Academic Press.

Stolz, L. (1954). *Family relations of war-born children.* Stanford, CA: Stanford University Press.

7
Commentary:
The Role of Conflict
in Adolescent-Parent
Relationships

Catherine R. Cooper
The University of Texas at Austin

Whether we consider developmental change in adolescent-parent relationships as emancipation or as renegotiation from asymmetrical to more mutuality-oriented relationships, the expression and resolution of conflict play a key role in accounts of this transition. This commentary focuses on three issues central to understanding conflict in adolescent-parent relationships: first, the sources of such conflict and how they operate in the interdependence of individual and relational functioning; second, under what conditions conflict is functional or dysfunctional; and third, the analysis of conflict through microsocial and developmental time. The discussion then turns to the two chapters directly concerned with conflict, those of Hill and Smetana, and consider implications of these chapters for future work.

SOURCES OF CONFLICT

A group of social, developmental, and clinical psychologists led by Kelley (Kelley, Berscheid, Christensen, Harvey, Huston, Levinger, McClintock, Peplau, Peterson, 1983) have recently proposed a framework for conceptualizing psychological and social interdependence in family and other close relationships. Their model is helpful in considering the different accounts of adolescent-parent conflict presented in this volume and in differentiating sources of influence in such conflict.

Two levels of interdependence in close relationships are delineated in the model. As elaborated by Huston and Robins (1982), the first level emphasizes the reciprocal patterns of influence between *relationship properties,* which summarize cumulative patterns of actual behavioral or psychological events, and *subjective conditions,* which refer to relatively stable beliefs, such as trust or satisfaction, about the self, the partner, or the relationship, that emerge from their interaction. For example, recurrent patterns of a mother's criticism and her adolescent daughter's psychological withdrawal may result in the daughter making increasingly frequent attributions of nonsupport ("she doesn't understand me") and hostility toward her mother and ultimately avoiding her. These distinctions illuminate the ways in which parents' and adolescents' attributions about themselves, one another, and their relationship intertwine with their overt behavior, and how they in turn affect and are affected by more stable subjective conditions. Such subjective conditions have been linked to personality development in childhood and adolescence.

The second useful feature of the Close Relationships framework lies in its approach to causal analysis, which focuses on conditions that affect both relationship properties, such as chronically conflictual interaction, and subjective conditions, such as mistrust. These causal factors include relatively stable properties of the individual (in this case, the adolescent), including biological, cognitive, and affective characteristics; properties of the other person in the relationship; and the interaction between them, such as the similarity or discrepancy in their attitudes. The social and physical environments include distal as well as proximal features of school, peers, work, and family structure.

This framework is not itself a theory; rather, different theories can be used to account for the interplay of causal conditions and relationship properties. Such a system brings order to the many variables and sources of data about adolescent-parent relationships considered in this volume. For example, Hill's account of such conflict emphasizes its sources in the interaction between adolescent and parental characteristics—the timing of adolescent girls' pubertal onset with parents' gender. Smetana's analysis of conflict focuses on the mismatch between parents' and adolescents' social-cognitive reasoning about conventions. The chapters of Elder on historical conditions and Simmons on school structures suggest features of the social and physical environment that could play significant roles as sources of influence in adolescent-parent conflict.

The core question for which this framework is useful is in tracing how variations in such causal conditions are expressed in behavior and subjective conditions. For example, with pubertal change, a key question is how biological change at puberty is expressed through self-evaluations, attributions of others, and in actual interaction in relationships. The Close Relationships framework keeps us from viewing properties of relationships, such as conflict, in terms of only one variable, when such properties function in the nexus of a complex multivariate system. Finally, it is useful in monitoring the continuing interdependencies in relational and individual development.

CONFLICT: FUNCTIONAL OR DYSFUNCTIONAL?

Thus far we have considered conflict primarily as a product of various causal conditions, that is, as an outcome. We now turn to the question of under what conditions conflict has functional or dysfunctional consequences for adolescent-parent relationships.

The key point is that functional and dysfunctional properties of conflict depend on the context in which it is expressed, that is, with what other behaviors it co-occurs. Although conflict is often considered an indicator of incompatibility, current research provides evidence that conflict can function constructively when it co-occurs with the subjective conditions of trust and closeness and their behavioral expressions (Cooper, Grotevant, & Ayers-Lopez, 1987).

An illustration of this can be drawn from the work my colleagues and I have conducted in developing a model of relationships that focuses on the construct of *individuation,* which can be seen in the transactive interplay of individuality and connectedness in relationships. Our studies investigate the way that children's and adolescents' experiences of these qualities in the family serve as a context for the development of attitudes and skills carried beyond it, such as identity formation, perspective taking, and conflict resolution skills with peers. We have pursued these questions with high school seniors (e.g., Cooper, Grotevant, & Condon, 1983; Grotevant & Cooper, 1985) and with sixth-grade children (Cooper & Carlson, 1986). In this work, we assess individuality and connectedness in family communication by asking family members to plan a fictitious vacation together for which they have 2 weeks and unlimited funds. This allows but does not, of course, ensure non-zero-sum interactions or power sharing. The interactions are audiotaped in the families' homes and later coded for expressions of individuality, including self-assertions and disagreements, as well as connectedness, including agreement, acknowledgments, and compromise.

A central finding from this work is that family members' expressions of their own points of view as well as their disagreements with others appear to be predictive of qualities of adaptive identity and relational skills in their adolescents. In such interactions, the adolescent can hear, consider, and integrate differing points of view, and decisions are made through negotiation rather than by the unilateral imposing of a solution by a parent or through indifference and default. What we see, then, is a cooccurrence of conflict and cohesion, which parallels the finding in cognitive developmental research that when friends disagree and discuss their disagreements, they make the greatest cognitive gains (Bearison, Magzamen, & Filardo, 1986; Nelson & Aboud, 1985).

In contrast, as studies of Olweus (1978) and Patterson (1986) have shown, when family conflict is hostile, impulsive, and inconsistent, and prone to escalating to high intensity, children feel neglect and lack of love, and avoid interaction with their parents. Thus, contentiousness alone may not be the distinctive feature of dysfunctional conflict, but whether or not conflict occurs within a context of relational cohesion. In fact, such co-occurrence may lead to significant individual and relational gains.

Of course, families, as well as mothers and fathers, differ in their styles of expressing and resolving conflict, and heat and contentiousness are given meaning by the contexts in which they occur (Youniss & Smollar, 1985). Nonetheless, dealing with conflict in adolescence may be the analogue of changing diapers in infancy: although the proximal cues may be aversive, the interactive context is one of great potential intimacy.

CONFLICT THROUGH TIME

The third core issue in the analysis of adolescent-parent conflict concerns the role of time, both as measured in minutes, and as measured in months and years which Cairns and Cairns(1986) have called *interactive time* and *developmental time,* respectively. When we consider interactive time, we increasingly see the need to open up the temporal window on our analysis of interaction. Instead of a focus on individual behaviors, such as frequencies of disagreements, interaction, even argument, is increasingly viewed as an extended cooperative social process (Clark, 1985).

Our findings suggest that in families who can sustain engagement in the expression, negotiation, and resolution of their differences, adolescents are more able to engage productively in conflict resolution with peers. In contrast, the families in which parents cut off discussions or disagreement by imposing their solutions are more likely to have adolescents who either dominate or passively acquiesce in peer conflict situations.

With regard to developmental time, it is important to remember that adolescence is but one period in the history of the parent-child relationship. Maccoby and Martin (1983) have pointed out that parent-adolescent dyads with a history of low-intensity conflict resolution, in which conflicts of interest are resolved communally, may engender subjective conditions of mutual trust and confidence so that the adolescents subsequently may be responsive to their parents' moderately expressed demands. Such a long-term perspective may account for findings that in both early and later adolescence, more conflict and more closeness are reported by adolescents and their mothers. Although they see their issues as serious, they do not see conflict itself as a threat to their relationship, whose meaning is based on years of interaction and mutual knowledge (Montemayor, 1983; Youniss & Smollar, 1985).

At the level of individual development, the major cognitive, biological, and social changes of early adolescence may render it a sensitive period for the impact of relational experience on the adolescent's sense of self. Thus just as periods of rapid physical development constitute periods of vulnerability in biological development, so early adolescence may be a period of vulnerability to the sense of self, and experiences in relationships involving the interplay of individuality and connectedness may have special impact.

THE ROLE OF CONFLICT IN INDIVIDUAL AND FAMILY RELATIONAL DEVELOPMENT IN ADOLESCENCE: TWO ACCOUNTS

The chapters in this volume by Hill and Smetana each concern the role of conflict in adolescents' relationships with their families. Hill has pioneered the examination of pubertal development as an individual difference variable in the study of adolescence. Rather than see puberty as a monolithic event, Hill's work has stimulated us to attend not only to the stage of pubertal development but also to the timing of pubertal onset as a key element of adolescent-family relationships. At a time when others may have slipped away from traditional questions regarding the role of gender in family conflict, his work has kept us engaged in defining and refining these constructs in adolescent and family development. Finally, Hill's work on the sequential analysis of conflict episodes brings us closer to identifying mechanisms of relational functioning than we were viewing communication in terms of frequencies of individual communication behaviors.

In a different way, Smetana's work helps integrate adolescence research with other domains of developmental psychology by considering the events of adolescence in a life span cognitive-developmental framework. Her chapter makes two major contributions. The first is its joining of cognitive development, traditionally seen as an internally self-regulating system, to life experiences in close relationships. This contrasts with much Piagetian research on the role of social interaction in development, which has traditionally been conducted using dyads of unacquainted children. Second, Smetana's concurrent assessments of adolescents, parents, their views of one another, and their interactions will be a major contribution.

These two chapters reflect the continuing utility of psychoanalytic and cognitive developmental theory in capturing significant issues in adolescence, as well as the renewed focus on individual development in transactive relational contexts. Adolescents are viewed neither as entities launched into isolated emotional autonomy nor as solitary cognizers. A number of questions, of course, remain to be addressed. For example, it would be fruitful to examine the issues raised by Hill and Smetana in the context of individual differences in parental cognitive and behavioral characteristics (e.g., power assertion, permissiveness, and so on). A second question concerns the chronic challenge in linking reasoning, as a property of the individual, to the behavioral interactions the individual has with others in relationships. The chapters in this volume demonstrate how many factors mediate, insulate, or instigate the behavioral expression of the adolescents' reasoning.

CONCLUSIONS

In this volume a diverse array of conditions that affect adolescents' relationships with their families has been considered—qualities of the wider social environment such as economic conditions, family members' experiences and attitudes concerning work and school, attributes of the adolescents and their parents as individuals, and qualities of their interactions and mutual attributions. The issues discussed lead to three conclusions regarding conflict. First, the study of conflict as a quality of individual and relational experience will come of age as we trace the impact of these conditions on specific relationship properties and subjective conditions. Second, we need to differentiate the construct of conflict noting origins, consequences, and contexts rather than assume that conflict and its expression are inherently dysfunctional and aversive. Discriminant and predictive validity work is needed to assess the consequences of different patterns of conflict resolution for the attributions parents and adolescents make of one another and their relationships. Finally, as the chapters in this volume illustrate, we will benefit from interdisciplinary work that brings to bear cognitive, affective, linguistic, and contextual perspectives on our understanding of the ways conflict functions in the development of individuals and relationships.

REFERENCES

Bearison, D. J., Magzamen, G., & Filardo, E. K. (1986). Social-cognitive conflict and cognitive growth in young children. *Merrill-Palmer Quarterly, 32*, 51–72.

Cairns, R. B., & Cairns, B. D. (1986). The developmental-interactional view of social behavior: Four issues of adolescent aggression. In D. Olweus, J. Block, & M. Radke-Yarrow (Eds.), *Development of antisocial and prosocial behavior: Research, theories, and issues* (pp. 315–342). Orlando, FL: Academic Press.

Clark, H. (1985). Language use and language users. In E. Aronson & G. Lindzey (Eds.), *The handbook of social psychology* 3rd ed., (pp. 179–231). Reading, MA: Addison-Wesley.

Cooper, C. R., & Ayers-Lopez, S. (1985). Family and peer systems in early adolescence: New models of the role of relationships in development. *Journal of Early Adolescence, 5*, 9–21.

Cooper, C. R., & Carlson, C. (1986). *Family process antecedents of children's competence and vulnerability in the school context.* Grant funded by Spencer Foundation, University of Chicago.

Cooper, C. R., Grotevant, H. D., & Ayers-Lopez, S. (1987, April). Discourse perspectives on individuation: Gender-related patterns of carryover in adolescents' family and peer interactions. In M. Zahaykevich (Chair), *Adolescent gender formation and individuation in family discourse.* Symposium presented at the meetings of The Society for Research in Child Development, Baltimore, MD.

Cooper, C. R., Grotevant, H. D., & Condon S. (1983). Individuality and connectedness in the family as a context for adolescent identity formation and role taking skill. In H. D. Grotevant & C. R. Cooper (Eds.), *Adolescent development in the family: New directions in child development* (pp. 43–59). San Francisco: Jossey-Bass.

Grotevant, H. D. & Cooper, C. R. (1985). Patterns of interaction in family relationships and the development of identity formation in adolescence. *Child Development, 51,* 415–428.

Huston, T., & Robbins, E. (1982). Conceptual and methodological issues in studying close relationships. *Journal of Marriage and the Family, 44,* 901–925.

Kelley, H. H., Berscheid, E., Christensen, A., Harvey, J. Huston, T. L., Levinger, G., McClintock, E., Peplau, L. A., & Peterson, D. (1983). *Close relationships.* San Francisco: Freeman.

Maccoby, E. E., & Martin, J. A. (1983). Socialization in the context of the family: Parent-child interaction. In E. M. Hetherington (Ed.), *Handbook of child psychology: Vol. 4. Socialization, personality, and social development* (pp. 236–271). New York: Wiley.

Montemayor, R. (1983). Parents and adolescents in conflict: all families some of the time and some families most of the time. *Journal of Early Adolescence, 3,* 83–103.

Nelson, J., & Aboud, F. E. (1985). The resolution of social conflict between friends. *Child Development, 56,* 1009–1017.

Olweus, D. (1978). *Aggression in the schools: Bullies and whipping boys.* Washington, DC: Hemisphere.

Patterson, G. R. (1986). Performance models for antisocial boys. *American Psychologist, 41,* 432–444.

Youniss, J. & Smollar, J. (1985). *Adolescent relations with mothers, fathers, and friends.* Chicago: University of Chicago Press.

8 Commentary: Developmental Issues in the Transition to Early Adolescence

J. Brooks-Gunn
Educational Testing Service

The theme that traditionally has unified and motivated research on adolescence is that of the impact of the normative life events that delineate this life phase. Until recently, however, we have focused on a limited set of biological and social changes, believing them to be age-related and to characterize all adolescents. As exemplified in this volume, our focus is changing. In addition to the life events themselves, the timing and sequencing of these events that mark the progression toward adulthood are now seen as critical in defining adolescence and in our understanding of how individuals adapt to adolescent life changes. The normative approach is being replaced by a sensitivity to individual differences in the timing and sequencing of the events of adolescence. Nowhere is this change in focus more evident than in research on early adolescence. Indeed, early adolescence is often defined in terms of transitional events: puberty (in itself a series of events), school moves, dating, alterations in achievement demands, and, more and more frequently, sexuality, smoking, and drinking. Examining sequences of events, however, does not mean that their temporal ordering is invariant across individuals. The early adolescent may move into a middle school in 5th, 6th, or 7th grade. If she dates, she may begin as early as 5th or 6th, as late as 11th or 12th grade, or not at all. Interindividual differences in the onset and completion of pubertal processes abound; for example, normal breast development may be initiated anywhere between 8 and 13 years and be complete as soon as age 12 or as late as age 18.[1] Intraindividual variability also is common; for example, although breast buds supposedly appear before pubic hair, the opposite is seen in

---

[1] However, some girls never reach Tanner Breast Stage 5 (Marshall & Tanner, 1969).

189

one third of all girls (Harlan, Harlan, & Grillo, 1980; Marshall & Tanner, 1969). The same is true for deviations from the so-called norm in timing and sequencing of other pubertal events—menarche, rises in gonadotropin levels, penile growth, spermarche, voice changes, and the growth spurt.

This cacophony of temporal ordering is one reason early adolescent research languished for so long (other possible reasons include beliefs about the inflexibility of development after childhood and the primacy of early experiences). However, the current zeitgeist augurs well for research on this life phase with the acceptance of a broader definition of child development (or more accurately, human development), renewed interest in continuity across life phases, concerns about the development of pathology and the pathology of development, and the portrayal of development as an interaction between the organism and the environment (Baltes & Brim, 1980, 1981; Brim & Kagan, 1980; Bronfenbrenner, 1985; Cicchetti, 1984; Lerner, 1985; Scarr, 1985). Also, early adolescent research has encouraged interdisciplinary collaborations, most specifically with sociologists who look at the timing and patterning of role changes and with endocrinologists who examine links between physiological processes and behaviors. Finally, patronage also is opportunist, in that early adolescence allows for the investigation of certain issues with a clarity or elegance not furnished by other life phases. As evident in the chapters in this volume, early adolescence offers the possibility of elucidating the relative effects of biological and social factors upon development, the emergence of certain forms of psychopathology, the changes in self-definitions that occur as the individual is transformed physically and socially from a child into an adult, and the reorganization of roles in families as the legitimate, and sometimes not so legitimate, demands of a young adult are negotiated. Each of these themes is touched upon in the present volume.

The enthusiasm with which a relatively new field goes about its business sometimes obscures the assumptions underlying much of the research. Two assumptions that plague research on early adolescence have to do with the possible distinctiveness and uniqueness of this life phase. Is early adolescence unique, in the fact either that the context in which development occurs is different or that the processes underlying development are different from other life phases? And, is early adolescence distinct from those life phases that precede and follow it, and if so, in what ways? Most researchers take an implicit stance on these issues without making explicit the unspoken premises that influence design and interpretation of their work as well as their choice of models.

In the following discussion, the chapters in the present volume are used to illustrate questions related to the issues of distinctiveness and uniqueness. In addition, conceptual frameworks that directly test assumptions of similarity and differences across life phases are presented. Such frameworks are necessary if we are to understand how the events of early adolescence influence development.

UNIQUENESS OF EARLY ADOLESCENCE

Several issues related to the uniqueness argument are examined: (1) the meaning of behavior across life phases (specifically adolescence and its adjacent phases); (2) the prevalence of certain behaviors in early adolescence, vis-à-vis earlier life phases; (3) the antecedents of early adolescent behaviors and the emergence and maintenance of behaviors making their debut in early adolescence; (4) the activation effects of hormones during this life phase; and (5) the interaction of environmental and person characteristics such as the timing of pubertal events.

Meaning of Behavior Across Life Phases

The issue of possible changes in the meaning of any particular behavior over the life course has frequently been discussed (cf., Brim & Kagan, 1980; Harmon & Emde, 1983; Sroufe, 1979). However, such discussions are notably lacking in the early adolescence literature. At least two questions may be put forth. First, are the behaviors thought to tap a specific construct analogous to those seen in childhood and/or in late adolescence and young adulthood? Until the past decade, it was believed that many behaviors emerged in early adolescence that were quite dissimilar to those seen earlier (see, for notable exceptions, temperament characteristics and conduct disorders; Buss & Plomin, 1984; Kellam, Ensminger, & Turner, 1977, Rutter, 1979; Thomas, Chess, & Birch, 1968). Additionally, whether behaviors first seen in early adolescence were analogous to behaviors exhibited by adults or even older adolescents has not been extensively explored. Although beliefs have changed about possible continuities in behavior across different ages, few procedures have been designed to assess the meaning of behaviors across ages. Second, even if continuity in behaviors is not seen prior to and after adolescence, we can question whether the organization of behaviors representative of any specific construct is similar or different across these life phases. Differences in relations among behaviors at different life phases would be evidence of a change in organization (cf. Sroufe, 1979). Several of the contributors to this volume have begun to examine comparability in meaning of behavior across adolescent subphases. Smetana (Chapter 4) is tracing cognitive processes and social cognitive attributions for one's own and others' behavior from late childhood through late adolescence. Simmons has considered whether self-images change during adolescence and how such changes may be linked with the normative events of adolescence; indeed, both her early work (Simmons, Rosenberg, & Rosenberg, 1973) and her more current research (chapter 5) are illustrative. Although Hill's work (chapter 3) on changes in parent-adolescent relations may not be perceived as directly addressing this issue, his focus on the meaning of menarche to the young girl and her parents and how it may influence interactions differently as a function of pubertal status and timing, takes into account such changes.

Comparability of constructs does not rule out the possibility that the relative importance of a construct, or behavior thought to tap a construct, may not be influenced by chronological age, cohort, or context. That is, researchers need to demonstrate not only constancy, but the instances in which change occurs (Brim & Kagan, 1980). Several investigators have examined both constancy and change over the adolescent period (Brooks-Gunn, Rock, & Warren, 1987; Dusek & Flaherty, 1981; Nesselroade & Baltes, 1974). For example, we (Brooks-Gunn et al., 1987) asked early to late adolescent girls to complete self-report scales that were believed to tap constructs associated with the rise in psychopathology seen in early adolescence. Models were tested using maximum likelihood factor analyses to see if the same pattern of factor loadings would be found and whether the salience of each factor would be similar across grade. The results showed that although the meaning of behaviors was similar across grades, the relative importance of some factors differed. For example, body image declined in importance from early to late adolescence. Body image may be most salient during the pubertal years when the body is rapidly changing from child to adult form. Numerous studies have demonstrated that pubertal youths are very concerned about their bodies, that physical attractiveness is a major dimension of their self-image, that body changes are viewed ambivalently, and that body image is influenced by pubertal status and maturational timing as well as contextual factors (Brooks-Gunn & Warren, 1985, in press; Duncan, Ritter, Dornbusch, Gross, & Carlsmith, 1985; Gargiulo, Attie, Brooks-Gunn, & Warren, in press; Tobin-Richards, Boxer, & Petersen, 1983). That Simmons and her colleagues have reported alterations in girls' self-image as a function of both the move to middle school and pubertal status is not surprising, given the salience of this construct in early adolescence (Blyth, Simmons, & Zakin, 1985; Simmons, Blyth, & McKinney, 1983). Hill's focus on the meaning of body changes for understanding early adolescent interactions also is congruent with the salience of body image for this age period.

Prevalence of Certain Behaviors

Many believe that the prevalence of certain behaviors increases during early adolescence. For example, Rutter, Graham, Chadwick, and Yule (1976) reported a 10-fold increase in aggression from age 10 to 15, and a 4-fold increase in mild depression over the same span. In our study mentioned earlier, we (Brooks-Gunn et al., 1987) found that depressive affect was more characteristic of younger than older adolescents. In order to make such statements, construct comparability must be demonstrated across life phases. Indeed, depressive affect in late childhood seems to be similar to that exhibited by adolescents and adults.

Moderate levels of stability in the self-report of depressive affect have been reported from late childhood to early adolescence (Seligman & Peterson, 1986), and 10- and 11-year-olds report patterns of depressive emotion and attributions of negative events similar to those of adults (Blumberg & Izard, 1985). The demonstration of continuity presupposes construct similarity, as was demonstrated for depressive affect in these two studies.

To return to the question of increased prevalence (given similarities in meaning of a behavior), several approaches may be taken. One tack would be to look at the factors that might presage such an increase. The elegant work of Simmons and her colleagues is a case in point. That the simultaneity of life-event changes, rather than any particular change, predicts lowered school achievement and social competence could be interpreted as a demonstration of the similarity of process across life phases. That is, the adult literature is replete with examples of the untoward negative effects of the occurrence of multiple life events. Simmons' Milwaukee Study results may be seen as confirmation of this relation in young adolescents. In early adolescence the number and/or salience of stressful life events may increase, resulting in a higher incidence of negative behavior than seen previously.

Another approach would be to test directly alternative models of the relation between life events and negative outcomes. For example, we have proposed four different models to test the influence of negative life events and pubertal change on the experience of depressive affect during early adolescence. As seen in Table 8.1, the first assumes similar relations in early adolescence and adulthood such

TABLE 8.1
Four Possible Models for Predicting Negative Affect
in Early Adolescence

Model	Prediction
Similarity Model	Negative life events but not pubertal change or pubertal status associated with depressive affect (similar to findings in studies of adults).
Difference Model	Pubertal change or pubertal status but not negative life events related to depressive affect (different from findings in studies of adults).
Additive Model	Negative life events and pubertal change or pubertal status each are independently associated with depressive affect
Interaction Model	Negative life events are associated with depressive affect in some stages of pubertal development but not in others, or negative life events are more associated with depressive affect in some pubertal stages than in other stages.

that negative life events, not pubertal processes, will be associated with depressive affect. The second is a difference model, postulating that pubertal processes, but not negative life events, will be linked to depressive affect. The third model is an additive one based on the premise that both factors will account for some of the variance in depressive affect. The final model states that depressive affect will be linked to negative life events in some stages of pubertal development but not others or will be differentially associated with pubertal stages. In a study of 120 fifth- to seventh-grade girls, these possible models were tested using the Youth Behavior Profile to obtain a measure of depressive affect (Achenbach & Edelbrock, 1979, 1981), the Early Adolescent Life Event Scale to document the occurrence of positive and negative events in the family, school, and peer arenas (Brooks-Gunn, Rosso, & Warren, 1987), and Tanner ratings of secondary sexual development to assess pubertal status (Marshall & Tanner, 1969). The four models were tested via a series of hierarchical regressions: Negative (but not positive) life events were directly associated with depressive affect as was the interaction of pubertal status and negative life events, whereas pubertal processes (in this case, menarcheal status, timing of maturation, and breast growth) were not. The interaction of pubertal status and negative life events, as illustrated in Fig. 8.1, indicates that the occurrence of negative school events was more likely to be associated with depressive affect in the prepubertal and early stages (Tanner Stages 1 and 2) than in the middle to late stages of development (Tanner Stages 3 and 4). Thus, the similarity and interactive models, but not the additive and difference models, were found to explain the relation of negative life events and puberty to depressive affect. In this study, like that of Simmons and her colleagues, puberty, in and of itself, did not account for negative outcomes. However, the occurrence of negative events at the earlier rather than the later stages of puberty were more likely to presage an increase in depressive affect.

Another framework for addressing the issue of increased prevalence might characterize a life phase as particularly conflictual. Early adolescence has been a prime candidate for such "storm and stress" appellations (Blos, 1979; Deutsch, 1944; Hall, 1904). Interestingly, partly in reaction to overdeterministic psychodynamic theories, researchers initially emphasized the fact that storm and stress was not normative and that individual differences in adaptation to early adolescence predominated (cf. Hamburg, 1974; Hill, 1982; Offer, 1969). More recently, attention is being given to those particular situations that may be conflictual as well as the timing of these possible conflicts. Hill's work is illustrative of this new approach, and even his use of the word "perturbations" implies a temporary change. Even if increased prevalence of certain behaviors, especially negative ones, can be attributed to perturbations in interactions, feelings, or behaviors occurring at early adolescence, such findings do not address the rise in certain forms of psychopathology at early adolescence, nor their maintenance of higher prevalence in later life stages.

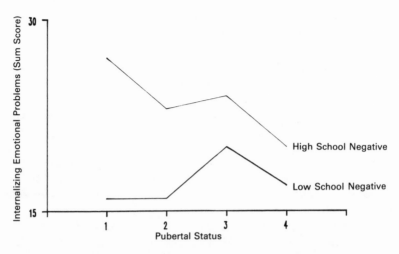

FIG. 8.1. The relation of negative school events and pubertal status, as measured by Tanner Breast Stage, to internalizing emotional problems, as measured by the Youth Behavior Profile.

Antecedents of Early Adolescent Behaviors

Although the researchers contributing to this volume are all interested in transitional processes, little interest has been shown in the antecedents of individual differences in adolescence, nor in the maintenance of certain behaviors first seen in early adolescence. That is, knowing that the simultaneity of events occurring at the time of early adolescence increases the likelihood of maladaption, as Simmons has demonstrated, does not mean that some adolescents may not be predisposed, either because of early experiences, individual characteristics, or some combination of the two, to react negatively to transitional events. For example, if attributional style is moderately predictive of depressive affect from late childhood to early adolescence (Seligman & Peterson, 1986), then children who attribute negative events to stable, internal, and global causes may be most likely to have difficulty negotiating pubertal, school, and peer transitions. The experience of a number of negative life events in late childhood also may predispose the early adolescent to be more vulnerable to the occurrence of multiple events. Hypotheses such as these remain to be addressed in early adolescence. It is unlikely that such relations are specific to early adolescence, as examples exist for other life phases (with regard to the aforementioned hypotheses, see Seligman, in press; and Garmezy, Masten, & Tellegren, 1984). What may be unique is the role that puberty plays in terms of specific adaptations to particular events.

Antecedents of particular behaviors or styles of adaptation also may be explored by looking at their correlates in different subphases of adolescence or by initiating short-term prospective investigations across adjacent life phases. A related approach is to examine the different predictors of the emergence and maintenance of certain behaviors to see whether they differ. Our work on the emergence of compulsive eating during adolescence is illustrative of these strategies. Two short-term longitudinal studies are being conducted, one from late elementary school to middle school and one from middle school to high school. We have hypothesized that compulsive eating (e.g., dieting and binge-diet cycles not severe eating disorders such as anorexia nervosa and bulimia) emerges as the adolescent encounters the conflict between cultural demands for thinness and pubertal increases in body fat, and hip and breast size (Attie & Brooks-Gunn, 1987; see also Crisp, 1984). Although compulsive eating may begin as a response to physical maturational change, given the context in which such changes now occur, different factors are hypothesized to account for its persistence in the years after pubertal change is complete. We have tested the relative effects of physical maturation, body image, psychopathology and family relationships upon compulsive eating patterns in the middle and high school years (both concurrently and longitudinally). In the middle school years, physical maturation, most specifically body fat, explained the greatest proportion of variance in compulsive eating scores, with negative body image also having a significant association. In contrast, by high school, physical indices played no role, whereas psychopathology (most specifically depression), negative family relationships, and poor body images did (Attie, 1987). Thus, compulsive eating emerges in the context of pubertal processes, which lays the foundation for eating problems in later adolescence (given high continuity between compulsive eating patterns across the two life phases). However, other factors contribute to its maintenance.

Hormonal Influences and Early Adolescent Behavior

Another question is whether certain biological factors operate during early adolescence and not at any other times. Hormonal changes have been thought to be a good candidate for uniqueness in process. As discussed by Coe (chapter 2), hormones may exert influence upon behavior prenatally (termed organizational efforts) or at the time of puberty (termed activation effects). Coe takes the strong position that in primates, as opposed to lower species, organizational but not activational effects operate. Unfortunately, testing this premise is not easy for several reasons.

First, gonadotropins rise at several different points in the life course, most particularly in the first months of fetal life, at around 2 to 4 months of age (boys), and in late childhood and early adolescence. Why the levels of gonadotropins level in early infancy are sometimes as high as those in adults is not understood (Faiman & Winter, 1974; Winter & Faiman, 1973). After this period, however, a negative feedback cycle keeps endocrine levels low until age 8 or 9, when gonadotropins increase (Faiman & Winter, 1971). The gonad's dampening effect upon the hypothalamic-pituitary axis is released, although the role of releasing mechanisms is still being studied (Warren, 1983). What follows are increases in the amplitudes and frequency of pulses of luteinizing-hormone releasing hormones (LHRH), increased responsiveness of gonadotropins to LHRH, increased secretion of follicle-stimulating hormone (FSH) and luteinizing hormone (LH) and nocturnal rises in the secretion of LH in a pulsatile fashion, increased responsiveness of the gonads to the pulses of LH and FSH, and increased secretion of gonadal hormones (Grumbach, Grave, & Mayer, 1974; Grumbach & Sizonenko, 1986).

Prenatal exposure to androgen secreted by the male testes in chromosomally male fetuses may be unique in that permanent, irreversible effects on brain structures occur. This results in gender differences in the organization of the hypothalamic-pituitary axis. How these structural differences and the hormonal patterns associated with them translate into later behavioral organization is the topic addressed by Coe (chapter 2). Typically, animal models are used to look at the long-term effects of prenatal exposure to androgens and estrogens because experimental manipulation of the prenatal and postnatal hormonal environment is possible. In a few cases, humans provide evidence about the primacy of prenatal exposure: Anomalous conditions such as andrenogenital, androgen-insensitivity, and testicular feminizing syndromes, and male pseudohermaphrodites with 5 α-reductase deficiency, all of which alter secondary sexual characteristic development, allow for an examination of the behavioral effects of the presence or absence of fetal androgen upon chromosomally male and female fetuses (cf. Imperato-McGinley, Peterson, Gautier, & Sturla, 1979; Money & Ehrhardt, 1972; Mulaikal, Migeon, & Rock, 1987). A related approach examines personality and intellectual functioning of children who were exposed to synthetic hormones prenatally but who did not have sexual characteristic structural changes (cf. Reinisch, 1977, 1981). The case studies suggest that so-called reproductive behavior almost universally is associated with assigned gender, rather than with hormonal status or chromosomal sex. The exception may be "tomboy" behavior or, more neutrally, increased activity levels in children reared as females who are exposed prenatally to androgenic hormones. Human sex-differentiated behavior, then, may be less dependent on prenatal organization of the hypothalamic-pituitary axis than is that of lower primates and other species. Of course, controversy exists as to what may be legitimately called gendered behavior in humans over and above childbearing, childbirth, and lactation, and some gender-related behavioral studies focus on behaviors such as rough-and-tumble play, age of sexual initiation, and time spent in contact with same-sex and opposite-sex individuals.

A similar argument has been made from examining findings phylogenetically. That is, the activation effect of hormonal rises at puberty may be more pronounced (and/or may influence more behaviors) at the lower ends of the phylogenetic scale. That fewer activation effects are seen in monkeys than rats or mice could be interpreted as evidence for such a statement. Indeed, this is the premise of Coe's chapter given his findings of activation effects on certain behaviors in squirrel monkeys. The premise that hormonal activation effects are less influential for primates than other species is not controversial. The suggestion by Coe that no activation effects may exist in primates is less likely to be accepted. Indeed, recently collected data on early adolescent humans indicate that some effects probably exist (Susman et al., 1985; Udry, Billy, Morris, Groff, & Raj, 1985). What is important in light of Coe's argument is that the hormonal activation effects in humans are not pervasive (i.e., occurring across many sets of behaviors), are not large (i.e., many account for a very small portion of the variance), are often overridden by environmental events, and interact with environmental events. Coe's hypothesis, however, is intriguing, and the extent of hormonal activation effects in humans and lower primates has not yet been well established.

Second, prenatal brain organization typically manifests itself in gender differences in levels of gonadal hormones and in the cyclic release of gonadotropins.[2] The most obvious evidence of the differences in hormonal release is secondary sexual characteristics and menstrual cycles in females but not males. Within each gender, the organizational effects of prenatal hormones lay the groundwork for the activation of the hypothalamic-pituitary-gonadal system in late childhood, when mean levels of gonadal hormones rise dramatically. However, the levels of circulating gonadal hormones do not show a one-to-one correspondence with secondary sexual chracteristics, in part because of individual differences in tissue sensitivity to hormones. Therefore, a great deal of overlap in hormonal secretions across Tanner stages is seen (Faiman & Winter, 1974). And, the gonadal hormones themselves do not rise in unison, in part because they are controlled by different gonadal-releasing factors with their own genetic timetable. Therefore, the activation effects, if they exist, would not be totally synchronized across hormones as the changes in gonadal hormones do not exhibit perfect concordance with the secondary characteristic they initiate. For example, in an analysis of the relation between gonadol and hypothalamic-pituitary hormones and affective expression in 100 early adolescent girls, estradiol but not other hormones (LH, FSH, testosterone) or secondary sexual characteristics (breast growth, pubic hair growth) was associated with depressive affect (Brooks-Gunn & Warren, 1987).

---

[2]However, other prenatal environmental conditions also may influence pubertal processes. For example, timing of maturation has been shown to be influenced by prenatal nutritional status (Ellison, 1981; Liestol, 1982).

Third, as Coe has mentioned, the hypothalamic-pituitary-gonadal system is exquisitely sensitive to environmental conditions. This is true for humans as well as other primates. For example, when weight loss is large (as in the case of anorexia nervosa), levels of gonadotropic secretions are suppressed in women, with the most obvious manifestation being amenorrhea and anovulatory cycles (Vigersky & Loriaux, 1977; Warren, 1986). In some adolescents with anorexia nervosa, a reversion to the prepubertal pattern of low LH secretion, lowered amplitude pulsatile secretion, and nocturnal spiking occurs (Boyer et al., 1972, 1974). The changes are reversible with weight gain. Also, the genetic program for the timing of puberty may be partially overridden through environmental factors such as nutritional intake, weight, and intensivity and extensivity of exercise (Brooks-Gunn & Warren, in press; Brooks-Gunn, in press; Malina, 1983; Warren, 1980). The presence of others also may affect the secretion of gonadotropins, just as has been reported for primates. Women who have sexual intercourse regularly (weekly) may have more regular menstrual cycles than those who do not, and women who reside together tend to synchronize their cycles; in both cases, pheromones have been implicated as a causal mechanism (McClintock, 1971, 1978). The point here is that models of hormone-behavior relations must consider bidirectional effects, or at least be circumspect in making causal inferences about directionality.

Given these caveats, several interdisciplinary teams are studying potential links between hormones and behavior during early adolescence, or what Coe and others have called activation effects. The working assumption of those studying hormones is that there is an influence on some behaviors and that such effects are more pronounced in boys, probably because of higher levels of androgen. Indeed, some support for these premises is forthcoming (Nottelmann, Susman, Inoff-Germain, & Chrousos, 1987; Susman et al., 1985). For example, levels of testosterone are related to sexual activity in boys, independent of secondary sexual development (Udry et al., 1985). However, whether engagement in sexual intercourse increases androgen levels or androgen levels influence sexuality is not known. Additionally, contextual effects, if entered into the equation, might account for more of the variation in sexual activity than hormonal levels. Initiation of sexuality is highly associated with what is normative in one's peer group (Furstenberg, Moore, & Peterson, 1986), so it is likely that although very early sexual initiations may in part be hormonally influenced, by the time the behavior is normative, social factors account for the sexual initiation (cf. Gargiulo et al., in press, for a similar argument about dating behavior). Thus, even if hormonal effects are demonstrated, they must be evaluated relative to contextual and interactive effects.

Directions for further research on possible activation effects of hormones in humans and other primates include the following. First, hormonal effects may not be linear nor even concurrent. Sensitivity to hormones may only occur when the "system" is being turned on (see Fig. 8.2) or when very rapid rises occur, as we (Brooks-Gunn & Warren, 1987) have found for early adolescent girls' report of depressive affect. It follows that short-term changes in hormones may be more predictive of behavior than current levels. It is even possible that such links may

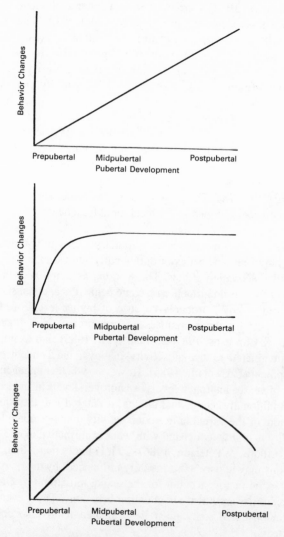

FIG. 8.2.   Three possible models of the relation between pubertal status and behavior; the top one is a linear model typically tested; the middle one suggests that behavior is more sensitive to hormonal alterations at the time when hormones first begin to rise, the bottom one indicates that hormonal associations may be temporary perturbations.

be temporary, only occurring during the period of change (i.e., in a similar sense to Hill's conceptualization of perturbations in parent-child relations during specific phases of puberty). Second, the fact that no perfect correspondence exists between secondary sexual characteristics and hormonal levels allows for a comparison of pubertal events that do and do not have social signal value. That is, breast growth is related to behavior but pubic hair growth is not (Brooks-Gunn, 1984, in press); we have hypothesized that breast growth is imbued with cultural meaning (vis-à-vis pregnancy, lactation, and sexuality) for the individual child (who may alter her self-definition as a function of such growth), as well as for others (who may treat the child differently). The same type of analyses may be done comparing hormones and secondary sexual characteristics, or examining the hormonal changes that occur prior to secondary sexual characteristic development (as in the case of LH night-time spiking). Third, how environmental events alter hormonal levels needs to be addressed more comprehensively, over and above the work on timing of puberty and on weight loss and exercise.

Interaction of Environmental and Physical Characteristics

Although perhaps not a unique characteristic of early adolescence, the possible interactions between environmental and physical characteristics may be profitably studied during this life phase. Indeed, Bronfenbrenner (1985) has conceptualized development as a function of person and environment, and several behavioral geneticists (Plomin, De Fries, & Loehlin, 1977; Scarr & McCartney, 1983) have proposed three different types of genotype-environment relations to describe development. Research using these frameworks has focused on early childhood, examining temperament or cognitive abilities as the "person characteristics." In early to middle adolescence, another set of personal characteristics may be examined, specifically pubertal processes or their timing. To date, most of the developmental research has focused on the behavioral effects, or correlates, of the timing of physical maturation or on the psychological significance of puberty (Brooks-Gunn, Petersen, & Eichorn, 1985; Hill, 1982).

If behavioral correlates of puberty are studied in different environmental contexts, then it is possible to investigate physical characteristic-environment interactions. First, personal characteristics may influence behavior differently depending on the environment in which they occur, given differences in expectations or demands that characterize a particular social milieu. An example is the findings of Simmons and her colleagues; the effects on body image of being an early-maturing sixth-grade girl depend on whether the girl attends an elementary or middle school (Blyth et al., 1985; Simmons et al., 1983). Second, an individual who possesses certain physical characteristics may actively seek or reject a certain social milieu. The work by Magnusson and his colleagues (1985) in

Sweden is a case in point. Although early-maturing girls were more likely than later-maturing girls to drink and to be sexually active, the effect was carried by early-maturing girls who had older friends. Having older friends, a phenomenon that was more prevalent in the early than later maturers, was the causal factor (Magnusson, Strattin, & Allen, 1985). In Hill's work, one might hypothesize that early-maturing adolescents actively avoid spending time with their parents (Hill, Holmbeck, Marlow, Green, & Lynch, 1985). These data fit nicely the active or evocative genotype-environment model described by Scarr and Mc-Cartney (1983). Finally, pubertal children may have chosen environmental contexts that become inappropriate as their bodies grow (in contradistinction to the elementary versus middle school example where contexts were not actively chosen). In this instance, the match between person and environment is altered as a function of changes beyond the control of the individual. The most obvious example involves activities in which body shape and size are critical, as in athletics, modeling, or dancing. It was hypothesized that in a context such as dancing, for example, which negatively values pubertal growth, individuals who develop pubertal characteristic may be more affected than similar individuals who are in a context that does not negatively value pubertal growth (e.g. Gargiulo et al., in press).

IS EARLY ADOLESCENCE A DISTINCT LIFE PHASE?

If early adolescence is distinct from other life phases, it is probably due to the fact that pubertal change alters the body from that of a child to that of an adult and that this change is associated with a myriad of social expectations, as Collins suggested (chapter 1). The question is whether this life phase may be demarcated from other life phases. The strong position is that early adolescence is a distinct life phase; the weak position is that since development is gradual, there may be no need to discuss the distinctiveness of early adolescence or any other life phase. The truth is probably somewhere in between, since distinctiveness becomes blurred when multiple markers or transitional events are used to delineate a particular life phase.

The three main markers of early adolescence are age grading, biological changes, and social events (interestingly, alterations in self-definitions are not used to ''mark'' the boundaries of this life phase; reliance on external rather than internal or intrapsychic events suggests that markers have social signal value for others as well as for the developing individual). Age grading still acts as the main marker of life phases, especially in the first 20 years of life. Examples include the stratification of schools and the conferring of social maturity by age to drive and to vote. Age becomes the implicit marker of developmental status. In early adolescence, age may be a particularly poor contender, given individual variation in biological growth, cognitive skills, and life events such as dating and sexuality. Biological markers often are seen as a better choice than age-graded ones, given the former's perceptual salience. The onset of pubertal change has been defined as the onset of secondary sexual characteristics, and puberty and early adolescence often are considered interchangeable terms. Problems with reliance on biological markers include (1) prepubertal children often are faced with social pressures similar to those of their more mature friends because of age-grouping; (2) biological changes precede the onset of secondary sexual development; and (3) girls and boys are discrepant in their pubertal timetables. Social events may be particularly relevant markers, given increasing expectations and demands for more adult behavior—the move to middle school, the onset of dating, the granting/earning of more independence from parents, and first intercourse. Like biological change, however, social demands occur in a highly age-graded society. Given such problems, early adolescence is now portrayed as a series or cluster of social, biological, and age-graded events in which variations in occurrence, timing, and sequencing are expected.

More profitable may be an examination of developmental trajectories across life phases in terms of both continuities and the likelihood of change due to environmental events. An especially fruitful approach is that taken by Elder, who, in his ground-breaking study *Children of the Great Depression* (1974), demonstrated that the experience of a major life crisis had very different long-lasting effects on children as a function of their age at the time of the event. As presented in this volume, Elder focuses on the timing and sequencing of events in order to explain long-term adaptations. Another example is the study of alterations in families as a function of divorce and remarriage (Hetherington, 1987; Hetherington, Cox, & Cox, 1985). Changes in family composition have profound effects on some children, which may be most likely to evidence themselves at early adolescence. In general, such longitudinal studies may address the question whether developmental trajectories may be more likely to be altered by environmental events in early adolescence than at other times, or whether preceding life events are likely to have more effects during early adolescence than during other life phases. If particular experiences in early adolescence result in great diversity in later outcomes, what is the mix of life events that might account for divergences?

CONCLUSION

Having examined some of the data presented in this volume and more generally issues raised by the study of early adolescence, we may return to the questions of whether this life phase is distinct or unique. The work in the present volume demonstrates that early adolescence is neither unique nor distinct in the strict sense (i.e., that the processes underlying development are unique or that boundaries between early adolescence and adjacent life phases are clearly delineated).

However, this life phase is distinct with regard to the timing and sequencing of the biological and social events that occur, and unique with regard to the role that physical and social changes play in the formation of self-definitions and the symbolic meaning of puberty. Whether relationships in early adolescence are more conflictual than at other times, or whether conflicts that do occur are predictive of later adaptation, are unresolved issues. Additionally, the antecedents of early adolescent behaviors (including possible activational effects of hormones) have not been extensively explored. Finally, whether developmental trajectories are more open to change at early adolescence than at other times is a particularly tantalizing question related to the timing, sequencing, and interpretation of events during development.

ACKNOWLEDGMENTS

Support for the writing of this chapter was provided by the National Institute for Child Health and Human Development and the W. T. Grant Foundation; their funding of the Adolescent Study Program at Educational Testing Service and St. Luke's-Roosevelt Hospital Center is greatly appreciated. Michelle P. Warren's is to be thanked for her critique of this chapter. Portions of this chapter were delivered at the Minnesota Symposium, October, 1986.

REFERENCES

Achenbach, T. M., & Edelbrock, C. S. (1979). The Child Behavior Profile: II. Boys aged 12–16 and girls aged 6–11 and 12–16. *Journal of Consulting and Clinical Psychology, 47*(2), 223–233.
Achenbach, T. M., & Edelbrock, C. S. (1981). Behavioral problems and competencies reported by the parents of normal and disturbed children aged 4 through 16. *Monographs of the Society for Research in Child Development, 46* (Serial No. 188, Vol. 461).
Attie, I. (1987). *Development of eating problems in adolescence: A follow-up of girls at risk.* Unpublished doctoral thesis, Catholic University.
Attie, I., & Brooks-Gunn, J. (1987). Weight-related concerns in women: A response to or a cause of stress. In R. C. Barnett, L. Biener, & G. K. Baruch (Eds.), *Gender and stress* (pp. 218–245). New York: Free Press.
Baltes, P. B., & Brim, O. G., Jr. (Eds.). (1980). *Life-span development and behavior* (Vol. 3). New York: Academic Press.
Baltes, P. B., & Brim, O. G., Jr. (Eds.). (1981). *Life-span development and behavior* (Vol. 4). New York: Academic Press.
Blos, P. (1979). *The adolescent passage.* New York: International Universities Press.
Blumberg, S. H., & Izard, C. E. (1985). Affective and cognitive characteristics of depression in 10- and 11-year-old children. *Journal of Personality and Social Psychology, 49*(1), 194–202.
Blyth, D. A., Simmons, R. G., & Zakin, D. F. (1985). Satisfaction with body image for early adolescent females: The impact of pubertal timing within different school environments. *Journal of Youth and Adolescence, 14*(3), 207–225.
Boyar, R. M., Finkelstein, J., Roffwarg, H., Kapan, S., Wertzmen, E., & Hellman, L. (1972).

Synchronization of augmented luteinizing hormone secretion with sleep during puberty. *New England Journal of Medicine, 287*, 582–586.

Boyar, R. M., Katz, J., Finkelstein, J. W., Kapen, S., Weiner, H., Weitzman, E. D., & Hellman, L. (1974). Anorexia nervosa: Immaturity of the 24-hour luteinizing hormone secretory pattern. *New England Journal of Medicine, 291*(17), 861–865.

Brim, O. G., Jr., & Kagan, J. (1980). *Constancy and change in human development.* Cambridge, MA: Harvard University Press.

Bronfenbrenner, U. (1985, May). *Interacting systems in human development. Research paradigms: Present and future.* Paper presented for the Society for Research in Child Development Study Group, Cornell University, Ithaca, New York.

Brooks-Gunn, J. (1984). The psychological significance of different pubertal events to young girls. *Journal of Early Adolescence, 4*(4), 315–327.

Brooks-Gunn, J. (1988, in press). Antecedents and Consequences of variations in girls' maturational timing. *Journal of Adolescent Health Care.*

Brooks-Gunn, J., Petersen, A. C., & Eichorn, D. (1985). The study of maturational timing effects in adolescence. *Journal of Youth and Adolescence, 14*(3), 149–161.

Brooks-Gunn, J., Rock, D., & Warren, M. P. (1987). Similarity of behavioral constructs across the adolescent years. Submitted for publication.

Brooks-Gunn, J., Rosso, J., & Warren, M. P. (1987, April). *Pubertal girls' psychological adaption: The role of stressful life events.* Paper presented in a symposium at the Society for Research in Child Development Meetings, Baltimore: MD.

Brooks-Gunn, J., & Warren, M. P. (1985). Effects of delayed menarche in different contexts: Dance and nondance students. *Journal of Youth and Adolescence, 14*(4), 285–300.

Brooks-Gunn, J., & Warren, M. P. (1987, April). Biological contributions to depressive and aggressive affect in young adolescent girls. Paper presented in a symposium on Hormonal Status at Puberty, Society for Research in Child Development Meetings, Baltimore, MD.

Brooks-Gunn, J. & Warren, M. P. (1988, in press). The psychological significance of secondary sexual characteristics in 9- to 11-year-old girls. *Child Development.*

Buss, A. H., & Plomin, R. (1984). *Temperament: Early developing personality traits.* Hillsdale, NJ: Lawrence Erlbaum Associates.

Cicchetti, D. (1984). The emergence of developmental psychopathology. *Child Development, 55,* 1–7.

Crisp, A. H. (1984). The psychopathology of anorexia nervosa: Getting the "Heat" out of the system. In A. J. Stunkard & E. Stellar (Eds.), *Eating and its disorders* (Pp. 209–234). New York: Raven.

Deutsch, H. (1944). *Psychology of women.* New York: Grune & Stratton.

Duncan, P. D., Ritter, P. L., Dornbusch, S. M., Gross, R. T., & Carlsmith, J. M. (1985). The effects of pubertal timing on body image, school behavior, and deviance. *Journal of Youth and Adolescence, 14*(3), 227–235.

Dusek, J. B., & Flaherty, J. F. (1981). The development of the self-concept during the adolescent years. *Monographs of the Society for Research in Child Development, 46,* (4, Serial No. 191).

Elder, G. H. (1974). *Children of the Great Depression.* Chicago: University of Chicago Press.

Ellison, P. T. (1981). Morbidity, mortality, and menarche. *Human Biology, 53,* 635–643.

Faiman, C., & Winter, J. S. D. (1971). Sex differences in gonadotropin concentrations in infancy. *Nature, 232,* 130–131.

Faiman, C., & Winter, J. S. D. (1974). Gonadotropins and sex hormone patterns in puberty: Clinical data. In M. M. Grumbach, G. D. Grave, & F. E. Mayer (Eds.), *Control of the onset of puberty* (pp. 32–61). New York: John Wiley.

Furstenberg, F. F., Jr., Moore, K. A., & Peterson, J. L. (1986). Sex education and sexual experience among adolescents. *American Journal of Public Health, 75*(11), 1331–1332.

Gargiulo, J., Attie, I., Brooks-Gunn, J., & Warren, M. P. (in press). Dating in middle school girls: Effects of social context, maturation, and grade. *Developmental Psychology.*

Garmezy, N., Masten, A. S., & Tellegren, A. (1984). The study of stress and competence in childen: A building block for developmental psychopathology. *Child Development, 55,* 97–111.

Grumbach, M. M., Grave, D., & Mayer, F. F. (Eds.). (1974). *Control of the onset of puberty.* New York: Wiley.

Grumbach, M. M., & Sizonenko, P. C. (1986). *The control of the onset of puberty II.* New York: Academic Press.

Hall, G. S. (1904). *Adolescence: Its psychology and its relations to physiology, anthropology, sociology, sex, crime, religion and education.* Englewood Cliffs, NJ: Prentice-Hall.

Hamburg, B. A. (1974). Early adolescence: A specific and stressful stage of the life cycle. In G. V. Coelho, B. A. Hamburg, & J. E. Adams (Eds.), *Coping and adaptation* (pp. 101–124). New York: Basic Books.

Harlan, W. R., Harlan, E. A., & Grillo, G. P. (1980, June). Secondary sex characteristics of girls 12 to 17 years of age: The U. S. Health Examination Survey. *Pediatrics, 96*(6), 1074–1078.

Harmon, R., & Emde, R. (1983). *Continuities and discontinuities in development.* New York: Plenum.

Hetherington, E. M. (1987). Family relations six years after divorce. In Pasley, K., & Ihinger-Tollman, M. (Eds.), *Remarriage and stepparenting today: Current research and theory* (pp. 185–205). New York: Guilford Press.

Hetherington, E. M., Cox, M., & Cox R. (1985). Long-term effects of divorce and remarriage on the adjustment of children. *Journal of the American Academy of Psychology, 24*(5), 518–530.

Hill, J. P. (Ed.). (1982). Special issue on early adolescence. *Child Development, 53*(6).

Hill, J. P., Holmbeck, G. N., Marlow, L., Green, T. M., & Lynch, M. E. (1985). Menarcheal status and parent-child relations in families of seventh-grade girls. *Journal of Youth and Adolescence, 14*(4), 301–316.

Imperato-McGinley, J., Peterson, R. E., Gautier, T., & Sturla, E. (1979). Androgens and the evolution of male-gender identity among male pseudohermaphrodites with 5 α-reductase deficiency. *New England Journal of Medicine, 300*(22), 233–237.

Kellam, S. G., Ensminger, M. E., & Turner, R. J. (1977). Family structure and the mental health of children. *Archives of General Psychiatry, 34,* 1012–1022.

Lerner, R. M. (1985). Adolescent maturational changes and psychosocial development: A dynamic interactional perspective. *Journal of Youth and Adolescence, 14*(4), 355–372.

Liestol, K. (1982). Social conditions and menarcheal age: The importance of early years of life. *Annals of Human Biology, 9,* 521–536.

Magnusson, D., Strattin, H., & Allen V. L. (1985). A longitudinal study of some adjustment processes from mid-adolescence to adulthood. *Journal of Youth and Adolescence, 14*(4), 267–283.

Malina, R. M. (1983). Menarche in athletes: A synthesis and hypothesis. *Annals of Human Biology, 10*(1), 1–24.

Marshall, W. A., & Tanner, J. M. (1969). Variations in pattern of pubertal changes in girls. *Archives of Diseases in Childhood, 44,* 291–303.

McClintock, M. K. (1971). Menstrual synchrony and suppression. *Nature, 229,* 244–245.

McClintock, M. K. (1978). Estrons synchrony and its mediation by airborne chemical communication. *Hormones and Behavior, 10,* 264–276.

Money, J., & Ehrhardt, A. A. (1972). *Man and woman, boy and girl.* Baltimore: Johns Hopkins University Press.

Mulaikal, R. M., Migeon, C. J., & Rock, J. A. (1987). Fertility rates in female patients with congenital adrenal hyperplasia due to 21-hydroxylase deficiency. *New England Journal of Medicine, 316*(4), 178–182.

Nesselroade, J. R., & Baltes, P. B. (1974). Adolescent personality development and historical change: 1970–1972. *Monographs of the Society of Research in Child Development, 39,* (1, Serial No. 154).

Nottelmann, E. D., Susman, E. J., Inoff-Germain, G., & Chrousos, G. P. (1987, April). *Concurrent and predictive relations between hormone levels and social-emotional functioning in early adolescence.* Paper presented at the meeting of the Society for Research in Child Development, Baltimore, MD.

Offer, D. (1969). *The psychological world of the teen-ager.* New York: Basic Books.

Plomin, R., De Fries, J. C., & Loehlin, J. (1977). Genotype-environment interaction and correlation in the analysis of human behavior. *Psychological Bulletin, 84,* 309–322.

Reinisch, J. M. (1977, April 7). Prenatal exposure of human fetuses to synthetic progestin and oestrogen affects personality. *Nature, 266*(5602), 561–562.

Reinisch, J. M. (1981, March 13). Prenatal exposure to synthetic progestins increases potential for aggression in humans. *Science, 211,* 1171–1173.

Rutter, M. (1979). *Changing youth in a changing society.* London: Nuffield Provincial Hospital's Trust. Cambridge, MA: Harvard University Press.

Rutter, M., Graham, P., Chadwick, O. F. D., & Yule, W. (1976). Adolescent turmoil: Fact or fiction. *Journal of Child Psychology & Psychiatry, 17,* 35–56.

Scarr, S. (1985). Constructing psychology: Making facts and fables for our times. *American Psychologist, 40*(5), 499–512.

Scarr, S., & McCartney, K. (1983). How people make their own environments: A theory of genotype-environment effects. *Child Development, 54,* 424–435.

Seligman, M. E. P. (in press). Explanatory style: Risk factor for depression in children, adolescents and adults. In M. Levine & E. R. McAnarney (Eds.), *Early adolescent transitions.* MA: Lexington Books.

Seligman, M. E. P., & Peterson, C. (1986). A learned helplessness perspective on childhood depression: Theory and research. In M. Rutter, C. E. Izard, & P. B. Read (Eds.), *Depression in young people: Developmental and clinical perspectives* (pp. 233–249). New York: Guilford Press.

Simmons, R. G., Blyth, D. A., & McKinney, K. L. (1983). The social and psychological effects of puberty on white females. In J. Brooks-Gunn & A. C. Petersen (Eds.), *Girls at puberty: Biological and psychosocial perspectives* (pp. 229–272). New York: Plenum.

Simmons, R. G., Rosenberg, F., & Rosenberg, M. (1973). Disturbance in the self-image at adolescence. *American Sociological Review, 38,* 553–568.

Sroufe, L. A. (1979). The coherence of individual development. *American Psychologist, 34,* 834–841.

Susman, E. J., Nottelmann, E. D., Inoff-Germain, G. E., Dorn, L. D., Cutler, G. B., Jr., Loriaux, D. L., & Chrousos, G. P. (1985). The relation of relative hormonal levels and physical development and social-emotional behavior in young adolescents. *Journal of Youth and Adolescence, 14*(3), 245–264.

Thomas, A., Chess, A., & Birch, H. G. (1968). *Temperament and behavior disorders in children.* New York: New York University Press.

Tobin-Richards, M., Boxer, A., & Petersen, A. C. (1983). The psychological significance of pubertal change: Sex differences in perceptions of self during early adolescence. In J. Brooks-Gunn & A. C. Petersen (Eds.), *Girls at puberty: Biological and psychosocial perspectives* (pp. 127–154). New York NY: Plenum.

Udry, J. R., Billy, J. O. G., Morris, N. M., Groff, T. R., & Raj, M. H. (1985). Serum androgenic hormones motivate sexual behavior in boys. *Fertility and Sterility, 43*(1), 90–94.

Vigersky, R. A., & Loriaux, D. (1977). Anorexia nervosa as a model of hypothalamic dysfunction. In R. Vigersky (Ed.), *Anorexia nervosa* (pp. 109–121). New York: Raven.

Warren, M. P. (1980). The effects of exercise on pubertal progression and reproductive function in girls. *Journal of Clinical Endocrinology Metabolism, 51,* 1150–1157.

Warren, M. P. (1983). Physical and biological aspects of puberty. In J. Brooks-Gunn & A. C. Petersen (Eds.), *Girls at puberty: Biological and psychosocial perspectives* (pp. 3–27). New York: Plenum.

Warren, M. P. (1986). Metabolic factors and the onset of puberty. In M. M. Grumbach & P. C. Sizonenko (Eds.), *The control of the onset of puberty II*. Baltimore: Williams & Wilkins.

Winter, J. S. D., & Faiman, C. (1973). The development of cyclic pituitary- and gonadal function in adolescent females. *Journal of Clinical Endocrinology and Metabolism, 37,* 714–718.

Author Index

Subject Index

Page numbers followed by (f) refer to figures. Page numbers followed by (t) refer to tables.